KT-499-139

Fashion
REVIVALS
from the Elizabethan age to
the present day

Barbara Burman Baines

B.T. Batsford Ltd, London

To 27 July 1937, with love.

First published 1981

ISBN 0 7134 1929 6

Filmset by Servis Filmsetting Ltd, Manchester
and printed in Great Britain by
The Anchor Press Ltd, Tiptree, Essex
for the publishers
B.T. Batsford Ltd
4 Fitzhardinge Street
London W1H 0AH

Frontispiece 'Hon. Louisa O'Callaghan,' *c.*1810, artist unknown (*Trustees of the Chatsworth Settlement*).

Contents

List of Illustrations

40 *Aglaia*, The Journal of the Healthy and Artistic Dress Union. No. 1, July 1893.
41 'Nature proposes but the corset disposes,' *Aglaia*, July 1893.
42 'The Empire Dress,' *Aglaia*, July 1893.
43 'Private View at the Royal Academy,' 1881, by W.P. Frith (detail; collection of C.J.R. Pope/photograph: A.C. Cooper).
44 'The Pavlova Influence in our Back Gardens,' *Daily Mirror*, 3 July 1912 (*British Library, London*).
45 Isadora Duncan. *The Sketch*, 29 May 1912 (*Victoria and Albert Museum, London*).
46 Kate Greenaway. St Valentine's Day frontispiece to supplement of *Illustrated London News*. 15 February 1879 (*Victoria and Albert Museum, London*).
47 Peach evening dress by Fortuny *c.*1912. Museum no. T 193+A1974 (*Victoria and Albert Museum, London*).
48 Greek dress. Liberty and Co. Ltd, spring 1915 catalogue (*Victoria and Albert Museum, London*).
49 Evening gown from Carven Collection, Paris 1963 (*photograph: Keystone Press Agency*).
50 Drawing by Cecil Beaton, London *Vogue*, May 1930 (*Museum of Costume, Research Centre, Bath*).
51 Tunic and culottes by Jean Muir, 1975 (*by kind permission of Jean Muir*).
52 'Unknown Young Man,' *c.*1590, by Isaac Oliver (*by gracious permission of Her Majesty the Queen*).
53 Detail of 'Unknown Girl,' 1587, by John Bettes the Younger (*St Olave's and St Saviour's Grammar School Foundation/photograph: J.F. Burman*).
54 'Unknown Lady,' 1557, by Hans Eworth (*Tate Gallery, London*).
55 'Lady Elizabeth Pope,' *c.*1615, attributed to Robert Peake the Elder (*Tate Gallery, London*).
56 Title Page from Robert Greene, *A Quip for an Upstart Courtier*, London, 1592 (*British Library, London*).
57 'Portrait of a woman as a shepherdess,' *c.*1660, by Sir Peter Lely (*Ashmolean Museum, Oxford*).
58 'Catherine of Braganza,' *c.*1660–61, by D. Stoop (*National Portrait Gallery, London*).
59 'Catherine of Braganza,' *c.*1662, by Jacob Huysmans (*by gracious permission of Her Majesty the Queen*).
60 Skirt panel. English. Museum no. 114+A–1873 (*Victoria and Albert Museum, London*).
61 Waistcoat panel. English. Museum no. 878–1891 (*Victoria and Albert Museum, London*).
62 'Duchess of Queensberry,' *c.*1740, after C. Jervas (*National Portrait Gallery, London*).
63 'The Montagu Family on the terraces of Sandleford Priory, near Newbury,' 1744, by Edward Haytley (*Leger Galleries, London*).
64 'Elizabeth Pennefather as a shepherdess,' *c.*1735, by Thomas Hudson (*The Earl of Antrim*).
65 'A Dame's School,' 1845, by Thomas Webster (detail; *Tate Gallery, London*).
66 Plate 16, *Ackermann's Repository*, Vol. X, *c.*1810 (*Victoria and Albert Museum, London*).
67 'Cheltenham Dress,' *La Belle Assemblée*, 1828 (*Museum of Costume, Research Centre, Bath*).
68 'Man in a Smock,' undated, by James Ward (*Tate Gallery, London*).
69 Child's silk smock, *c.*1918. Museum no. T 213–1972 (*Victoria and Albert Museum, London*).
70 Day and evening dresses, *Englishwoman's Domestic Magazine*, February 1866 (*Victoria and Albert Museum, London*).
71 Hats and trimmings. Woodland Bros catalogue, *c.*1911 (*Museum of Costume, Research Centre, Bath*).
72 'The Smiling Woman,' *c.*1908, by Augustus John (*Tate Gallery, London*).
73 Liberty and Co. Ltd, catalogue, spring 1938 (*Museum of Costume, Research Centre, Bath*).
74 Coat from Wallis Fashion Group Ltd, 1970s.
75 Dresses from Laura Ashley Ltd, 1970s.
76 Working dress, *Aglaia*, July 1893.
77 'Original Western jeans'; shirts, jackets and shoes all by Levi's (UK). 1980.
78 'Are you one of Chloé's *recherché* gardeners?' Photograph by Guy Boudin, London *Vogue*, 1 March 1977.
79 'George Clifford, 3rd Earl of Cumberland,' *c.*1590, by Nicholas Hilliard (*National Maritime Museum, London*).
80 English troops, Plate VIII, John Derricke, *The Image of Irelande*, 1581 (*Crown Copyright reproduced with permission of the Controller of Her Majesty's Stationery Office/photograph: Department of the Environment*).
81 'Portrait of a Lady,' *c.*1600, artist unknown (*City of Bristol Museum and Art Gallery*).
82 Lovers in a garden. Early fifteenth-century French manuscript illumination. Harley, MS. 4431, f, 376 (*British Library, London*).
83 'Robert Rich, Earl of Warwick,' *c.*1630, by Anthony van Dyck (*The Metropolitan Museum of Art, The Jules S. Bache collection, 1949*).
84 English dress. Abraham de Bruyn, *Habitus Variarum Gentium*, Antwerp, 1581 (*Victoria and Albert Museum, London*).
85 Old-fashioned courtiers. Designs by Inigo Jones for Sir William d'Avenant's *Britannia Triumphans*, 1638 (*Trustees of the Chatsworth Settlement/photograph: Courtauld Institute*).
86 Title page from James Taylor, *The Needles Excellence*, London, 1631 (*Victoria and Albert Museum, London*).
87 'Dame Elizabeth Pettus,' *d.*1653, artist unknown (*Norfolk Museums Service, Castle Museum, Norwich*).
88 'Mary, Mrs Rowe,' 1752, by Henry Pickering (*York City Art Gallery*).
89 Fourteenth-century dress. Joseph Strutt, *A Complete View of the Dress and Habits of the People of England*, London, 1796.
90 'George, Prince of Wales and Frederick, later Duke of York,' 1764, by Johan Zoffany (*by gracious permission of Her Majesty the Queen*).
91 'Helene Fourment,' *c.*1630, by Peter Paul Rubens (*Gulbenkian Foundation, Oerias, Portugal*).
92 'Mary Panton, Duchess of Ancaster,' 1757, by Thomas Hudson (*by permission of Grimsthorpe and Drummond Castle Trustees*).
93 'Thomas and Isabel Crathorne,' 1767, by Francis Cotes (*Henry E. Huntington Library and Art Gallery, San Marino, California*).
94 'The Bradshaw Family,' *c.*1769, by Johan Zoffany (*Tate Gallery, London*).

95 '3rd Marchioness of Salisbury and her son,' *c.*1870, by George Richmond (*Hatfield House/photograph National Portrait Gallery, London*).
96 Dress and shawl. *Ackermann's Repository*, March 1824 (*Museum of Costume, Research Centre, Bath*).
97 'Queen Victoria and Prince Albert as Queen Philippa and Edward III,' 1842, by Sir Edwin Lanseer (*by gracious permission of Her Majesty the Queen*).
98 Seventeenth-century dress. F.W. Fairholt, *Costume in England from the Earliest Period till the Close of the Eighteenth Century*, London, 1846.
99 Fourteenth-century dress. F.W. Fairholt, *Costume in England from the Earliest Period till the Close of the Eighteenth Century*, London, 1846.
100 'George IV and trainbearers,' 1821, engraving by E. Scriven (*Museum of London*).
101 'Sir Francis Sykes and his Family,' 1837, by Daniel Maclise (*by permission of F.J.B. Sykes/photograph: National Portrait Gallery, London*).
102 Photograph by Lady Harwarden, *c.*1861 (*Victoria and Albert Museum, London*).
103 The Mutual Admirationists,' by George du Maurier, *Punch* 22 May 1880.
104 Dress in Liberty Indian silk, *c.*1881. Museum no. T 171–1973 (*Victoria and Albert Museum, London*).
105 Good and bad historical dress. *Aglaia*, July 1893.
106 Velvet dress, *c.*1900. Museum no. T 202–1962 (*Victoria and Albert Museum, London*).
107 Photograph of a wedding, Bourne, Lincolnshire, 1950.
108 'The Past Meets the Present After Dark.' London *Vogue*, May 1930 (*Museum of Costume, Research Centre, Bath*).
109 Photograph of Queen Mary, 1902 (*Victoria and Albert Museum, London*).
110 Cotton dresses, 1979. Laura Ashley Ltd.
111 'Princess Louise,' 1865 by F.X. Winterhalter (*by gracious permission of Her Majesty the Queen*).
112 Evening dress with crinoline petticoat, 1953. Peter Russell photograph (*Keystone Press Agency*).
113 Princess Alexandra. *The Times*, 4 May 1978.
114 Teddy boy at London dance hall, 1954 (*Photograph: Keystone Press Agency*).
115 Teddy boys at Wembley Stadium for Rock'n'Roll revival show, 5 August 1972 (*Photograph: Keystone Press Agency*).
116 Professional ballroom dancers, photograph by Ron Self, 1970s.
117 Wool coat, 1978. Wallis Fashion Group Ltd.
118 Dress and jacket, 1977, by Thea Porter. Photograph by Van Pariser.
119 Femme Turque. Nicholas de Nicolay, *Les Quatres Premiers Livres des Navigations et Pérégrinations Orientales,* Lyon, 1567 (*British Library, London*).
120 'Portrait of a Lady,' *c.*1590–1600, by Marcus Gheeraerts the Younger (*by gracious permission of Her Majesty the Queen*).
121 Persians. J.-J. Boissard, *Habitus Variarum Orbis Gentium*, Maline, 1581 (*British Library, London*).
122 'Elizabeth I,' *c.*1600. The 'Rainbow Portrait' by Marcus Gheeraerts the Younger (*Hatfield House/photograph: Courtauld Institute*).
123 'Sir Robert Shirley,' 1622, by Anthony van Dyck (*Petworth House/photograph: Courtauld Institute*).
124 'William Feilding, 1st Earl of Denbigh,' *c.*1633, by Anthony van Dyck (*National Gallery, London*).
125 'Samuel Pepys,' 1666, by J. Hayls (*National Portrait Gallery, London*).
126 Persian youth. Costume design 1635 by Inigo Jones for Sir William d'Avenant's *The Temple of Love* (*Trustees of the Chatsworth Settlement/photograph: Courtauld Institute*).
127 Dressing gown, 1770–80. Museum no. 58.40 (*Museum of London*).
128 'Lady Mary Wortley Montagu,' *c.*1717, attributed to J.B. Vanmour, (detail; *National Portrait Gallery, London*).
129 'Unknown Lady,' *c.*1770, studio of Jervas (*National Portrait Gallery, London*).
130 'Captain John Foote,' *c.*1761–5, by Joshua Reynolds (*York City Art Gallery*).
131 Captain John Foote's Indian costume (*York City Art Gallery*).
132 Embroidered muslin apron, early eighteenth century. Museum no. T 9–1952 (*Victoria and Albert Museum, London*).
133 'Edward Lane,' 1829, by his brother R. Lane (*National Portrait Gallery, London*).
134 'Colin Mackenzie,' 1844, by James Sent, RA (*National Army Museum, London*).
135 'Hon. Margaret Elphinstone,' *c.*1815, by George Sandars (*Marquess of Lansdowne, Meikleour*).
136 'Exhibition of Bloomers in Hyde Park,' 1852, by George Cruikshank.
137 Burnous and other fashions. *The Englishwoman's Domestic Magazine*, April 1862.
138 Printed silk; pattern in use from *c.*1900 onwards (*photograph by Mike Sossick by permission of Liberty and Co. Ltd*).
139 Judo suits, 1975. Photograph by David Finch.
140 'Hints to Holiday-Makers,' *Punch*, 21 August 1929.
141 Evening skirt and jacket. Allwyn's fashion show. London, April 1951 (*Photograph: Keystone Press Agency*).
142 Shop front, 1980. The Tibet Shop, Coptic Street, London W1. Photograph by J.F. Burman.
143 Vali with a lamb, *c.*1965 (*Photograph: Keystone Press Agency*).
144 Shop front, 1980. Mitsukiku Ltd, Old Brompton Road, London SW7. Photograph by J.F. Burman.

Those photographs without credits are from the author's collection.

The reader is advised that in a few cases, for reasons of space, and in order to show the detail of the costume as clearly as possible, illustrations have been slightly trimmed.

Preface

This book is a general survey of revived styles as they came into male and female dress in England from the mid-sixteenth century to the present day. It is not limited to high fashion: where revivals occurred in other sorts of dress, and where indicative of a wider trend, they have been included here, such as the pseudo-Elizabethan suits worn for the coronation of George IV in 1821, or the various revived styles employed in masques during the later sixteenth and the seventeenth centuries.

In order to make this survey broad enough to demonstrate the pattern of such revivals, but not so broad that it would curtail adequate discussion of the main examples, it seemed best to begin the book at the reign of Elizabeth I and so to be sure, too, that most interested readers would have an image of the dress of the period in their mind's eye. It may be difficult to retain an accurate memory of the period before the mid-sixteenth century without recourse to frequent visual reminders, and the book would have then developed into a warren of references and illustrations darting back and forth in time. However, since historical revivals by their very nature make use of various features from the dress of previous eras, in the following pages there are some illustrations of dress from before the reign of Elizabeth I, but these are placed, for comparison, at the point in the book where their revived or revised versions occur. Thus an illustration of fourteenth-century dress occurs in the discussion of nineteenth-century historical revivals because some Victorians, being very partial to such dress, copied it for themselves.

The book is arranged and illustrated thematically, but the reader is invited to refer at any point to illustrations of a similar date in another part of the book to add to the sense of the particular period being discussed.

In interpreting the meaning, and the function, of revivals in dress as widely as possible, four separate themes emerge: classical, rural, historical and exotic. The principal unifying characteristics of each of these are discussed in the introduction, after which each theme is surveyed and illustrated separately.

Exotic apparel has been included in this book so that the amount of inventive English dress could be fully recognized. It has not been possible or necessary to give more than a basic sketch of this last theme, but this provides some idea of the range and richness of borrowings and reanimation which have revitalized English dress. For the purposes of this book, any search, manifest in dress, for a paradise lost by time or place, qualifies as a revival. Thus the use of certain exotic features is seen to be in the same spirit as that which leads an English townswoman to assume rural overtones in what she wears or a Victorian aristocrat to appropriate mediaeval features of dress. There are many visions and many paradises, and as many ways of regaining and realizing them. Revivals, being more romantic and effervescent than other sorts of dress, are an anomaly within conventional dress history which, if they are a genre at all, suggest rewards in a more errant treatment than usual.

This book can only be an introductory and general survey, so of course there are omissions and limitations, but by presenting various examples of revivals in their settings of contemporary attitudes to dress and fashion, it is hoped the reader will get an impression of the overall patterns of the subject. Butterfly-like the subject may be, but anyone with a special interest in any one aspect can make use of the enlarged chapter notes and annotated guide to further reading which is at the end of the book.

Acknowledgments

To the following individuals I owe my very grateful thanks for their varied kindnesses and help: Jane Ashelford, John Burman, Penelope Byrde, Alan and Hazel Fletcher, John Hawkins, Diana de Marly, Jean Muir, Stella Mary Newton, Thea Porter, Pauline Ridley, David Sassoon, Mike Sossick and Jessica York.

My thanks are due to the staff of the following libraries: The Research Centre, The Museum of Costume, Bath; The British Library; The Devonshire Collection, Chatsworth; The London Library; The National Art Library in the Victoria and Albert Museum; The Library of St Martin's School of Art; The Westminster City Victoria Library; The Witt and Conway Libraries of the Courtauld Institute of Art, The University of London.

For their assistance, I also thank Laura Ashley Ltd, Liberty and Co. Ltd, Liberty of London Prints Ltd and Selfridges Ltd.

Paula Shea and Tim Auger, my editors, I thank particularly for their guidance, enthusiasm and tact, and Pauline Rainford for so doggedly typing a wayward manuscript.

During preparation of this book, John Baines my husband supplied patience, excellent coffee and skilful encouragement; to John I owe my greatest debt, but neither he nor anyone else on whom I have leaned in this work is responsible for its inevitable vagaries, which are all my own.

Introduction

Clothes are expressive of an individual's personality as well as of their own time and their own place; in 1757 Thomas Jefferys noted in his book *A Collection of the Dresses of Different Nations*: 'the Habit is become a Kind of Index to the Mind, and the Character is in some Particulars as easily discovered by a Man's dress as by his Conversation.' Indeed we often strive consciously for self-expression in this way, balancing practical considerations with a need to assert some inner aspects of ourselves. In a book simply called *Dress*, in 1878, Mrs Oliphant described the balance in this way: 'No dress can be good which is not useful and adapted to practical necessities, nor can any dress be perfect into which the element of individuality does not enter.' But when we look back on 1878, or on the dress of the time of Thomas Jefferys in the mid-eighteenth century, or further back into the past, we may wonder how much self-expression there really was, when, by and large, to the casual observer *now* everybody *then* seems to look the same, however distinct they may have felt at the time. Nowadays, we feel, we are unfettered and may wear whatever we choose, but in the past the individual was lost in a cloud of conformity and, so it seems, the personality outweighed by time and place.

Fortunately, as more people begin to look at the dress of the past and present with the care and attention it deserves, this view is changing. Fashion and dress historians, for example, are beginning to reveal more of the picture and more of its detail, and we are learning that at any given period in English dress there were more options and versions than had previously been described. Not only were there class and occupational differences, but within what was thought of as high fashion itself at any time there were likely to be sub-fashions and variations within the dominant taste. The knack lies in our learning to see differences instead of expecting conformities. To the range of possibilities and inflexions within dress and fashion, revivals add another rich dimension, either as the result of individual invention and idiosyncrasy, or as a result of a widely shared inclination producing a sub-fashion.

In Maurice Chevalier's famous song 'I remember it well' his partner reminded him that he didn't remember it at all well and that time had rearranged his fond memories. So it is with revivals in dress which

1 We like to conform, but not this much. In reality fashion thrives on subtle distinctions, and rewards those with ingenuity. 1913.

Beauty and Health go hand in hand—

*For beauty cannot live but with health,
whilst health of itself creates beauty.*

Beauty and grace of form, a clear, healthy complexion, a free and graceful carriage, personal charm and superb vitality, all, to a large extent, depend upon health; and health in its turn depends upon the human system receiving the best nourishment for body, brain and nerve.

Ordinary food does **not** contain sufficient brain and nerve nourishment. It is necessary to reinforce our ordinary diet with a special food for brain and nerve.

Visem, the new tonic food, is the most concentrated form of nourishment known. It supplies the nerve and brain cells with new energy and vigour, and the body with nutriment which can be immediately and effectively assimilated.

Visem is the culmination of many years of research on the part of the leading scientists of the day, but there is no mystery about its composition. It is just a simple wholesome food, consisting mainly of pure milk proteid combined with organic phosphorus derived from yolk of egg, known to the medical profession as lecithin. Milk proteid feeds the body—lecithin the nerves and brain.

Excellent milk proteid preparations have been obtainable for years, but Visem has all their merits and the additional advantage of containing lecithin which **every** medical man will tell you is the finest nerve food known to science.

VISEM
(Seed of Strength)

Visem is made up in the form of little tablets which are eaten like biscuits. It is sold at all high-class chemists in tins of 24 tablets, 1/6.

If any difficulty in obtaining, send 1/6 to St. Ivel, Ltd., Yeovil, and a tin will be sent you post free.

stem from historical memory or visions of how things used or ought to have been. They are, we should be thankful, overlaid with fresh style and rearranged by affectionate nostalgia. In many cases revivals alter the originals sufficiently to turn them into *arrivals*, and some old favourites, never out of use, are as much *survivals* as revivals. In short, revivals are not a neat grouping, for they are both nebulous and specific, both elusive and insistent. They do not take kindly to classification, any more than other forms of human fantasy do, but in an attempt to catch these butterflies of fashion, it was helpful to look for some underlying patterns.

Broadly speaking revivals fall into four types: first, revivals of styles and types of dress originally established by the Greeks and Romans of classical antiquity; second, dress known to have been worn at periods of more recent history, from mediaeval times and after; third, dress drawn from rural life; and fourth, dress of exotic origins, transplanted and revised for English usage. Some revivals, of any time, are made with deliberate archaism, such as the attempt by nineteenth-century dress reformers to reinstate classical dress as a healthier alternative to modern dress; others stem from some unorganized configuration of factors, in which a latent or partially developed taste might be triggered off by external events such as films or exhibitions; some other revivals seem to be part of a more or less permanent nostalgia, such as the nostalgia for rural life.

The revival of classical dress has, like that of exotic dress, been based on an interest in clothes which were structurally very different from traditional English types, but, unlike that of exotic origin, it has always attracted a good deal of criticism. The civilian dress of antiquity, or classical dress, is taken here to be that of the Hellenic Greeks, and the Romans. Ancient Egyptian dress is also mentioned because it has on occasion been absorbed into English dress either on its own, or has been fused with a general idea of antiquity. The characteristic of classical dress which distinguishes it from most of later European dress was its assembly from rectangles of cloth, draped over the body or fitted to the body by wrapping and girdling. In contrast, in post-classical times European dress has been made of cloth cut and sewn into connecting shapes to enclose the body, and with the use of buttons or bias-cut cloth, the fit has been very close and exact.

Hellenic Greek clothing was chiefly of two types: first a garment roughly equivalent to a tunic, called a chiton, which was partially sewn together, or a peplos which was a garment made by folding cloth and then pinning and girdling it; secondly, a piece worn loosely over the body somewhat in the manner of a cloak, wrap or poncho, called a himation. This could have weighted corners to hold it in place. These garments were knee or ankle length, dyed or natural colours, patterned or plain; over the centuries and from region to region there were variations and changes, but these were the basic methods for clothing both men and women. The Romans used the same system, with a tunic and an over-wrap called a toga, for men, and a long tunic, a stola, with an over-wrap called a palla for women. Like the Greeks, the Romans wore a variety of colours and decorative additions, and social rank was easily discernible; they also had a number of variations and additions to their basic system. Both the Greeks and the Romans, at various periods, used wool, linen and cotton, leathers and furs too; even silk was known. Silk and cotton were known to the later ancient Egyptians, but their characteristic cloth was linen, woven in varying weights. They had wool too. Their system of dress was likewise based on shapes taken directly from the loom, the men using a short, wrapped loin cloth, and the women a long wrapped sheath; on these basic garments a very varied range of appearance was achieved.[1]

The span of history occupied by these people was vast, and there are still difficulties in establishing details of certain aspects of ancient dress; for example, the origin and uses of knitted garments are still obscure. However, the revised use of the attire of antiquity as it has occurred in England has been dependent less on exact archaeological research than on impressions gained from very diverse sources. Statues, pictorial vases, bronzes, medals or isolated fragments could all play on the imagination, regardless of whether or not they were accurately dated or identified. Regional, historical and social differences within the antique world were of less importance in the revival of the dress than the fact that the basic system of clothing was dramatically unlike the established English one. Indeed, part of the English view of the classical world was a second-hand one, through the already transformed images of the Renaissance; in England in the sixteenth century, for example, a fifteenth-century Italian depiction of Venus or Mars was probably as fascinating and as curious as a first-century original, and no fine distinctions are required when people search the past, consciously or unconsciously, for alternative sorts of dress to express inner needs.

Because the classical past was seen only in partial glimpses, particularly before the advent of readily accessible illustrated books, and often through works of art of great beauty, there was an association of the classical world with a high degree of physical beauty.

2 Health and beauty went hand in hand with classical dress; a traditional association continued in advertising long after dress reformers had ceased trying to convert followers of fashion to the idea.

3 Part of fifteenth-century 'Triumph of Caesar,' The Corselet Bearers, by Mantegna, imported into England by Charles I. Renaissance views of antiquity shaped its other later revivals.

4 Rigidity meant rectitude. The re-shaped body in corset, bustle and frills militated against reformers' attempts to reinstate classical dress. 1873.

This was also confirmed by later Renaissance versions. The great 'Triumph of Caesar' which came to England after being sold to Charles I in 1627, showed a procession of handsome figures in beautifully draped robes, bearing all manner of rich and historical treasures; it was indeed a tempting glimpse into antiquity. It was the product of a Renaissance imagination, that of Andrea Mantegna who did this series of paintings some time during the 1480s and nineties, for the Marchese Gonzaga of Mantua, and it demonstrates the strength of a later vision of antiquity overlaying its original, interpreting it in a new idiom [3].

Whilst looking at the antique world through its own art, or the art of later cultures, the English have also created their own model of it, interpreting it in their own style. For example, in the late sixteenth century, the antique world fused with a pastoral idea, creating an Arcadian past; in Edmund Spenser's *Faerie Queene*, he posed this past as a proper confirmation of Queen Elizabeth's reign:

And thou, O fairest Princess under sky,
In this faire mirrhour maist behold thy face,
And thine owne realmes in lond of Faery,
And in this antique Image thy great aunchestry.[2]

English male education over the centuries has relied heavily on the literature and language of ancient Greece and Rome, and has so woven these cultures

into our own that as much significance is invested in the English response to the classical past, at the level of dress revivals for example, as in that to the English past. Lord Chesterfield, in 1748, warned against the more comical, worse effects of this educational dominance by the classics; he described a species of men 'who have contracted such a familiarity with the Greek and Roman authors, that they call them by certain names or epithets denoting intimacy. As *old* Homer; that *sly rogue* Horace;'[3] Chesterfield advised that a man should wear his learning, like his watch, in his pocket. Women, not usually subject to, or privy to, this style of education, have probably taken to classical types of dressing with less nervousness than men, having less invested, from the point of view of their status, in its cultural background.

Men, however, have never been reluctant to wear classical military garments and armour; for English sculptors and painters it became an established mode for heroes and would-be heroes, and there were male civilian fashions which borrowed various features of imperial-looking Roman armour for ordinary use.

There has been a tendency to resist revivals of full classical dress; spurious arguments about our unsuitable climate often masked concern that these clothes would be too revealing, too immodest, and that women, being traditionally thought of as morally infirm, would be unable to resist the inevitable dangers. A balance or compromise has been the usual solution, so that classical revivals appear as occasional alternatives to normal dress, or as selected features superimposed on it, and as temporary interludes, as for instance a fashionable woman in the 1930s might have worn a closely tailored suit of heavy fabric during the day, but a classically draped gown of satin for an evening occasion. London *Vogue* commented in January 1934: 'We were wrong in thinking speed and practicality the most important demands of the day; the need of variety outweighs them both.'

Organized efforts to reinstate classical dress as a permanent alternative to modern styles have never succeeded on any scale; the reform societies pushed this idea, amongst others, during the second half of the nineteenth century, but gained only partial victories. They were fully aware of the power of fashion: 'We consider the old Greeks the most artistic of nations; but if a lady were sending measurements for a dress for herself, and her proportions were those of an ancient Venus, she would probably be ashamed of them, and would squeeze in her waist to proportions as inartistic as unhealthful, and perhaps use padding to alter her feminine proportions further.'[4]

The revival of rural themes seems a perennial activity, closer to the heart than the question of classical dress and its various advantages, and rural revivals have been part of an unfaltering response to the countryside. In 1667, Samuel Pepys took a trip to the countryside and recounted in his diary on 14 July that a shepherd and his boy, with a flock of sheep on Epsom Downs was 'the most pleasant and innocent sight that ever I saw in my Life.' A hundred years later, in June 1770, when Horace Walpole saw morris dancers outside the window, he leaped up and danced for joy.[5] The anonymous author of *The English Courtier and the Cutrey-gentleman* wrote in 1586 that 'our Country habitacion is more godly, more honourable, more holesome, more quiet, more pleasant and profitable, than it can be in any Cittie or Burrough.' In short, the English have repeatedly affirmed an affection for country life which has had a deep and abiding influence on dress. Throughout the period studied in this book, various expressions of a fond but complex relationship between city and country have found their way into the clothes of fashionable people, despite the fact that England has been remarkable among European countries for its lack of distinctive regional, rural dress. Where rural dress has been assimilated by fashion it has been therefore largely concerned with supposed occupational dress, such as that of foresters or shepherdesses, and not with the local displays of status and style which used to abound in peasant dress elsewhere in Europe.

Rural imagery in fashionable dress almost always associates rusticity with the historical or recent past. Laura Ashley once said that everybody wants to live in the country in the past, and this has probably been so, not just in the twentieth century, but throughout the period covered in this book; at any rate *part of* everybody wants to live in the country in the past. When this association of rural with historical features centres on the notion of a simple past in which people were assumed to be living a better life, to some extent outside current social systems, in other words in Arcadia, it is best described as pastoral rather than merely rural. Innocence has been seen as a characteristic of this Arcadian England. The eighteenth-century poet, William Cowper, mourned those 'golden times,' and expressed the essence of pastoral nostalgia as it has existed from before the sixteenth century to the present; as urban life for us grows more crowded and more violent so this essential idea takes on more meaning.

. . . Innocence it seems
From courts dismiss'd, found shelter in the groves.
The footsteps of simplicity impress'd
Upon the yielding herbage (so they sing)
Then were not all effaced. . . .[6]

Cowper, whilst calling this a 'gay delirium for a truth,' still acknowledged it to be an enviable dream; turning to the inhabitants of the countryside themselves, like so

5 Fashion can recreate a country life. This *Punch* cartoon of 1920 parodies the rural atmosphere thought necessary for fashionable weddings.

many have before and since, he found they did not quite square with the dream:

> . . . The rural lass
> Whom once her virgin modesty and grace,
> Her artless manners and her neat attire
> So dignified, that she was hardly less
> Than the fair shepherdess of old romance,
> Is seen no more. The character is lost.
> Her head adorn'd with lappets pinn'd aloft
> And ribbands streaming gay, superbly raised,
> And magnified beyond all human size,
> Indebted to some smart wig-weaver's hand
> For more than half the tresses it sustains. . . .[7]

In the later eighteenth century Cowper was worried that 'the town has tinged the country;' this concern, and the corresponding nostalgia for a supposed previous age when the town had *not* tainted the country seem to be permanent. If we look back on nineteenth-century life as simpler and closer to Arcadia than our own, we are looking back on people who were also looking back, longing for the golden age *they* supposed to have preceded *them*. In this general survey of five centuries of revived and revised rural dress, the ache for Arcadia plays a formative role.

Inherent in nostalgia for a country life outside the court and the city has been the urban belief that country people possess an enviable capacity for happiness founded on their contact with the seasons and the earth. 'Earthy' has other connotations to add to the image; the city and the gentry attributed a bawdy sensuality to working country people, especially in the spring. Maypoles and morris dancers, or haymaking and harvest-home, all have been seized on by moralists as licentious and dangerous aspects of country life.

Again, constant to the period under review, has been the habit of fashionable people to see the countryside as the cradle or the arena for the sporadic enactment of their various ideals and dreams whilst frequently finding the real inhabitants not merely un-Arcadian, but boorish as well. *The Spectator* commented, in 1711, on the futile efforts of provincial people to attain

6 Nineteenth-century vagrants. Real rural poverty never had a place in fashion's reconstructed Arcadia. Picturesque shepherdesses were preferred.

modishness; if they stayed, said the paper, in unchanging dress and waited for the wheel of fashion to turn their way, they would occasionally, by coincidence, be properly fashionable, instead of always chasing the wrong novelty as at present: 'I could wish, for the sake of my Country friends, that there was such a kind of *everlasting Drapery* to be made use of by all who live at a certain distance from the Town. . . .'[8]

As in most revivals of dress, wishful thinking often clouds the original reality, and current tastes modify those of other eras or places; in looking at rural revivals through the years, it is as if the countryside has been peopled twice over, once with those who work the land, in the brutish historical truth of short lives, dispossession and Enclosure Acts, sweating summers and frozen winters, and then peopled all over again by fashion, with golden lads and lasses, gentle swain piping to their flocks in the valleys and contented milkmaids festooned with flowers in never-ending sunshine. Just as Cowper discerned in the city dweller's spoutless teapot planted with flowers, an ardour for 'a peep at nature,' so dress reveals the same 'inextinguishable thirst of rural scenes.'

In addition to searching for the classical past, and for Arcadia, English dress has also shown a continual taste for the historical past. There has been an endless variety of past styles undergoing revision and revival. In the later 1960s there was a boom in clothes redolent of the Depression years, clothes which provided the longer, softer lines to replace the hard-edged mini which was by then becoming jaded. The focus of a historical style from forty years before helped to direct taste during a period of transition in the dress of both men and women. To Victorian women, Mary Queen of Scots seemed a heroine, and there was a long-lived vogue for having hats, dresses and hoods modelled on those in her portraits. Paintings were an important source of historical images, and these were supplemented by a vigorous output of history paintings from the mid-eighteenth century onwards which sought to recreate past scenes and characters in vivid detail. Much of the Mary Queen of Scots revival was based on later imaginative reconstructions, exhibited at the Royal Academy and elsewhere; these images tended to supersede the few original sixteenth-century

7 Fashionable rustication – beribboned straw hat, a basket of flowers and a walking stick. It was observed that the gentry had *houses* in London but *homes* in the country.

portraits, as popular films seemed to oust original images of the Depression.

The extensive array of such historical revivals in English dress is not surprising if revivals elsewhere are taken into consideration; for example, a partiality for Gothic architecture so strong as to produce a nineteenth-century railway terminus like St Pancras was almost bound to effect more ephemeral items such as dress. Like St Pancras, these shorter-lived products of revived taste could mix styles and features at will. In the 1850s and sixties attention was centred on the width of women's skirts, held out by crinolines, and any Gothic additions had to be superimposed over this central item, despite its incompatibility with the shape of original Gothic dress. In May 1861, the *Englishwoman's Domestic Magazine* demonstrated how a revival may do as it wishes with its original source, for authenticity is not the aim; 'The Tudor, or hat with broad, turned-up brim, will be worn of a rather more elongated shape than it was last summer; it is made in every variety of straw. . . .' Since an individual may have several suits or sets of clothes and change them at least once or twice during the day (this diminishing practice was, until fairly recently, common amongst people of leisure and fashion) it has been possible to wear a variety of styles, exchanging a revival of one historical period for another, being 'early mediaeval' in

8 Popular history painting brought the past to life. Vivacious but not always strictly accurate depictions of historical dress aided its influence and revival in fashion. This scene from the life of Mary Queen of Scots took place in 1566, and was painted in 1833.

the afternoon and 'Tudor' in the evening. In this way at the peak, for instance, of the nineteenth-century's flirtation with history, a fashionable woman's wardrobe might echo the interior of this house: 'Every room is in masquerade. . . . They sleep in Turkish tents, and dine in a Gothic chapel. . . . The mitred chairs and screens of the chapel . . . so very upright and tall, and carved and priestly, were mixed up oddly enough with the squat Chinese bronzes, whilst by some strange transposition a pair of nodding mandarins figured amongst the Egyptian monsters. . . .'[9]

The ability to cast about and pick out carefully chosen samples of past dress and then to modify and mix them at will has produced many inventive, endearing revivals, all illustrative of varying degrees of nostalgia. A writer on Romanticism, in 1802, observed the duality of which we are all conscious: 'As a sentient being man is set as it were in time, however as a spontaneous being he carries time within him, and this means that he can live in the past and dwell in the spirit wherever he pleases.'[10]

In some periods the choice of a past in which to 'live' has inclined more towards antiquity; for instance, although for much of the seventeenth century archaic dress was employed in ceremonial, fashion was chiefly concerned in reviving classical dress. In our own time the past is popular but appears to be revived at rather shorter intervals. This may be an illusion due in part to a division of the market for clothes; up until the end of the Second World War the monopoly was held by the mature age group, and 'teenage' was still a newly imported word, but since then a fragmentation of the market has occurred so that quite distinct groups can be catered for more or less separately; in this way those who were only very young children during the 1960s can enjoy revivals of dress from that period, whilst those who were adult during the same period and have had enough of it can pursue a separate course. It seems likely therefore that historical revivals are not happening in shorter cycles, but that several cycles are revolving simultaneously. There seems no reason why the rate of these cycles should remain constant. What does remain, however, is the fact that no style plucked out of the past and dusted down for a revival will survive its role if it does not conform to the dominant taste of its new owners. It would be a telling exercise to select from the illustrations in this book dress which one simply could not bring oneself to wear for more than a few minutes and to examine the reasons: whilst our choice might be different from one made in the last century, or only a generation or decade ago, our reasons would be just as heartfelt and as un-negotiable as those which have led to one historical style being passed over in favour of another at any period in English dress.

Anyone currently nostalgic for the look of the Edwardian era is probably focusing longingly on the elaborate needle skills which adorned a petticoat or blouse rather than on the bother of keeping a skirt hem free of dirt, and if we wistfully think of a smart Edwardian hat it is likely to be one trimmed with roses rather than the dead stuffed birds so popular then; nor would we wish for the longer working week, or the struggle for suffrage which surrounded those elegant clothes. As Pope said of the fashion for pastoral poetry: 'We must therefore use some illusion to render a Pastoral delightful; and this consists in exposing the best side only of a Shepherd's life, and in concealing its miseries.'[11] We do this, naturally enough, in each of the areas of dress revivals; when exotic dress is in question, we have no need for too much detail of its background or context.

9 Opinions of the past often alter. Clothes such as these from the 1930s seemed drab to fashionable people of the fifties, but in the later sixties and the seventies they were widely revived.

Exotic dress is taken here to include the dress of the rest of the world which is or has been substantially different in construction or shape from that of traditional English dress. A random list of some articles of clothing, fabrics or methods of construction soon indicates how widely and readily we have borrowed: jodhpur, moccasin, poncho, anorak, dirndl, caftan, dungaree, bandana, shawl, pyjamas, khaki, seersucker, cotton, silk, puttee, djibbah, kimono, parka. Not all of these differ in construction from English garments; an anorak in its original sense was made on similar lines to English overgarments, but from warmer parts of the world we have over the centuries helped ourselves gladly to many useful and fresh ideas. By and large, the influences described here centre on the Near, Middle and Far East, and it is from those areas that English men in particular have borrowed the sartorial freedom they were shyly reluctant to take from classical dress. For example, Benjamin Disraeli always had a taste for more flamboyant dress than was wholly acceptable in the London circles he frequented, and he caused

eyebrows to rise by his purple trousers, scarlet waistcoat, black velvet jacket and bright rings worn *over* white gloves;[12] but he could more easily express his true self in dress bought locally on a trip to Egypt in 1830, at the very time when men's dress in England was starting to disown its former colourfulness and to settle into a more uniform primness: 'You should see me in the costume of a Greek pirate. A blood-red shirt, with silver studs as big as shillings, an immense scarf for girdle, full of pistols and daggers, red cap, red slippers, broad blue striped jacket and trousers.'[13] Sadly Disraeli had to return 'properly' dressed to London in the following year.

In England there has been a broad knowledge of what foreigners wore throughout the period under discussion, and it has been based on direct experience relayed or written of by travellers, illustrations in the several books of costume compiled during the sixteenth century,[14] embassies and merchants coming into England, and actual garments and fabrics imported either as collectors' items or on a commercial basis. These various means of knowing about exotic dress have been available since the sixteenth century, but not always commonly or freely so. Our present-day familiarity with the dress of all corners of the world is a recent phenomenon, due in some part to colour photography and to the opening up of previously inaccessible regions. Nevertheless, even when they have had only a partial and uncertain knowledge, the English have been notably curious and enthusiastic about strange dress. They have also translated it easily from one purpose to another; pyjamas, for example, were regular daywear in their native India, but usefully filled a gap in English nightwear; and then by the 1920s they were back in daytime use for women at the seaside and promoted to evening wear at about the same time.

One of the main attractions of oriental dress has been the misguided but tenacious belief that it was not subject to the ceaseless change which afflicted European dress. It was often thought that in the East people had no notion of fashion, and that by wearing the apparently unchanged dress of their ancestors they gained in dignity and commonsense.[15] English use of oriental dress has taken the form of borrowing whole garment constructions or attractive decoration, but has also involved numerous individual cases of the temporary abandonment of English dress altogether in favour of some oriental guise; men in particular have seemed susceptible to this, and not always wholly for the practical reasons they usually declare. There is something altogether more magical: '. . . one will feel oneself projected into another world of being, another age of the earth's history. . . .'[16]

10 In sixteenth-century Europe there was a vogue for costume books, whose fanciful illustrations of foreign clothes helped extend the horizons of English dress. J.-J. Boissard, 1581.

11 Edward Cross, dealer in foreign creatures to George IV – sombre beside the visiting Egyptians. Eastern costume has often been revived by Englishmen glad to escape their suits.

PART I Classical Revivals

12 To entertain a private banquet, Diana with attendants and torch bearers. Music accompanied both processional entry and the subsequent dancing. Such depictions of sixteenth-century masques are rare. *c.*1596.

1 *Of Gods and Goddesses*

THE SIXTEENTH CENTURY

The Elizabethan episode in the long sequence of English revivals and revisions of classical dress depended, like other revivals of the period, on literate and educated circumstances; particularly it was part of court life, often making a sartorial excursion for expressions of faith and delight in Elizabeth herself, and her reign. There were links made with Elizabeth and Astraea,[1] and no doubt Elizabeth was fully alert to the significance of the welcome she received from the city of Norwich in 1578, when at 'an excellent princely maske brought before hir after supper . . . gods and goddesses, both strangely and richly apparelled' complemented her and offered protection and praise. Six musicians and ten torch bearers had marched round the chamber to accompany Mercury, Jupiter, Juno, Mars and Venus and others in the event. '. . . Jupiter spoke to the Queen and presented her with a riding wand of whale's fin curiously wrought.'[2] Juno gave a purse, and at least eight more such offerings were made. Thus Norwich made the monarch welcome, and she was seen to be very well satisfied with their efforts.

Although the exact appearance of the 'richly apparelled' participants is not known, Norwich was exhibiting a fashionable taste echoed in other events of the reign.

In 1560 there had evidently been some difficulty in distinguishing between Greek heroes in a masque dressed by the Office of the Revels for a court occasion, because their names had to be prominently displayed on their garments, not for storage purposes, but obviously for the benefit of the guests. There were six 'longe garments the upper bodies and upper baces of white clothe of siluer stayned with colours and on the backes & brestes the names of hercules Iason percius Pirothus Achilles and Theseus writen.'[3] In Edmund Spenser's *Faerie Queene* (published between 1589 and 1596) a figure portraying Ease, at a masque, had to have his name in golden letters on his robe, but that would have been an understandably difficult portrayal, particularly as he was accompanied by Fancy, Hope, Desyre and others equally abstract. Hercules and Jason have obvious attributes to identify them, but no doubt their names were decoratively applied and added to the spectacle as well. The Hercules-porter figure who greeted the Queen with mock confusion on her arrival at Kenilworth in July 1575 carried a club and keys, and was 'wrapt also all in silke.'[4]

On the occasion of this famous visit, Queen Elizabeth was treated to extremely lengthy and elaborate entertainments and events, and the entire castle and grounds were given over to the recreation of a fantastic miniature kingdom; there was Neptune, and an 18-foot long mermaid popped out of the moat, and there was jousting and a mock rural wedding. Officially it was reported that during the visit, excessively hot weather kept the Queen in her private rooms until late in the day, but it is not unreasonable to guess that she was also sheltering from some of her host's zealously full timetable of 'showes' and 'inventions'; she was clearly expected to exchange words with the various figures. When the Queen and her retinue had first arrived they had been greeted by 'one of the ten Sibills,' who, meeting them at the gates, was 'cumly clad in a pall of white silk.'[5] This comely figure, we can assume, was wholly recognizable to the Queen and her accompanying courtiers; its glimmering appearance was quickly succeeded by the complaining porter 'wrapt also all in silke,' and even before the arrival was completed, the Queen then found herself in conversation with 'the Lady of the Lake, (famous in King Arthurz book) with too Nymphs waiting upon her, arrayed all in sylks.'[6]

The inauguration of this 1575 visit demonstrates something of the range of erudite imagery and often very creative dress available at the time, and also the capacity of an educated, if tired, audience to identify and interpret it. One breathless narrator of the Kenilworth events may perhaps have been over generous about the allocation of silk, but he was obviously searching to describe the unusually loose and flowing garments he saw in and around the castle that July, clothes quite unlike the more familiar mainstream fashions of court or city.

In the second half of the sixteenth century the most sought-after features in male and female fashion were a firm, even harsh outline, sometimes bulbous in sleeves and trunk-hose, padded and extensively garnished and stiffened by embroidery; much taste and pleasure was concentrated in the starchy ruffs, great and small, at the neck and wrists. Decorative use was made of the otherwise functional lacing and points which held parts of suits together. There is mention of a dapper and jaunty tailor in 1592 of a fashionable appearance characterized by restricted movement and an extreme silhouette: he was 'quaintly attired in velvet and sattin, and a cloake of cloth rash, with a cambricke ruffe as smoothly set, and he as neatly spũged as if he had been a bridegrome, only I gest by his pace a farre off he should be a Tailor: his head was holden uppe so pert, and his legges shackle hamd, as if his knees had been laced to his thighes with points.'[7]

Philip Stubbes had earlier singled out ruffs as one of the worse follies of women's dress, in his *Anatomie of Abuses* in 1583. They were of paramount importance to a fashionable outline, and no doubt they were considerable symbols of status: 'Some are wrought with open worke downe to the midst of the ruffe and further; some with close worke, some wyth purled lace so cloied, and other gewgawes so pestered, as the ruff is the least part of its selfe; Sometimes they are pinned

13 Even Juno, Pallas and Venus pale before Elizabeth's power. Using 'antique' dress, in 1569, this closely resembles events put on to entertain the Queen on her Progresses or at court.

upp to their eares, sometimes they are suffered to hang over theyr shoulders, like windemill sailes fluttering in the winde, and thus everyone pleases herselfe in her foolish devises. . . .'[8] Double portraits such as Hans Eworth's 'Frances Brandon and Adrian Stokes' in 1559, or 'Sir John and Lady Mary Harington,' attributed to Custodis in the 1590s, demonstrate that men as much as women enjoyed the 'foolish' ruff. The neck ruff began to sprout rather shyly in the 1540s and was well established by the fifties and sixties; it achieved its deepest and most pneumatic shapes in the 1590s. So entrenched was the taste for extensive neck decoration that over the following twenty years it evolved into spikey, upstanding collars, with or without front openings, sometimes as wide as the shoulders themselves.

As at later periods, the fundamental principles of classical dress did not come easily to the English mainstream taste. The draped, unfitted mode of dress such as the simple 'pall' of soft fabric worn by the welcoming sibyl at Kenilworth in 1575 has been said to be unsuitable for a northern climate, yet in July 1575 there was sweltering heat. Indeed, anyone who has visited Greece in the winter knows that it can be bitterly cold; the ancient Greeks, and the Romans too, has a range of warm fabrics at their disposal, as well as an understanding of the effectiveness of layers of cloth in preserving body heat. But there was more than the insistence about our unsuitable climate ranged against acceptance of such simplicity in dress. An unchanging, economical mode of apparel is not good commercial sense, and was as subject to pressure and ridicule in the sixteenth century as it was in later centuries, and would be today. Clothiers, tailors and other merchants had a strong interest in the continuation of complicated and novel garments for both men and women: 'what Poet hath so many fictions, what Painter so many fancies, as a Taylor hath fashions, to shew the varietie of his art? changing every week the shape of his apparrel into new

14 Simple woodcuts illustrated continental source books of classical imagery used in England during the sixteenth and seventeenth centuries.

forms, or els he is counted a meere botcher.'[9] It was suggested tailors did this not only to create new needs to satisfy, but in order to falsify their bills, for if their clients 'were tyed to one fashion, then stil might they know how much velvet to send to the Taylor, and then would his filching abate.'[10] Undoubtedly commercial interests weighed against any emergent English taste for simplicity in dress outside the experimental and creative possibilities of court events.

So too did strong and stern voices make themselves heard, sometimes from the pulpit, whenever dress looked set to reveal the body, especially the female body.

> It was the mischaunce of a homely maide, that, belike, was but newly crept into the fashion of long wasted peticotes tyde with points, and had, as it seemed, but one point tyed before, and comming unluckily in my way, as I was fetching a leape, it fell out that I set my foote on her skirts: the point eyther breaking or stretching, off fell her peticoate from her waste, but as chance was, thogh hir smock were course, it was cleanely; yet the poore wench was so ashamed, the rather for that she could hardly recover her coate againe from unruly boies, that looking before like one that had the greene sicknesse, now had she her cheekes all coloured with scarlet.[11].

It was Kemp, the actor, on his prodigious dance from London to Norwich in 1599, who stepped on this petticoat, or 'coat' as he also called it, and brought about the confusion. The account conveys something of the Elizabethan sense of appropriate and inappropriate dress, as well as the manner of holding together the substantial parts of a suit of clothes. To people of lesser rank a suit of clothes made of a waistcoat and petticoat were sought-after signs of status and sufficiency; a loose smock or chemise-like garment was not. When the courtiers enjoyed the freedom of such clothes, long, white and loose, at a masque or 'invention,' they were within the confines of their own rank, and distinguished by silk and spangles and other luxury decorations, and could not be confused with the poor. The relative simplicity of the dress of the goddesses in the masque procession in the 'Life of Sir Henry Unton' (*c.*1596), in the National Portrait Gallery, London, is still far grander than the clothes worn by the poor who wait at Sir Henry's gate.

A painting known as 'Elizabeth and the Three Goddesses' was made in 1569 [13] and is attributed to Hans Eworth. It shows considerable inventiveness in the dress of the goddesses, Juno, Pallas and Venus; they, however, have been put to shame by Queen Elizabeth in the role of Paris, who possesses in her own stately presence all of their attributes. In this painting are details of how far sixteenth-century taste wished to embrace classicism in dress. Venus is naked, sitting on her discarded garment which is not a Roman tunic but an exquisite Elizabethan chemise or smock, embroidered and ruffled at the neck and wrists like those of high fashion. Juno and Pallas are, in effect, in contemporary undress, in something of the state of the embarrassed girl who lost her petticoat to Kemp's careless foot. By leaving off the sleeves and skirt, or petticoat, of usual over-dress, they are left with a loose undergarment, or smock, and a stout bodice, but without ruffs; Pallas's bodice has been overlaid with the features of armour. The great floating cloaks fringed and scalloped at the edges, and the loose sleeves of Juno's chemise or smock, would denote antiquity to a sixteenth-century eye, as would the sandals and head-dresses; but it is necessary to look at only the squared necklines of the bodice and armour of Juno and Pallas, and the positions of the lower edges of these garments, to see how classical effects have been expressed within fashionable shapes which echo those of the fully dressed Queen and her attendants on the left. It has been pointed out that the dress of Pallas resembles that described by Sir Philip Sidney, in *Arcadia*, as worn by an Amazon, in that it consists of revealing but rich garments related to those of Italian theatrical designs.[12] If Sidney's words are taken in conjunction with the appearance of both Pallas and Juno, the Elizabethan sense of the classical past begins to emerge: the Amazon's hair was partially

> drawne into a coronet of gold richly set with pearls, and so joined all over with gold wires, and covered with feathers of divers colours, that it was not unlike to a helmet, such a glittering show it bare, and so bravely it was held up from the head . . . a kind of doublet of sky-colour satin, so plated over with plates of massy gold . . . sleeves of the same, instead of plates, was covered with purled lace . . . and the

nether part so full of stuff and cut after such a fashion that . . . one might well perceive the small of the leg which, with the foot, was covered with a little short pair of crimson velvet buskins, in some places open (as the ancient manner was) to show the fairness of the skin. . . .[13]

During Elizabeth's reign a number of illustrated books of costume were published on the continent most of which must almost certainly have been known in England, and which could have provided ideas for a rich range of alternatives to the north European tailored and fitted garment. What these books lacked in accuracy they were able to make up for in imagination, and in addition to the high fashions of urban Europe, they showed Turks, Africans and European peasants in loose, comfortable, unpadded clothes. By their linear and monochromatic engravings, they certainly added to a simplified image. The Ethiopian of Vico,[14] who appeared in Breton as 'la Barbare,' and came back in Ferdinando Bertelli as an Ethiopian again, was shown in a long, unshaped over-robe with fringed edges similar to the painted goddesses of 1569. Similar complex, swept-up hairdressings appear in other books of costume. Vecellio showed Roman dress and also a Chinese original of the kimono, in 1590, thus adding to the range of known options for loose, wrapped forms of dress.

15 Panel, *c.*1600, displays perfect confidence in current ideas of 'antique' dress for men and women. Did 'showes' and masques at court look something like this?

Exoticism and antiquity were fused, and transformed by current taste into a creative form of dress which gave the court or its hosts a wider range than that available in normal dress. The pen portraits in the literature of the period are convincing and detailed; for example, in *Arcadia*:

Pyrocles came out, led by Sympathus, clothed after the Greek manner in a long coat of white velvet reaching to the small of his leg, with great buttons of diamonds all along upon it. His neck, without any collar, not so much as hidden with a ruff, did pass the whiteness of his garments, which was not much in fashion unlike to the crimson raiment our Knights of the order first put on. On his feet he had nothing but slippers which, after the ancient manner, were tied up by certain laces which were fastened under his knee, having wrapped about (with many pretty knots) his naked leg.[15]

He wore a white ribbon rolled round his long hair.

The tone of this, and other literary scenes, suggest familiarity, as well as a likely wish to develop the already imaginative sights seen at courtly enactments of classical scenes; there was a 'showe' of 'Diana and Pallas' in 1564, 'a pastorell of historie of a Greek maide' in 1578, and in 1584 a 'history of Aggmemnon and Ulisses,' put on by the court.[16] Amazons, dressed in

1578 by the Office of Revels, for a particularly elaborate masque, had extremely rich dress, but such that it must have allowed a certain freedom of movement, because after a masque of knights, and some dancing, they had to fight the knights, at the barriers.

Their kirtles were of Crymson cloth of gold being indented at the skirte and Laied with silver Lace and frindge with pendauntes of golde Tassells gold Knobbes and set on with Broches of golde plated uppon the skirte with plates of silver lawne with tassells of gold Laid under belowe in steed of petticotes with white silver rich tincle fringed with golde fringe Buskins of oringe cullor velvet Antick ffawcheons and shieldes with A device painted thereon. . . .[17]

They were accompanied by torch bearers whose long sleeveless gowns were decorated with fringes and tassells. These Amazons were much more elaborately dressed than the Amazon who vanquished the knight in Spenser's *Faerie Queene*; there she had a 'camis light,' or a light shift-like garment, which was, despite its silver and ribbons, practical and 'short tucked for light motion Up to her ham,' but she could wear it down to her feet if she wished.[18]

16 Classical allusions – Lady Chandos in 1589 wore seed pearl embroidery of altars and butterflies. On her breast and left sleeve she put jewelled pendants of mythological figures.

2 *Order in a Sweet Neglect*

THE SEVENTEENTH CENTURY

During the seventeenth century people of fashion developed a widespread taste for revivals of both military and civilian features of the dress of antiquity. By the 1660s a loose, relaxed form of clothing was well enough established to provide fashionable women with a common alternative to the more structured clothing of formal appearances, and came to show elaborate classical detail [17]. By the seventies men were seen portrayed in varying degrees of classical dress, from full armour with imperial overtones [see colour plate of James II] to rather senatorial details such as a pseudo-toga and tunic. These revivals allowed both men and women appearances which were previously confined to the depiction of mythological figures in painting or in masquing [55]; for instance, Sir Peter Lely's portrait of Jane Bickerton, Duchess of Norfolk, done in the late 1670s, or his slightly earlier

17 Roman dress evoked, *c.*1670, by jewelled bodice resembling armour, with girdled sleeves, raised waist and elaborate hair ornament (compare with 'The Tichborne Dole," Plate 19).

portrait of Diana Kirke, Countess of Oxford, show a type of voluminous, billowy *deshabillé* which had been seen a hundred years earlier in Hans Eworth's 1570 'Allegory of the Wise and Foolish Virgins,' worn, significantly, by the foolish virgins.

By 1648, in his famous poem *Delight in Disorder*, Robert Herrick had observed the predeliction for soft meandering lines in women's dress [18] which was to become one of the hallmarks of seventeenth-century fashion.

A sweet disorder in the dresse
Kindles in cloathes a wantonnesse:
A Lawne about the shoulders thrown
Into a fine distraction:
An erring Lace, which here and there
Enthralls the Crimson Stomacher:
A Cuffe neglectfull, and thereby
Ribbands to flow confusedly:
A winning wave (deserving Note)
In the tempestuous petticote:
A carelesse shooe-string, in whose tye
I see a wilde civility:
Doe more bewitch me, then when Art
Is too precise in every part.

18 A sweete disorder in the dresse *c.*1637.

The relative restraint in fashionable dress which had prevailed in the previous century and at the start of the seventeenth century, partially sustained by affection for embroidery and its display in both male and female dress, did not suddenly recede; the later versions of classical dress were arrived at by gradual change, and formality in high fashion remained, literally, tight-laced [19]. However, even a queen could eventually find occasion to be seen in the freedom of an antique style. It is interesting to compare the portrait, painted in *c.*1685, of Mary of Modena [20] with a painting of more than a hundred years earlier [13], in which Elizabeth I remained stiffly dressed in great formality, whereas Juno and Pallas wear costume very close in spirit of that of Mary, wife of James II. Something of the changes which brought about the new notions of propriety which Mary's portrait manifests can be seen in masques and pageants of the earlier part of the century; vehicles of entertainment such as these were often most indicative of change because they provided an outlet for imaginative experiment and fantasy which was denied in the normal routine of life.

Late Elizabethan masquing dress seems to have been quite fluid already; in the procession in Sir Henry Unton's house [12] the masquers have let their hair down, and it flows in bright and probably artificial abandon down their backs. At the end of the century Francis Bacon had said of masques and triumphs: 'As for rich embroidery, it is lost and not discerned. Let the suits of the masquers be graceful, and such as become the person when the vizards are off. . . .'[1] When Ben Jonson wrote in 1606 of the masque of Hymena, he celebrated the spectacle of luxury combining with grace and ease in dress and, incidentally, acknowledged the role of statuary in providing models for this sort of garb: 'The manner of their habits came after some statues of Juno, no less airy than glorious. The dressings of their heads rare; so likewise of their feet: and all full of splendor, sovereignty and riches.'[2]

The impact of imported classical images helped to promote a taste already seeking expression in masques. Nowhere is the contrast between early seventeenth century fashion and classical statues more dramatically evident than in a portrait of the Earl of Arundel, done about the year 1618 [21] in which the seated Earl points our attention to part of his collection of statues, some of which he had imported from Italy in 1614. They stand in various types of draped clothing, in unfettered, graceful poses whilst the Earl sits gravely in sombre tailored garb as Earl Marshal with a heavy fur-lined robe, and a deep ruff entirely hiding his neck, and

19 Gentry, their servants and tenants, 1670. In contrast to classical revivals the Tichborne family (in the middle) display more conventional high fashion of the time. Sir Henry (centre foreground) and others in the new knee-length English or 'Persian' vest.

20 Mary of Modena (1658–1718) wife of James II, in 'antique' mood *c.*1685 created by fringed sleeves, clasped bodice and burgeoning chemise. Elizabeth I had left such exposure to goddesses only, see Plate 13.

21 The Earl of Arundel (1585–1646) travelled in Italy with Inigo Jones. His imported classical statues at Arundel House emphasize the grace of draped clothing for both sexes. *c.*1618.

elaborate thick-soled shoes. A commentator noted that it was to Arundel's pioneering collection that England 'oweth the first sight of Greek and Roman statues, with whose admired presence' he adorned his property, and continued 'to transplant old Greece into England.' Charles I was also a major patron of art and 'hath amply testified a royal liking of ancient statues by causing a whole army of old foreign emperors, captains, and senators all at once to land on his coasts, to come and do him homage and attend him in his palaces. . . .'[3]

At a period of transitional taste, statues such as these offered solid original evidence of attractive alternatives to English traditional clothing, and added considerably to the possibilities in dress and art. Interestingly, by the end of the century it was possible unaffectedly to prescribe antique statues as aids for developing a proper dress sense: '. . . shew young Girls the Noble simplicity which appears in the Statues and in the other Figures which remain of the *Greek* and *Roman* women where they would see how Hair negligently ty'd behind, and draperies full, and carelessly hanging are agreeable and Majestick.'[4]

In the costume designs of Inigo Jones these new options became evident as they developed during the first half of the century; Jones was active in providing masque costume and scene designs from 1605 to 1640, during which years he travelled in Italy with the Earl of Arundel, in the forefront of new exploration of classical and Italianate taste. Source books were used by Jones: such as Valeriano's *Hieroglyphica* and Ripa's *Iconologia*, and the costume book of Vecellio. Using this background of classical sources, Inigo Jones produced designs, for example, for Ben Jonson's *Masque of Queenes* of 1609, in which twelve great queens of antiquity appeared in appropriate dress. The Countess

22 Costume design, 1609, for the Duchess of Derby by Inigo Jones. Raised skirts allowed dancing. Unlike formal dress, tiered, fringed hems and short sleeves denoted antiquity. Courtiers participated in masques rather than professional actors.

23 Interpretation of classical dress by Inigo Jones for a masque at court. Perhaps in imitation of half-draped antique statues.

of Derby was Zenobia [22], and the sketch for her dress demonstrates the extension of fashionable features into a much freer style than would have been usually seen at court or in high fashion. The waist and the hairline remained true to current expectations (these two facets of taste are seldom changed by even the most exotic intentions of wearer or designers); but both under- and overskirt were raised to facilitate dancing, and over both a shorter, open vest or coat was put, with a fringed hem. Fringed or scalloped edges had been well established by this time as antique features. This outer garment and the bodice were draped with extra lengths of cloth, festooned into shapes reminiscent of a wrapped stola. Long and closely fitted sleeves were retained, and shoes, but the splendid head-dress outweighed these features of ordinary seventeenth-century dress by its height and splendour. The impression was of a more vertical and free-falling use of fabric than that seen in high fashion, and of an appearance calculated to look at its best during any movement or dancing.

In the drawing of an unnamed lady masquer [23] Jones achieved a startling effect of freedom and airy lightness. The revival of the nudity or semi-nudity of classical statuary to this degree was not acceptable to everyone. The unfortunate William Prynne published his *Histriomastix* in 1632, and for suggesting a lack of decorum on the Queen's part in even appearing in masques he received an incredible combination of punishments. His objections to the idea of women dancers and performers were common amongst Puritans; perhaps if they had seen some of the designs of Inigo Jones they would have felt their fears confirmed. Thomas Fuller's 1648 description of a harlot was in one sense certainly also applicable to this lady masquer: '. . . she is commonly known by her whorish attire; as crisping and curling, making her hair as winding and intricate as her heart, painting, wearing naked breasts.'[5]

The last Inigo Jones designs, for the 1640 *Salmocida Spolia*, featured the Queen Henrietta Maria as an Amazon. She was seen in a more fitted costume than the previous examples, but one intended to suggest the Amazonian arms and armour. Distinct from usual dress, this antique impression was mainly achieved by a short, fringed overskirt. In this dress the Queen descended and danced with the King; 'The Queen's Majesty and her ladies were in Amazonian habits of carnation, embroidered with silver, with plumed helms, bandrickes with antique swords hanging by their sides, all as rich as might be, but the strangeness of the habits was most admired.'[6] King Charles, on this occasion, wore a silver embroidery, long white stockings, and a silver cap decorated with gold scrolls and plumes of white feathers.

Within the coterie of the court, revived classical dress for men and women was a fairly frequent sight in these years; it was developed and exploited by Inigo Jones in particular, who refreshed such imagery by his classical taste and Italian inspiration. Ordinary people, unless they were part of the workforce employed to make up and decorate these fanciful clothes, would more likely have based their idea of classical dress on the evocations seen in the Lord Mayor's pageants. In these annual events considerable effects were produced: 'Orpheus, habited in a silk robe striped with many colours, his shoulder adorned with a large scarf of cloth of gold, on his head a long and crispy hair, invested with a Caesar's wreath of laurel, all the leaves tip'd with gold; in his hands a lyre with strings of gold . . . on his legs are buskins, laced with silver, after the Roman mode. . . .'[7] The nineteenth-century costume historian, F.W. Fairholt, who edited the collection of reprints from which this extract is taken, would have thoroughly disapproved of a Greek wearing anything after the Roman mode, but in the seventeenth century the spirit of this sort of revival mattered more than authenticity, and these annual pageants, or the court masques, produced a bevy of imaginative evocations of classical themes.

Male fashion made use of military aspects in this revival. The grand portrait of James II when Duke of York [see colour plate] probably painted in the early 1670s, shows this use taken to its furthest extreme. When compared with men's more ordinary wear [19], the conversion of Roman into English taste becomes clear; James retained his full head of hair, probably a wig, to the same length as that being worn in the Tichborne Dole; his moulded lorica (trunk armour) had a sash, as worn by three of the gentlemen, and the boys, in the Dole picture, and his tunic, beneath his shorter imitation pleated-leather doublet, was worn to just above the knee, only fractionally shorter than the coats and vests of the day. James magnificently combined the fashionable stance and cane with a splendid over-mantle draped across his body rather like a toga, although the long train behind him had modern stately overtones. This rich mix of past and present was further compounded by the contrast between the pseudo-Roman armour and the suit of English armour lying at James's feet (the helmet, carried by his page,

24 As English field armour was reduced for speed and agility during the seventeenth century, so coincidentally the taste for decorative imitation Roman armour spread. Here James II's cuirass (1686) has proof mark over the heart. One riding gauntlet only, other hand set free for using a weapon.

was for the Roman suit). This English armour was by the 1670s obviously old-fashioned, and closer in date to the suits worn at earlier tournaments. In the portrait, James was seen in pseudo-Roman buskins of great splendour, and above them, most un-Roman, curtailed green stockings edged with gold. There is something about the inclusion of these improbable nether garments to support the argument that James's ensemble was real and not wholly the product of the painter's imagination. The figures in the background display a mixture of Roman and English armour.

James's own modern armour [24] shows that by the time he was king, in 1686, it was thought necessary in the interests of speed and efficiency to combine heavy protection with the much more flexible protection of leather garments; there is only one riding gauntlet, to leave the right hand free for using a weapon.

Male dress used these revived features in various ways always trimming them to contemporary taste, and usually in a less grandiose manner than in James's portrait. Sir Peter Lely's portrait of Sir Thomas Isham, painted in the 1670s, shows an example. A portrait of the 2nd Earl of Rochester [25] shows a more partial use of Roman features, in which the lace cravat was retained, and so too were the long, full shirt sleeves with lace cuffs. The loose drapery which disguises the exact nature of the body of the costume suggests deliberate vagueness on the painter's part, in an attempt to achieve a compromise between the modern and the antique. There is surviving costume to indicate that the armour costume worn by James could well have been real,[8] and portraits such as that of the Earl of Rochester are useful in indicating just how widespread the taste was, and how painters played a major role in promoting such appearances, real or otherwise.

A further use of classical dress was the creation of what came to be known as a civil vest; that is, of civilian rather than military origin. This was a tight-fitting vest, or, in modern terms, a knee-length jacket, fastened only at wide intervals at the centre front; wrist-length sleeves were similarly held together and revealed, like the centre front, a generous amount of loose undershirt. Over such a vest, or jacket, a full cloak or mantle was allowed to drift, an echo of the toga over the tunic of Roman civilians, or senators. Sir Peter Lely's portrait of the Cotton family [26], done in 1660, shows a male version. This clasping of sleeve or bodice seams together at strategic intervals was also a feature of women's loose pseudo-antique dress as the Lely portrait also shows, and was a variant of the slashing method of displaying chemises or shirts. It can be seen elsewhere in the same artist's work in, for example, the *c.* 1651 portrait of Elizabeth Murray, Countess of Dysart, or that of the Perryer family painted in 1655. The style developed from these simple versions of the 1650s and sixties, becoming more elaborate, and going out of fashion at about the end of the century.

25 Roman dress with a cravat and a full-length periwig, *c.* 1665–70. The Earl of Rochester, poet, was also noted as a dissolute courtier.

In 1667 Pepys noted how much he admired the appearance of an actress 'come out in her night-gown with no locks on, but her bare face and hair only tied up in a knot behind; which is the comeliest dress that ever I saw her in to her advantage.'[9] The same woman had appeared at a gathering of friends, Pepys noted, 'undressed.'[10] This was not to say she was naked, but that she was not formally dressed on either occasion, and it is this informal garb which came to display many classical features. In the 1630s van Dyck had painted Lady Venetia Digby posthumously as Prudence, a portrait in which a billowing shift and mantle buckled over the bust were placed in an allegorical setting.

Such settings were not always required; the pseudo-classical undress was to become a commonplace studio portrait dress, and Horace Walpole was later to call such costume in Sir Peter Lely's portraits 'a sort of fantastic night-gowns [sic], fastened with a single pin.' After this painter died in 1680, numerous pieces of silk and satin and whole garments were in his studio, and subsequently sold to other portrait painters; it is certainly clear that painters did often impose, by these aids, a loosely draped effect onto their willing sitters, in order, they thought, to avoid the most immediate effects of dating.

26 All the family in variations of the antique sleeve, 1660.

It is also the case that such dress was frequently worn in reality. In Pepys' diary we read of the occurrence of undress or nightgowns in social life. Evelyn, too, noted in 1671 that the lady who was to become the Duchess of Portsmouth 'was for the most part in her undresse all day.'[11] This style of dressing was equated here with unconventional and permissive behaviour, as it also may well have been when worn by the women known as the Windsor Beauties, in Sir Peter Lely's series of paintings from the 1660s.

Roman masque dress for men towards the end of the century had developed much more demanding detail and complex display than was evident in the easier 'undress' styles worn at home. For *Calisto*, a court masque in 1675, Roman habits had become an excuse for rich ornamentation, including a green-and-scarlet colour scheme garnished with gold fringe and helmets adorned with jewels, spangles and feathers. Sea gods had green breeches embroidered all over with red pearls.

3 *Simplicity and Freedom*

THE EIGHTEENTH CENTURY

Thou, who with hermit heart
Disdain'st the wealth of art,
And Gands and pageant weeds and trailing pall:
But com'st a decent maid
In Attic robe arrayed,
O chaste unboastful nymph, to thee I call!

William Collins (1721–59), *Ode to Simplicity*

By the first decade of the eighteenth century a new factor had emerged in women's dress: the hoop, which established a firm and conical outline, precluding free-flowing lines. It looked set to prevent any future moves towards a classical simplicity, for it had a strong and persistent hold on popular taste. Taste such as this, and its eventual conflict with the naturalness and simplicity of dress in the second half of the century, illustrated a typical pattern in historical attitudes to signs of loosening up of firmly structured dress for both sexes: when moral values have merged with sartorial values, any changes can be met with resentment or regret.

The hoop was a petticoat, an underskirt slotted around with whalebone or other concentric stiffeners from the waist to the ankle. Briefly, in mid-century it was replaced by bulky petticoats without extra structuring, but understructure returned in the fiercer shape of paniers or baskets, or pads of various materials, laced round the waist and resting on the hips. Although shallow, these understructures were often enormously wide, but viewed from the side, the skirt might only be a little wider than the bodice. These understructures sought, one way and another, to enlarge the span of the skirt and to present fine cloth or embroidery to advantage, and, by contrast, to emphasize a small waist and even smaller feet. On these devices centred much of the discussion of the nature of beauty and utility, issues which have been at the heart of English prevarication about classical attributes in their dress. The eighteenth-century form of this discussion illuminates that of other periods. Despite the fact that the fanciful, voluminous dress so beloved by a previous generation could hardly have been convenient or utilitarian, its looseness and apparent lack of understructure must have helped, by comparison, to make hooped skirts seem both grotesque and chaste, according to the point of view. Hoops meant that: 'a vivacious damsel cannot turn herself round in a room a little inconsiderately without oversetting everything like a whirlwind; stands and tea-tables, flower-pots, China-jars, and basins innumerable, perish daily by this spreading mischief, which, like a Comet, spares nothing that comes within its sweep. Neither is this fashion more ornamental than convenient. Nothing can be imagined more unnatural, and consequently less agreeable.'[1]

Others considered that anything restraining vivacious girls from inconsiderate activity was to be applauded; it was observed that the hoops beneath a robe were similar to the Elizabethan farthingale, and that contemporary prudes even boasted 'while they were in that circle, they were secure from temptation, nay, some of them have presumed to say it gave them all the chasity of that heroic Princess. . . .'[2] The same writer, critical of prudes, referred to the stay, or corset, as 'female armour,' and 'void of all grace and an enemy to beauty.'

Despite their critics, hoops, paniers and stays became so firmly established as a prerequisite of tasteful femininity, that women abandoning them towards the end of the century were open to charges of immorality. Hoops remained as court dress for longer than in

27 Many sorts of dress visible in St James's Park and the Mall, *c.*1745, foreign and English, rich and poor.

normal fashion, and so were associated with probity and formality. Gradually they fossilized, and eventually were viewed as an escape into a picturesque and quaint world embodying former values of elegance. It was on 24 May 1820 that *The Times* notified its readers of the official ending of the style for ladies attending court functions; two days later it added that hoops had been 'long felt very inconvenient.' They had certainly been at strange and often comical odds with the early nineteenth-century taste for high-waisted, close-skirted dresses, but their splendour outweighed their inconvenience, and it was only just over thirty years later that concentric hoops reappeared in the artificial crinolines of the 1850s.

The following description indicates clearly not only the problems of the fossilized hoops in the neo-classical era, but also exemplifies the splendour accompanying any court event at the time, whose characteristics were precisely those which the supporters of classical and natural dress would have to counteract: in February 1818, it took the American Ambassador and his party about three-quarters of an hour to ascend a staircase glittering with the participants at a Drawing Room for the aging Queen Charlotte's birthday; he greatly enjoyed 'the fanciful attitudes which the hoops occasioned, some getting out of position as when in Addison's time [in government a hundred years' before] they were adjusted to shoot a door; the various costumes of the gentlemen as they stood pinioning their elbows, and holding in their swords; the common hilarity, from the common dilemma.' To one who had never attended a function which required such rich and archaic dress, the sight in the Drawing Room itself was spectacular:

28 Hoops were worn at court until 1820 and spoiled the short-bodied, neo-classical line. This court dress, 1807, has 'Tudor' collar and sleeves.

Then the hoops! I cannot describe these. They should be seen. To see one is nothing. But to see a thousand – and their thousand wearers! I afterwards sat in the Ambassadors' box at a coronation. That sight faded before this. Each lady seemed to rise out of a gilded little barricade, or one of silvery texture. This, topped by her plume, and the 'face divine' interposing, gave to the whole an effect so unique, so fraught with feminine grace and grandeur, that it seemed as if a curtain had risen to show a pageant in another sphere. It was brilliant and joyous.[3]

So hoops, once a ridiculed novelty, were part of a fetching pageant. In between they had varied and modified, fostering the required appearance of width and bulk; they had been overlaid with all manner of ornament, and festooned and draped: 'her petticoat was black velvet embroidered with chemille, the pattern a *large stone vase* filled with *ramping flowers* . . . it was a most laboured piece of finery, the pattern much properer for a stucco staircase than the apparel of a lady – a mere shadow that tottered under every step she took under the load.'[4]

From elaboration and abundance such as this in women's dress, a new, daring version of classical dress emerged to dominate fashion from about 1780 to the 1820s. It gained surprisingly rapid hold, given that the previous dominant taste was so opposite, and by the turn of the century even those ladies who sought to display great rank or wealth outside court functions would choose to do so within the relative restraint of neo-classical taste.

For the principles of relative simplicity and freedom of movement to be established, the long-standing notion that 'armoured' dress for women was more chaste and more dignified had to be dispelled. When William Hogarth (1697–1764) painted women in states of undress to signify bawdiness or boudoir dramatics in the middle of the eighteenth century, their clothes were not so different from those worn by fashionable women of impeccable reserve at the turn of the century (compare the unhooped Countess in the fifth scene of Hogarth's 'Marriage à la Mode' with Plate 31). Hogarth approved of simplicity in dress, in other circumstances: in his *Analysis of Beauty* of 1753, he advocated it as a

29 Female form was effectively disguised by hoops which were bothersome when seated (see top right). Busy milkmaid has no hoop and brings her cows to her customers. *c.*1745. (Detail of Plate 27.)

necessary restraint to the need for variation in external decoration; in this book he also observed the process which was, after his death, to facilitate a simplicity in high fashion he could hardly have dreamed of: 'How gradually does the eye grow reconciled even to a disagreeable dress, as it becomes more and more the fashion, and how soon return to its dislike of it, when it is left off, and a new one has taken possession of the mind? – so vague is taste, when it has no solid principles for its foundation!'

Hogarth spoke up for simplicity as part of his scheme of perfect beauty; others did so because they felt a need to alter contemporary attitudes in which artificial and restrictive dress seemed an expression of more generally debased values. What Jean-Jacques Rousseau had to say on the subject encapsulates fragments of the arguments made by others both in France and England. In 1762 he published *Emile* in France, in which he not only condemned contemporary dress but he firmly established ancient Greece as the source of solutions to the problem of fashion. In this book and its framework of an alternative educational system, he asserted several novel ideas later to become routine, not least because Rousseau successfully married reactionary sexual rules with simplicity in female dress: he 'proved' that the release of the body, from stays and hoops, need not necessarily release anything else. (The Victorian dress reformers very much wanted this to be believed.) In arguing that nature and reason both prescribe a retired domestic life for women, Rousseau used the women of ancient Greece as examples of this pattern of life, and contrived to connect their virtue with their clothes:

> . . . their flowing garments, which did not cramp the figure, preserved in men and women alike the fine proportions which are seen in their statues. These are still the models of art, although nature is so disfigured that they are no longer to be found among us. The Gothic trammels, the innumerable bands which confine our limbs as in a press, were quite unknown. The Greek women were wholly unacquainted with those frames of whalebone in which our women distort rather than display their figures. It seems to me that this abuse, which is carried to an incredible degree of folly in England, must sooner or later lead to the production of a degenerate race. . . . Everything which cramps and confines nature is in bad taste; this is as true of the adornments of the person as of the ornaments of the mind.[5]

For Rousseau, and others who advocated reform, the classical past shone brightly with solutions to contemporary problems. *Emile* contains many examples of past art and life held up as models for present life, and like his predecessors, and successors such as the dress reform groups of the later nineteenth century, Rousseau seemed inclined to think that all an individual had to do to get rid of artificiality or fashion was to cross fingers and wish. 'The love of fashion is contrary to good taste. . . .'[6] 'If a young girl has good taste and a contempt for fashion, give her a few yards of ribbon, muslin, and gauze, and a handful of flowers, without any diamonds, fringes, or lace, and she will make herself a dress a hundredfold more becoming than all the smart clothes. . . .'[7] 'Good is always good, and as you should always look your best, the women who know what they are about select a good style and keep to it, and as they are not always changing their style they think less about dress than those who can never settle to any one style.'[8]

In these statements, Rousseau marked out beliefs which have often accompanied English interest in forms of classical dress at different periods; these are that a domestic life is woman's chief role, and it will incline her towards 'proper' dress because it not only raises her morally, but it restricts her access to the follies of pleasure-seeking women. Much of the concern expressed about women's dress stems from anxiety at shifting lifestyles and sexual patterns and 'proper' dress is seen as having a protective role to play for a sex supposedly lacking in moral muscle. There has also been a vigorous belief that fashion is bad, any fashion, just because it is fashion. It has also often been argued that the natural state of dress is simplicity, but obviously the later eighteenth century *fashionable* idea of simplicity belies Rousseau's attempts at timelessness! Muslin and gauze, ribbon and a few flowers—he could hardly have chosen more apposite components for a child's modish ensemble. In addition to these sometimes conflicting beliefs was the idea that any decent, reliable woman with scruples would demonstrate, even advertise, these characteristics by finding a becoming but simple style of dress and sticking to it ever after. In conjunction with concern for the unhealthy physical effects of tight stays or corsets, these various ideas have accompanied or perhaps caused the successive flirtations with classical modes in English dress.

Another eighteenth-century response to classicism in dress was that of artists: Sir Joshua Reynolds, for example, who between 1769 and 1790 as President of the Royal Academy delivered a series of lectures in which he asserted amongst other ideas that the ancients offered proper models of study in all forms of art. In his seventh lecture, given in 1776, he acknowledged their influence on taste in dress and sculpture:

> As Greece and Rome are the fountains from whence have flowed all kinds of excellence, to that veneration which they have a right to

30 Connoisseurs discuss points of antiquity amongst Charles Towneley's fine collection of original classical art. Neo-classical taste in dress was encouraged by such sights. *c.*1781–3.

31 'Classical' dress in artistic mood, 1793. Simple, soft, short-waisted gown and natural hair *à l'antique*. The painter has signed her own name on the classical-style brooch.

claim for the pleasure and knowledge which they have afforded us, we voluntarily add our approbation of every ornament and every custom that belonged to them, even to the fashion of their dress. For it may be observed that, not satisfied with them in their own place, we make no difficulty of dressing statues of modern heroes or senators in the fashion of the Roman armour or peaceful robe; we go as far as hardly to bear a statue in any other drapery.

Reynolds suggested among other reasons for our liking their dress, 'we may justly rank the simplicity of them, consisting of little more than one single piece of drapery, without those whimsical capricious forms by which all other dresses are embarrassed.' In the same lecture he pointed out that the professor of anatomy at the Academy had very recently proved how destructive 'to health and long life' was the English ladies' habit of strait lacing. In his 1784 lecture, Reynolds admonished his students 'never to lose sight of nature.'

The progression towards simpler dress for men and women was at first accompanied by similar ideals and tastes in other fields, and from about 1790 onwards dress can be seen as a full partner in the wider movement towards the antique and the picturesque, the whole to be later known as neo-classicism. Dress from the neo-classical era of taste could perhaps better be designated by borrowing the architectural terms of Romantic Classicism, for it did not stem solely from a concern for the antique world; it was overlaid in England particularly with elements from romantic and picturesque notions. There were of course many people who wore this dominant style with no sense of its wider connotations; a man's interest in antiquity might merely be limited to his barber's recommendation of a hairstyle *à la* Brutus.

In the sense that classicism became the dominant and principal style of fashion, this period is unlike any other in English fashion. Classicism was not adopted as a minority expression of dissatisfaction with mainstream style, for it was the mainstream style; nor was it solely a result of the artificial and painstaking efforts at reconstruction so characteristic of the reformers' classical dress of the 1880s and after. If the progressive steps towards an eventual dress equivalent to Romantic Classicism are set out, it becomes clear that the characteristics associated with the style grew from seeds sown several decades earlier. Their effect was cumulative, a relentless modification towards simplicity; the details are worth reiterating because they demonstrate a mechanism of modification common to many otherwise apparently isolated changes in fashion at any period.

Simplicity first dominated the clothes of children and young girls [94], who frequently wore pale or white dresses, plain but for a wide sash of soft colour at the waist. Such plainness was typical of the 1760s and can be seen in striking contrast to the dress of fashionable adults in such portraits as that of the Byan family, about 1764, and the Countess of Sussex and her niece, done in 1771, both pictures by Thomas Gainsborough. (Gainsborough's career spanned the change in question almost exactly. He lived from 1727 to 1788 and in his portraits, always sensitive to nuance in dress, the steps towards simplicity and softness can be conveniently charted.)

In women's dress, attention gradually rose from the narrow waist set low into swelling hooped skirts, towards the bust. The process began with a shortening bodice overlaid and softened with muslin, often seen in the 1760s, and then the broad sash which was taken from children's dress, and widely adopted by women by the later seventies, blurred the waist of the bodice beneath – attention focused on the top edge of the sash, and so accustomed the eye to a line high under the bust. In addition, the use of scarves or large handkerchieves, often of frilled muslin, tied crossways across the bust kept the attention there and on the upper arms, and was seen in chemise gowns of the 1770s and eighties. Even at their most popular, it is known that hoops had frequently been dispensed with when women were at home, and the nightgown, a loose, relaxing dress for informal wear at home maintained, in private at least, the sense of relaxation in clothes. Men, too, had become accustomed to their house gowns providing a less cluttered sensation than normal day wear.

As a popular fabric, muslin helped to create a softer and lighter appearance for women, and the fashion for aprons, especially narrow ones inserting a long shape from waist to floor, often of frail fabrics, accustomed the eye to the possibility of more slender shape.

There was, therefore, every indication that a taste for slimmer and plainer clothes was to emerge; the convergence of this inclination with classicism in other forms resulted in a style with a strong grip for thirty years or so, and with every possible reinforcement from architects, furniture makers, sculptors, painters and others involved in the neo-classical environment. Indeed, though such revealing clothes were not widespread in England until the 1790s they had been seen amongst the early *cognoscenti* of *le gout grec* in Paris three decades before: 'She immediately flung herself carelessly into an Elbow Chair, almost half reclined, with one leg thrown over the Knee of the other, and so she sat for 2 or 3 Hours; and being without Stays, in the loose, easy and negligent Dress of the French Women, she had more the Appearance of a Person just got out of Bed, with a Night Gown flung hastily over her, than a Person dressed to make a Visit in an Evening. However, her Company was very entertaining, and her Conversation spirited and agreeable. . . .'[9]

In England in that year, 1765, such a sight was unlikely in equivalent circumstances. Even by 1791 when Catherine Hutton was describing from Birmingham the new high-waisted dresses, she suggested they were still something sufficiently novel to warrant a detailed account and the subsequent revelation of more of the female form, bitterly complained of later, was evidently not a noticeable feature: '. . . the most elegant women . . . wore dark silk bodies, with long sleeves, and gauze skirts over white. Their gowns came very high over the shoulders and sides of the bosom; and instead of neckerchiefs they had only lace tuckers, standing up all round. They had sashes of black velvet sparkling with steel, and worn, not round the waist, but over the shoulder.'[10]

Although Catherine Hutton elsewhere considered the beau monde to be less elegant than in the past, she took the new short-bodiced style seriously, and captured the essential focus on the shoulders and bust. Short sleeves were later very common, revealing most of the arm. The new style, however, met with ridicule and disapproval in some quarters; the gown was associated with lack of morality or common sense. Many novel fashions come in for a share of criticism usually based on follies of inconvenience or expense, but at the end of the eighteenth and beginning of the nineteenth centuries, the critical focus was on the immodesty and permissiveness which the high-waisted gown was thought to encourage. It is as if the critics needed women to be tightly laced and safely hooped in order to believe their behaviour was also acceptably circumscribed; unlike Rousseau, they thought the control of firm and bulky clothes would compensate for the assumed lack of inner control, and women without these visible sartorial restraints, in the novel clothes inspired by Romantic Classicism, were often subject to gross caricaturization or charged with all sorts of folly. In a popular ballad from 1801, Miss Sally hankered after the new vogue:

The mother surpriz'd, only thought it a jest,
Saying 'Sally, your old fashion'd gown fits you best,
So leave this new fashion to folks in the town,
And don't waste your cloth in a short body'd gown.'

'O mother, you are a bad judge of the size,
The length that it takes, it would you surprize,
For the breadth of the waste is three inches all round;
That's just the full size of a short body'd gown' . . .

Both maids, wives, and widows, you'd think were all wild,
And all look as if they were got with child;
Neither baloons, nor turbans, or all fashions round,
Will fit them, unless they've a new body'd gown.[11]

The new tubular look did allow some women to dispense with the more obvious stays of the seventeen hundreds, but corsets or stays continued to be worn by many. As the waist rose so too did the restrictive whale boning, a restriction far more unpleasant as a narrow band high up the ribcage than a deeper undergarment

32 Cruikshank mockingly anticipated the final, over-ornate phase of neo-classical dress. 1818.

reaching to the natural waist. Inside the small bodice was often a far stouter construction than the flimsy appearance of some gowns would suggest, and art was required to aid nature: as the purer classical styles began to wane, in 1813 Jane Austen observed: 'I learnt from Mrs Tickars's young lady, to my high amusement, that the stays now are not made to force the bosom up at all; *that* was a very unbecoming, unnatural fashion. I was really glad to hear that they are not to be worn, so much off the shoulders as they were.'[12]

These artificial and firm versions of what had earlier been called female armour were ignored by the critics, who might have considered them the saviours of respectability. Largely ignored too were the expensive fabrics, bejewelled turbans, impossibly minute slippers: the possibility of the female form's revelation, if only its arms and a suggestion of the legs, was enough to occupy the conservative observers. However, to those who enjoyed clothes and style there was a sense of relief in rejecting old modes; in 1807 Malcolm noted in his book *Anecdotes of Manners* that dress was definitely improved:

The Ladies have at length, much to their honour, thrown aside those hateful attempts to supply Nature's deficiencies or omissions, the false breasts, pads, and bottoms; and now appear in that native grace and proportion which distinguishes an Englishwoman: the Hair, cleansed from all extraneous matter, shines in beautiful lustre carelessly turned round the head in the manner adopted by the most eminent Grecian sculptors; and the Form appears through their snow-white draperies in that fascinating manner which excludes the least thought of impropriety. Their Hats and Bonnets of straw, chip and beaver, are generally well-proportioned and handsome; and their velvet Pelisses, Shawls, and silk Spencers, are contrived to improve rather than injure the form.[13]

Malcolm, however, noted that some women indulged the new freedom too far, and showed themselves 'in a manner offensive to modesty.'

No doubt some of the concerns about impropriety arose from the fact that some neo-classical sculptors on the continent were putting modern sitters into the antique mode, in almost total nudity, and Princess

33 Festive swan-song for neo-classical dress. Women's heads dressed with turbans and flowers. Slim silhouettes remain for both sexes but fashion's demand for change is beginning to show. By Bristol artist Rolinda Sharples (1793–1838).

Pauline Borghese's famous nude pose to Canova seemed only part of her celebrated advertising of her attractions. This sort of behaviour must have alarmed the old guard; what if it spread from Italy to England? '. . . One evening the Princess was reclining in her drawing room in bed with a large assembly of people, among whom were several English ladies of distinction, when a page bearing a gold vase entered, she put her foot from under the silken cover. The page poured the perfume over it and then carefully dried it with a napkin. Pauline then turned to Lady Jersey and told her she might kiss it if she chose. Lady Jersey obeyed. This was going too far and various other such stories are told of her.'[14]

The Princess, in 1819, allowed Thomas Moore, when he was in Rome, to see her beautiful hands and kiss them twice, and to feel her foot, 'which is matchless.'[15]

Neo-classicism encouraged a new boldness in assessing figures and faces, as if a taste for antique status transferred itself to humans. Men, in following the slimming and sleeker silhouettes of women, did not actually take on togas or tunics, but their more tightly fitting breeches and cutaway jackets made their bodies less mysterious to women also accustomed to statuary: 'He is by far the most *beautiful* creature of his sex, I ever saw; so like the Antinous, that at Rome he went by that name. The exquisite regularity of his features, the graceful air of his head, his *antique* curls, the faultless proportions of his elegant figure, make him a *thing* to be gazed on, as one looks at a statue.'[16]

34 'Antique' dress used by Emma Hamilton in bringing classical figures to life, 1801. Walpole wrote in 1791, 'people are mad about her wonderful expression.'

These comments were made in the early nineteenth-century phase of classical dress, when the English were free to travel in Europe again after the restrictions of the Napoleonic wars. The insular years of the previous period had helped to fuse English neo-classicism with a native sense of the picturesque, an amalgam which was always obvious in the dress of the era, and one allowing a more eclectic taste in ornament than a strictly classical vision would have encouraged.

Those observers who took the chance to revisit Europe often commented on the peasant dress they saw, fitting it easily into the already familiar classical mode. The English sense of Romantic Classicism saw beauty everywhere: 'At Mola I remarked several beautiful women. Their headdress is singularily graceful: the hair being plaited round the back of the head, and there fastened with two silver pins, much in the manner of some of the ancient statues.'[17] This observer, Mrs Jameson, saw in the draped shawls of European peasants, something elemental and close to an original style of dress; she anticipated the search for an unchanging, classically draped attire which occupied some of the later Victorian reformers. In Genoa, she noted, 'a veil or shawl thrown over the head and round the shoulders, is universal and is certainly the most natural and becoming dress which can be worn by our sex . . . the effect is particularly picturesque and bewitching.'[18]

One patron of neo-classical arts was Thomas Hope (1769–1831). His house in Duchess Street became an acknowledged repository of furniture, vases, statuary and interior design, all in the most advanced and exquisite expression of the style, including its extension into the Egyptian and Indian. Hope's collection and patronage, and his own life, show the picturesque side of English classicism: in Chapter 19 his travels and oriental taste are illustrated, and he was also keenly interested in antique dress. In 1807 he published *Household Furniture and Interior Decoration*, but in 1809 his two-volume, profusely illustrated *Costume of the Ancients* [35] was concerned entirely with the translation of dress from vases and other antique sources into line drawings. Hope's main concern was to give English art students cheap printed access to antique forms; in France this was an easier matter, for there were more sources open to students. He hoped his book would prevent incorrect draping of figures in history painting; the common mistakes in that field, he claimed, were 'offering a masquarade instead of a

35 Page from Hope's very influential classical costume source book, 1809. He thought ancient Greece and Rome provided 'the happiest mixture of beautiful naked forms with grand features of attire and armour.'

historic subject, a riddle in place of a tale clearly told.' Hope may well have helped art students; he certainly produced a useful series of drapery details and decorative ideas for dressmakers, or for fashionable people searching for an ideal. His wife was painted by George Dawe in 1812 in a Greek-inspired dress, a pose based on an illustration from the 1809 book. Later, in 1812, Hope published *Designs of Modern Costumes*, and an enlarged edition was put out in 1823. The designs were drawn by Henry Moses, and this little book is a fascinating glimpse of a deep love of classical form fusing with modern taste: very careful reproductions of antique hairdressing appear over antique gowns with modern puffed sleeves, and the gentlemen's breeches are so tight, with such faint delineation of shoes, that apart from the cutaway jackets they show an imitation nudity. This book (now rare but re-published by the Costume Society in 1973) and *Costume of the Ancients*, both emanating from an impeccable arbiter of taste, added considerably to the vocabulary of classical dress in England in the early nineteenth century.

Something of the atmosphere of Hope's circle is present in the grand masked gala described in *A Winter in London*, a novel by T.S. Surr, published in 1807, set in 1804 and closely observant of the fashionable world. The interior of Rosedale House, scene of the gala, was like Hope's house in Duchess Street: '. . . a long gallery, which was formed into an Egyptian temple, the effect of which was truly grand and striking. . . .' In the gardens, made into a Turkish seraglio, were 'beautiful young ladies, in the dress of Grecian slaves . . . scattered in groups, some playing on musical instruments, while others danced, and others again were bearing refreshments or perfumes. . . .' The artificial cypress trees were made to sway in the air by machinery, there was a finely carpeted pavilion, all transforming the mansion into a picturesque mix of classical and arab features. The arrival of the masked guests produced:

All that diversify life's crowded field,
And all prolific phantasy can yield.

(There is a striking resemblance between the exotic

reconstructed fantasy of 1804 and the *couturier* Paul Poiret's extravagant '1002nd Arabian Night' held at his mansion in Paris in 1911 and attended by the most fashionable leaders of style in his day.)

Egyptian taste was frequently added to, or mixed with, the antique classical taste, and various echoes found their way into costume and textiles, as well as into everything else:

. . . I shall not be surprised if it were to become as fashionable, in a short time, to construe these Egyptian hieroglyphics, as it is now to decorate our apartments with them. In that case an Egyptian master will become as necessary as a French governess.[19]

Some of the freedom in English dress sought by people favouring various versions of classical taste became possible for women in this period; for men the desired ease and simplicity was partly achieved by the paring down of the existing garments, and, as in other revivals, their waistcoats played a central role for the display of classical themes [36].

Happily men had another escape route to freer and looser dress; it lay not towards antiquity but to the contemporary Middle East. In Chapter 19 this fanciful and rich addition to the Englishman's enjoyment of dress at this period is described and illustrated.

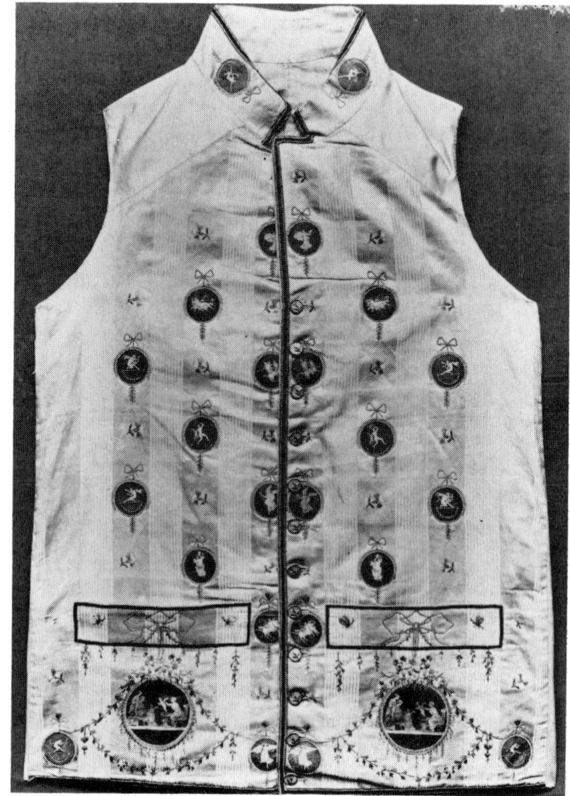

36 Man's satin waistcoat, late eighteenth century. Silk and chenille embroidery, painted 'antique' medallions.

4 *First Principles*

THE NINETEENTH CENTURY

To those who wish to work their way to fuller knowledge of the most perfect dress that has even been made (the *Greek* dress) a pure *clothing* for the human form beneath it, I recommend a course of study at the British Museum. There, by observation and comparison of statues and vases, one comes to understand by what simple and perfect appliance the logical Greek mind arrived at results in harmony with then existing conditions. One does not wish to parody these results under different circumstances, but only to profit by that which is unchanging in the fundamental idea.
The Rational Dress Society's Gazette, October 1888

At the start of the nineteenth century it seemed as if simplicity and classical taste in dress were unassailable components in a fashionable wardrobe. It could not have been foreseen that by the middle of the century fashion was once more being rebuked for its lack of simplicity, nor that the combined energies of societies later formed specifically to reform dress and re-educate the English back to sartorial sense would fail to establish again classical or romantic-classical styles as anything more than a minority eccentricity, or mere decoration to embellish other styles. However, by about 1809 or 1810 the purest form of classical dress for women, white, undecorated and tubular was, by and large, showing signs of disintegrating; from then on, although the waist remained high, there came an increasing amount of ornamentation, and terms began to diversify as the plain 'round' dress began to amplify.

In 1809 the *Ladies Monthly Museum* described a walking dress, as worn with 'Tyrolese cloak of lilac shot sarsnet, trimmed with Venetian binding and white lace. . . . The hair in the Grecian style. Veil à la Maltese, of the most transparent texture, edged in vandykes thrown with simple elegance over the whole. . . .'[1] In another description, in Ackermann's in 1818, as if pushed by the dilating hemlines and decorations, 'the skirt is finished at the bottom with a broad black *crape* flounce; over this is a very narrow flounce, which is *quilled* in the middle to correspond, and the whole is surmounted by a broad band of bias

37 Like hoops in the previous century, crinolines contradicted classicism in dress. This photograph was taken in *c.* 1865. More active roles for women meant twentieth-century revived crinolines were for evening only.

crepe.' Displaced by the gradually fussier skirt, classical features retreated upwards to the bodice and head. In 1818, 'a necklace and brooch of jet, put on in the Grecian style, partly shade the bust,' or 'it is ornamented round the top of the bust with a light silk trimming, both the back and the front are full but the *Athenian braces* which are worn with it, confine it to shape.' In 1822, 'the hair is parted, and a few light curls on the temple; the hind hair twisted and fastened on the crown of the head a l'antique.'

The *Ladies Monthly Museum*, a London magazine which included fashion commentary and illustrations as a regular service alongside other features such as 'The Fatal Effects of Jealousy,' serialized fiction, poems, historical anecdotes or 'The Advantages of Industry,' played a role, with its fellow publications, in the fragmentation of the unified classical vogue. Their copy became dotted with descriptions of clothes or hairstyles *à la Diana*, or *à l'antique* and it was to their advantage that readers and seekers of fashion should require explanations of these terms. The more diverse the paths to modishness, the more need for a guide in the form of a regular fashion publication. Some sense of satisfaction surrounds the *Museum*'s fashion comments charting the beginning of the break-up of the purely classical taste, as it was also anticipating a readership yet more anxious for advice:

> There was a time when in catering for our subscribers in this department, a very few words would suffice; in those times a dull uniformity pervaded their habiliments, a sombre colour dealt out a universal monotony; dress reigned in all the frippery of gauze and powder, and our task was comparatively light and easy; but now that the *couturieres* have availed themselves of the Grecian costume, the true standard of taste; now that they have had recourse to the artist and the antiquary, who have not disdained to render their assistance, what elegance has appeared! Unconfined even to the statues of antiquity, the genius of dress roves in endless variety; she steals her hue from the rainbow, and the whole habitable world is ransacked for bodily adornment.[2]

Indeed, all kinds of novelties and options were 'ransacked' to find alternatives to the, by now, increasingly unsatisfactory plainness of the short-bodied gown. Its survival was not helped by the climate; it had always required tippets and shawls and spencers and muffs and overgarments to make it serviceable out of doors. Miss Weeton, when a governess in the Lake District, and careful of her few clothes, wore a 'short mantle or fly' over her dress in 1810, with a grey bonnet. She had a coat as well, but it caused problems. 'One day, to preserve it from the rain, I put over it a new Scotch plaid of Mr Pedders', and the dye of it has stained the coat in such a manner that I cannot wear it again as it is; it must be dyed some dark colour, what do you think of dark bottle green?'[3]

By the 1820s the waistline dropped and by the end of that decade the waistband began to dip in the centre front. Skirts and sleeves began to expand and during the 1830s they belled out, the sleeves extensively so. Although sleeves then rather suddenly deflated in 1836, the bell skirt became fuller, and the typical mid-Victorian balance was established. Classical shapes with long falls of plain and unsupported fabric and uncluttered arms were now firmly *démodé*. By the 1840s, for instance, *à la Greque* had come to be applied to any bodice which was decorated by festooned or bunched fabric. It became possible to use 'Grecian' to describe a style based on modern Greek regional or peasant dress, instead of antique dress.

The *chignon* survived the changes, with its accompanying Grecian bands; it came to be elaborated and popular for use with dress which had no antique connections. 'Still the chignon grew and grew, until the maid-of-all-work appeared with locks distended by a mass of visible padding so appalling that the world turned with horror from the picture.'[4] In more moderate shapes, it became the focus for inventive variations. Ever practical and helpful, in 1865 *The Young Englishwoman* suggested its readers could make 'bandelettes' for the Josephine or the Antigone coiffures (by this time, the name of Napoleon's empress was often synonymous with an antique and classical style). 'They can be made of black or coloured velvet, according to taste, and studded with large round gold, steel or crystal beads. The bandelettes are worn either over plain bandeaux or rows of frizzed curls; the ribbon with which they are tied at the back should be concealed under the chignon'[5] [38].

In the late 1850s, the artificial crinoline came on the scene, as a more convenient addition to the numerous ways previously used to hold out the skirts. Stuffed pads and numerous petticoats had satisfied the taste for ever-expanding circumferences to skirts, and the artificial crinoline, with steel or cane concentric hoops allowed the expansion to continue; the huge spans of the 1860s would scarcely have been possible without it. Once more the vision of an unchanging simplicity had receded, and those who wished for its return had to repeat earlier arguments. Those in favour of classical

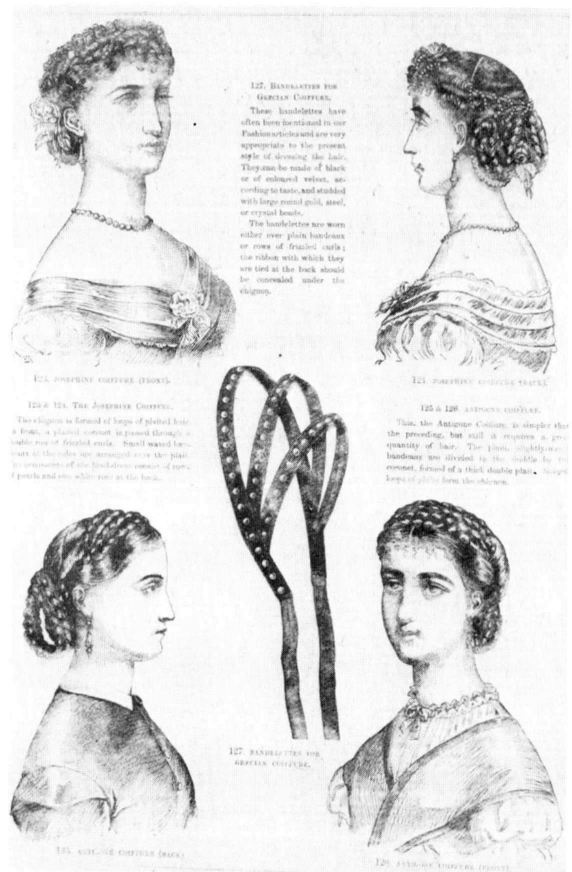

38 Do-it-yourself Grecian hairdressing, 1865.

and draped dress had several opponents: a new definition of femininity favouring helplessness; commercialism; and a tide of fashion which did not flow their way, as it had done for similar exponents of natural dress in the previous century; in the end the First World War forced it to turn towards at least some of their objectives.

What is considered to be feminine in any given generation is obviously variable. The Victorian sense of femininity involved helplessness, pliancy and dependence; of course there were exceptions, and women known as 'platform' or 'strong-minded' took part in the later dress reform activities. However, by the third or fourth decade of the century, generally fashionable femininity could be summed up with the words used by Mrs Gaskell in her novel *North and South* (1855) to distinguish flighty Edith from the stronger Margaret, heroine of the book: Edith curled 'into a soft ball of muslin and ribbon, and silken curls.'[6] Those arguing for clothes which would let girls be active and robust, healthier and less physically dependent, encountered many deaf ears. In another novel of almost the same date, Charles Reade gave a prominent role to peasant women unhampered by corsets, nor wrapped in muslin. In *Christie Johnstone* (1853), they had, and were meant to have, a dramatic impact. 'These women had a grand corporeal trait; they had never known a corset! so they were straight as javelins . . . every gesture was ease, grace and freedom. What with their own radiance, and the snowy cleanliness and brightness of their costume, they came like meteors into the apartment.'[7]

But for the most part, amongst the middle and upper classes, and the fashionable of both, a woman had to be dependent and lovable in a suitably modest way, for if she was not capable of evoking love, she would not be married, and in marriage and the home she should achieve her highest aspirations. Most men, unaccustomed to trousers on women, in any sense, did not seek strength in their wives; they preferred fragility. The dress reformers blamed this as one of the principal reasons for the continuation of unhealthy tight lacing and restrictive clothes:

> Strength of body is not an object for which women appear ready to make any sacrifice, nor indeed is robust health in women much admired by the young of either sex. Girls like to look upon themselves as ethereal beings, and care very little about their internal arrangements as long as they do not suffer acute pain. Young men like the sense of protecting a fragile, clinging creature, who will be like wife and child in one. . . . Indeed the feeble strength of women is one of the most crying disgraces of the age. Many cannot walk more than a few hundred yards without fatigue.[8]

So convinced by their experience that medical and health reasons rarely carried any weight in the argument against modern dress, the Rational Dress Society, begun in 1881, concentrated its efforts on promoting designs and ideas for attractive alternatives: 'the world must be convinced not only that modern costume is unhealthy, but that it is ugly, and public taste must condemn what is distorted from an artistic standpoint, before we can hope for any permanent improvement in the vagaries of fashion.'[9]

The business of reinstating classical dress in its rightful place, not only as a replica of antiquity, but in modern versions based on antique principles, had also to contend with commercial interests which, sensing the reformers' tastes to be in the minority, made no great efforts to heed them. Nevertheless the nineteenth century saw much genuine concern for sweated labour in the clothing industry and trades, and voices were raised against the profit-motive which was bullying the consumer as well as the worker. In 1885 the National Health Society heard this argument, put by Mrs Ada Ballin – it repays quotation, for we have to live with the same problem today:

> It is to the advantage of that large section of the people who make their livelihood by supplying the rest of the world with clothes, that fashions should change quickly, so that new clothes may be bought before the old have been worn out, because the latter have become *outré*. . . . Now, to devise a real novelty is something which requires

39 Jane Morris, 1865. An artistic search for freer style of dressing. D.G. Rossetti arranged this pose as part of a photographic series. Similar garments appeared in his paintings.

positive genius, and as this commodity is rare, the majority of the new fashions which are constantly appearing are, in reality, only modifications of bygone styles . . . why is it then, it may well be asked, that bad old fashions are generally revived in preference to good ones? The answer is to be found in the fact that revivals are the work of trade influence, and that as it is to the interest of those concerned in trade that fashions should be as extravagant as possible, there is no probability that they would attempt to revive styles which are simple and owe their healthfulness to following the lines of nature.[10]

The establishment of a possible relation between health and simplicity in dress has not been easily made in the history of English dress. Some earlier writers had made the connection, such as Stubbes in 1583 (see page 70) but generally it did not come easily to followers of fashion. (Today we have amassed extensive evidence on potentially unhealthy practices such as smoking, but we are irrational in our response, and are therefore well placed to understand the reluctance in the nineteenth century to discard restrictive dress on medical grounds.) An early individual effort to achieve comfortable dress was made by Jane Morris; surrounded by the attempts of her husband, William, to change the tide in the applied arts, and posed by their mutual friend. D.G. Rossetti, she was photographed in 1865 in a dress of voluminous character, with no construction at the waist, and a fall of free fabric at the back [39]. Whilst not part of mainstream fashion, this dress stemmed from a circle concerned with artistic ideals more than medical ones, yet it helped to generate an atmosphere of interest in alternative clothes.

In the search for a natural style, concerned individuals such as Mrs Merrifield, writing in 1854, often expressed strong opposition to the previous, neoclassical attempt at simplicity, on the grounds of immodesty, or sheer ugliness: 'waists so short, that the girdles were placed almost under the arms, and as the dresses were worn at that time indecently low in the neck, the body of the dress was almost a myth.'[11]

The Greek ideal was rejected by Mrs Oliphant in 1878 on the grounds that the English climate, and busy modern life, were both unsuited to loose and free drapery; she too rejected the earlier classical revival as a failure; although it had aimed at a 'lofty return towards the first principles of beauty,' it was not at all Greek, and even if it had been, it would have suffered the fate of the reformers to whom she addressed herself: 'The chyton on an Englishwoman would be like the toga on an Englishman; and persistently as Greek and Roman have been put before us, this has never been a successful suggestion. The fashion of close-fitting dresses must have sprung at first from special adaptation to the needs of the climate.' She added that 'revolutions are practicable in everything: in manners, morals, government, even religion, sooner than in clothes. . . .'[12]

Whether or not Mrs Oliphant and her fellow objectors to the Greek means of dress reform had correctly assessed the reasons for its lack of success, they certainly anticipated the fact that the English never did fully take to the reformers' suggestions, and neither before nor since have they been massed in classical garb. However, the idea persisted; it still generates interest, and in the twentieth century became a live issue again with dancers such as Isadora Duncan, in search of natural unfettered movement. In the twentieth century too, some of the underlying purposes of antique dress, to do with ease of movement, display of form and temperature control, have been tackled successfully in other ways.

Nine years after the formation of the Rational Dress Society, the Healthy and Artistic Dress Union came into being in 1890, and has left a legacy by which its aims can be assessed and something of the tone of the reform debates can be conveyed: its journal *Aglaia* was first published in July 1893 and survived for three issues. Of a very high standard [40], this elegant publication discussed and illustrated a range of topics considered central to reform, such as cycling costume, 'Corset Wearing: the medical side of the Attack,'

40 Aglaia was a goddess of beauty, one of the Three Graces and a daughter of Zeus. This is one of the journal's only three issues.

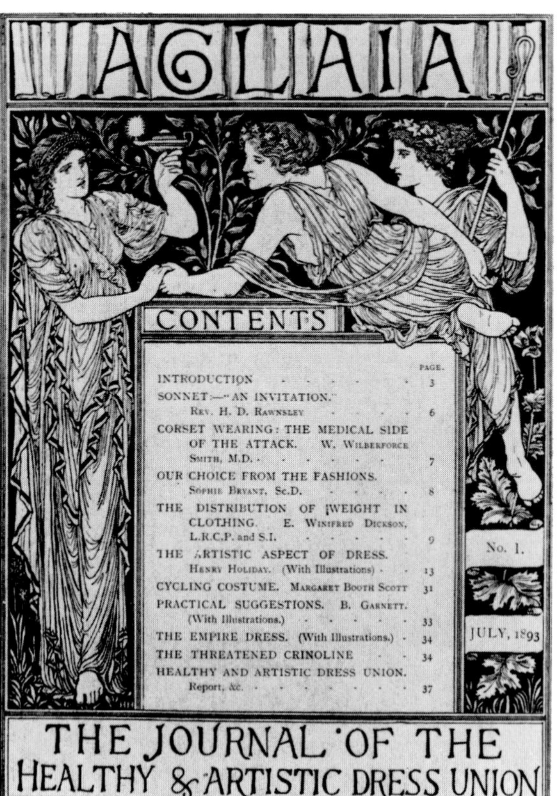

AGLAIA

CONTENTS

	PAGE.
INTRODUCTION	3
SONNET:—"AN INVITATION." Rev. H. D. Rawnsley	6
CORSET WEARING: THE MEDICAL SIDE OF THE ATTACK. W. Wilberforce Smith, M.D.	7
OUR CHOICE FROM THE FASHIONS. Sophie Bryant, Sc.D.	8
THE DISTRIBUTION OF WEIGHT IN CLOTHING. E. Winifred Dickson, L.R.C.P. and S.I.	9
THE ARTISTIC ASPECT OF DRESS. Henry Holiday. (With Illustrations)	13
CYCLING COSTUME. Margaret Booth Scott	31
PRACTICAL SUGGESTIONS. B. Garnett. (With Illustrations.)	33
THE EMPIRE DRESS. (With Illustrations.)	34
THE THREATENED CRINOLINE	34
HEALTHY AND ARTISTIC DRESS UNION. Report, &c.	37

No. 1.

JULY, 1893

THE JOURNAL OF THE HEALTHY & ARTISTIC DRESS UNION

picturesque and ultilitarian dress for men and children, suggestions for evening wear for men, all topics which would push reform in a constructive direction and give it a role in all areas of life. An article in the first issue, 'The Artistic Aspect of Dress' by Henry Holiday, exemplified the range of arguments proposed by reformers against the status quo; part of the article deals in detail with the negation of beauty caused by corsets: corsets obstructed the swaying of the torso from side to side, and they prevented the turning of the lumbar vertebrae: 'the central line down the front of the corset is always at right angles to its upper margin, but this is not the case with the central line of the body – it is only strictly true of a soldier standing at attention.'[13] In addition, corsets weakened the muscles they were supposed to support. Holiday also illustrated the injurious effect of high-heeled and pointed shoes and boots. The artistic side of the discussion centred on aspects such as harmony between interior surroundings and dress, and establishment of 'a fitness between the rooms and their occupants,' and on making the busy street a more joyous and attractive scene by allowing the pleasure of seeing human beings walking naturally in unfettered clothes. Convenience of dress for work was explored, and healthier forms of evening dress in which to dance more freely.

Asking why his contemporaries chose ugliness, and avoided beauty in their dress, Holiday produced a broad political answer: they were so busy making money and profit that art in all its forms had become spurious, handicrafts especially being divorced from beauty by the need for profit. It was not an argument to bear much examination, but Holiday's impassioned commitment, and his conclusion, were generally typical of those involved in reform:

> When we have all realised that it is more worth our while to make life a bright and beautiful thing than to amass the means of living by methods which destroy the beauty of life, then, and not till then, will beauty have a chance of recovering its former healthy growth. Then, and not till then, will our dress spontaneously, and by the simple action of natural forces, recover that beauty which was once so natural to it.[14]

Looking backwards for examples of 'natural' beauty in dress, Holiday and others found, in addition to the lightly draped garments of the Greeks and Romans, that the closely fitted mediaeval dress which 'displayed every beautiful curve' of the limbs was also a potential solution [105].

In Vernon Lee's novel of aesthetic life, *Miss Brown*, 1884, the artist Hamlin created a dress especially for his

41 Corsets hampered movement and grace. Careful analysis to accompany Henry Holiday's lecture on artistic aspect of dress, 1893. Modern revivals of nineteenth-century dress are more supple because the underlying structure is omitted.

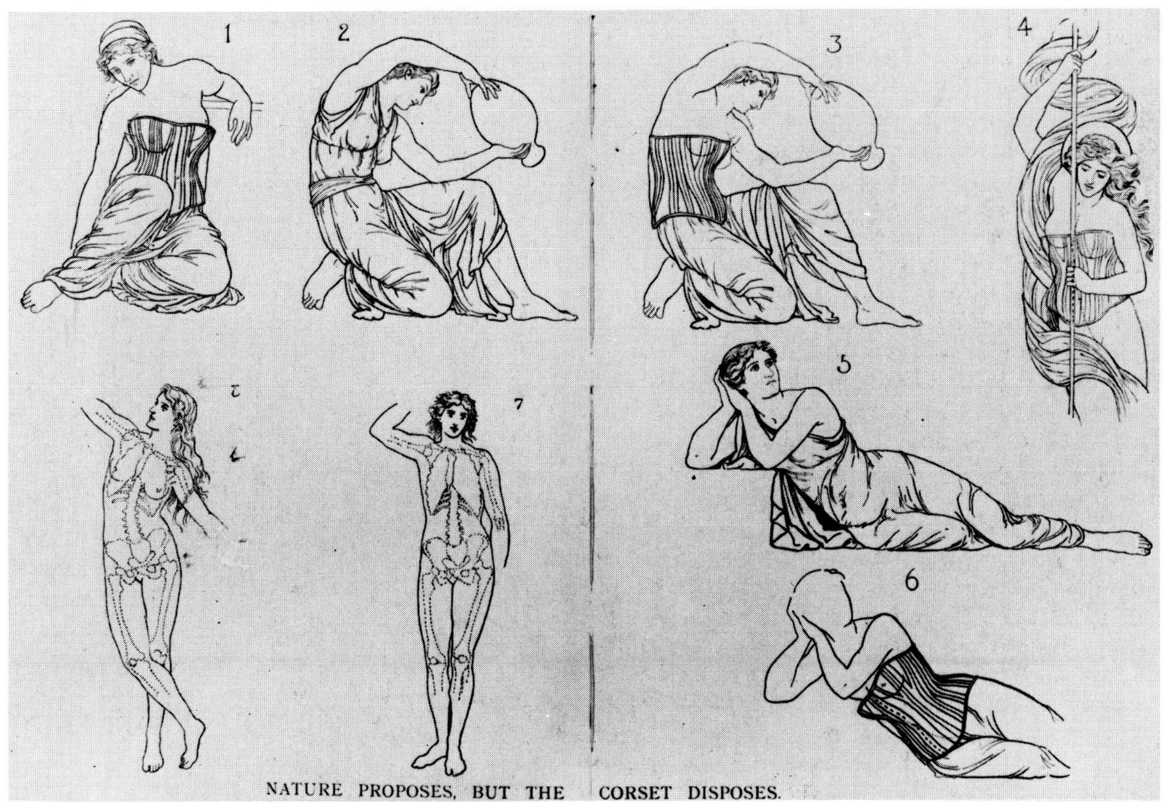

1

2

3

42 Reformers found previous attempts at classicism attractive and Empire styles were revived. 1893.

43 Softer colours, softer shapes. Historical features fused with classical ones in distinctive Aesthetic dress at the Royal Academy, contrasted with more fashionably restrictive styles.

beloved Anne Brown to wear at her important début in aesthetic circles. She shrank in dismay from the mirror in which she first saw herself; she had never worn such a dress before. 'It was of that Cretan silk, not much thicker than muslin, which is woven in minute wrinkles of palest yellowy white; it was made, it seemed to her, more like a night-gown than anything else, shapeless and yet clinging with large and small folds, and creases like those of damp sculptor's drapery, or the garments of Mantegna's women.' Miss Brown's pleas for a long petticoat to preserve her modesty were energetically refused by the dressmaker who considered that the one already worn was one too many, and she went off to the party accompanied by a friend in mediaeval garments of grey cashmere, wearing in her red hair a garland of gilt oak-leaves and parsley.

5 *A Beauty of its Own*

THE TWENTIETH CENTURY

It was one of the greatest achievements of the Greeks to perceive that the body had a beauty of its own that, in the best of cases, could be rendered but little more attractive by extraneous decoration.
J.C. Flugel, *The Psychology of Clothes*, 1930

The English summer of 1975 was one of the hottest on record. A newspaper interviewed four people 'who'd rather dress up than strip down' in their attempts to beat the heat that summer; they had chosen respectively tight shorts, baggy pyjamas and a cotton tank suit, and one man had tied rags into his hair claiming they kept his head very cool. It was rather defiantly, however, that Manolo Blahnik the shoe designer spoke of his home-made efforts to keep cool: 'I've made myself a Grecian tunic. Yes, with a little piece of yellow silk and some scissors, I've done it. People say how wonderfully cool I look. . . . Yes, everybody stares – but I don't care. I think it's appalling and horrible what most people wear in the hot weather.'[1] In the accompanying photograph, the loose, girdled silk tunic, over wide trousers, looked comfortable and relaxed. It seemed an excellent solution to prolonged heatwave conditions which made even barristers in a London court seek permission, unsuccessfully, to discard their traditional combination of wigs and robes over suits. Sadly, however, perhaps the general failure to take up antique dress at the very moment when one of its chief functions in keeping the body cool was most needed was indicative of the wavering English attitude to it. Revivals of antique dress have followed a career just as uncertain and as uneven during the twentieth century as they did in previous eras.

44 'The Pavlova influence in our back gardens.' Via modern dance, Greek styles found an extensive new following.

At the beginning of the century the vestiges of the earlier reformers' aims meant that classical styles for women could remain in use for formal wear under the aegis of such establishments as Liberty of Regent Street and their imitators. Liberty continued to produce a Grecian gown as one of their long-lived and popular series of 'Costumes never out of Fashion' and by subtle modifications sustained it until after the First World War, by which time in the 1920s it was in competition with a prevailing taste for bustless figures, ever-dropping waists, and uninterrupted angularity without ruffles or ripples. However, the crossed bands so reminiscent of a girdled Greek chiton were simply lowered so that they crossed the bodice at a central point level with the elbows instead of immediately below the breasts as they had previously done, and girdled the back of the dress well below the natural waist. This post-war model also sprouted a train at the rear hem, and cleverly appeared to taper at the front

45 Isadora Duncan promoted free love and free-form dancing.

hem, with very few folds: so it contrived to remain both Greek and perfectly modern.

In comparison with some classical revivals of the early century, Liberty's efforts could be said to be more purist than most. The dancer Isadora Duncan (1878–1927) [45], who established schools of dance in Berlin and Moscow and was rapturously received in London, developed a form of revived antique dress which earnestly sought to capture the original spirit, but which was in part based on Renaissance models, especially after her visit to Florence. Nevertheless, she achieved an appearance remarkably like the dancers on the Greek vases she had studied, and helped to popularize a more purist approach to the dress. 'I sat for days before the "Primavera," the famous painting of Botticelli. Inspired by this picture, I created a dance in which I endeavoured to realize the soft and marvellous movements emanating from it. . . .'[2] During her residence in Greece itself she and her entourage wore copies of ancient Greek tunics and sandals, 'much to the astonishment of the modern Greeks themselves.'[3] Such sandals and tunics, wool in winter and linen in summer, were her usual clothes wherever she was living; what she wore off-stage was not much changed from what she wore on the stage in her inimitable dancing career, although during a sojourn in Paris she succumbed to some *haute couture* models. Isadora Duncan's pupils and family wore these classical garments too. (When her two small children were tragically drowned in the Seine they were wearing little Greek tunics.) Isadora Duncan made a considerable impression on artists who attempted to draw her idiosyncratic dance movements. She was one part of a wider attempt in dance in the early years of the century to create fresh images; Leon Bakst's costume designs, for example, for the many appearances of the Russian Ballet in Paris and London and elsewhere also made new developments in forming a fluid and light attire capable of expression in movement.

There was a widespread following at amateur level of these new naturalistic forms and images based on the appearance of Isadora Duncan and others [44]. For example, at the Simple Life and Healthy Food Conference held at Caxton Hall in April 1913, a troupe of 'Grecian' dancers performed, and the previous August a *Daily Mirror* photographer snapped two women walking in the West End in Grecian dress, and the newspaper observed that they even wore sandals.

There was an association between classical dress and health, fitness and youth which was widely exploited by advertisers for many years.

It is interesting to note that Isadora Duncan was herself aware that she was also part of a curious situation in which a revival was revived: the early years of this century saw the beginning of the Empire or Regency revival. It concerned architecture, furniture and interior design and became what was known in the 1920s and thirties as 'Vogue Regency,' producing, for example, 'jazz-modern neo-Greek murals in silver-foil.'[4] In the pre-1914 days it was a dominant and acknowledged feature in dress. Isadora Duncan had spoken of reclining *à la* Recamier on a sofa (Madame Recamier, 1777–1849, was a noted leader of French neo-classical taste), and described some of her own clothes as 'Directoire.' Empire, Regency, Directoire, Josephine were all early twentieth-century names employed by fashion commentators to describe what is more recently called neo-classical style. For women the high-waisted, early nineteenth-century dress seemed a happy combination of relief from the stubborn curves of the 'S' bend corset and a chance to evoke something of what seemed coyer, more feminine times. On the day the suffragette Emily Davison went under the King's horse at Epsom, a dressmaker was quoted as saying she had never made so many gowns for girls wishing to attend Derby Day: 'And, strangely enough, I have made dresses for them in which they might be mistaken for their grandmothers. They are quite Kate Greenaway in effect, with round barrel-trimmed skirts and fichu bodices, and utterly different from the tortured draperies and slit side seams to which the mothers of my young customers object for their daughters.'[5]

Kate Greenaway's popular illustrations [46] seemed to assist the spread of the neo-neo-classical styles. At the grand wedding of Lady Marjorie Manners and Lord Anglesey in August 1912 the bride was attended by no fewer than fifteen children in a mixture of picturesque Greenaway and Tudor clothes. The high-waisted Empire dress remains a popular wedding dress shape for brides to the present day. It is so far removed from its neo-classical origins that it could no longer be referred to as a classical revival; it has become instead simply old-fashioned, quaint and traditional fare in bridal departments. What was written of this style in 1907 remains applicable today: 'Again, the "Empire," always more or less modified, is much to the fore. Nowadays, the "Empire" modes are so altered that, to be strictly accurate, they are hardly "Empire" at all, but a happy compromise between a high and low waist, and the graceful draperies in the way of sleeves which we now see are an improvement on the hard puff which one used to associate with the gowns worn by the Empress Josephine.'[6]

The French *couturier* Paul Poiret (1879–1944) was in some measure responsible for the raised waistline of the pre-1914 revival. He had by about 1906 come to the idea of rejecting the corset, and began making column-like straight gowns falling from the bust. Poiret also rejected fussy ornament, and entered what he called his Hellenic phase. One of his customers is said to have

46 Kate Greenaway's nostalgic illustrations in children's books greatly influenced current tastes in dress.

remarked that she felt like a Greek column,[7] much to his satisfaction. Although Poiret declared that women should follow their own inclinations and dress just as they pleased, his career clearly suggested that he considered his own taste to be impeccable, and that his creative ideas were best for his customers. Charles Frederick Worth (1825–95) had established the structure and status of *haute couture* as we know it today, and Paul Poiret added a dimension of theatricality and panache to the image of the designer himself. Madeleine Vionnet (1876–1975), arguably this century's finest designer, considered Poiret a *costumier* and not a *couturier*, but whatever his work methods, he established a classical line in expensive clothes for women who would have laughed at such events as the Simple Life and Healthy Food Convention.

The *couturiers* enter into the story of revivals in various ways. Some, like Vionnet, used former images as a starting point for an entirely fresh interpretation, some used them as additions or features to superimpose on current forms, and it became widespread practice to base the showing of a collection on some theme to help unify the event and aid publicity, and very often past eras of fashion were used in this way, as it were, for recognizable bait. Said London *Vogue* in January 1932, 'Fashion has picked up a bad habit; we adore to speak of style influence. "Renaissance" is the dada of the moment.'

Vionnet's design method was unusual; she worked out her ideas directly onto a half-size wooden mannequin, draping and easing the fabric into the eventual shapes, which would then be transferred to patterns. The fluid lines of much of her designs are partly attributable to this approach, and the finished dresses, characteristically cut on the bias, would seem to be both moulded and draped. Like the garments of antiquity, a Vionnet 'classical' style would appear limp and formless until it was worn, when it would take on the life of the wearer's body. With cloth on the bias, and a habit of using cowl necklines, Vionnet's products were not authentically antique in construction, but she, more than most this century, achieved the pliant and supple forms which both acknowledged and extended the spirit of classical originals. Many designers made use of classical ideas, but Vionnet and Madame Grès were the two who exploited the method of draping to its best results.

Grès, who worked as 'Alix' during the 1930s, had been trained as a sculptress, and is best known for her distinctive use of jersey and other soft fabrics which she draped into intricate configurations, with pleats and gathers which determined the final form of dress but which disappeared in the resulting impression of perfect simplicity. Fashion writers frequently referred to the sculptural quality of her designs, which were summed up in a famous photograph taken in 1937 by Man Ray for *Harper's Bazaar*: a model in a long white halter-neck dress, seemingly made of nothing but multifarious pleats, leans dreamily by an antique statue of winged victory attired in a long tunic of fluid folds.[8]

Some decades do not like other decades; the 1950s did not like the 1930s, and in Cecil Beaton's survey of the great fashion makers of this century which he published in 1954, he observed that the thirties were drab and uninspired, although he was wise enough to add, 'perhaps someone may be able to recapture the feeling of excitement that women's fashions engendered in their day.'[9] However, Beaton's criticism absolved Madeleine Vionnet, whom he recalled as a parrot-like little woman in rather masculine clothes and a trilby hat. She made, he said, a Greek dress in a way no Greek could ever have imagined, and turned her customers into moving sculptures. Grès did not achieve the Beaton stamp of approval; he was indeed harsh on the thirties. The climate of taste has since changed so that we have revived styles of the thirties in the last two decades, but have concentrated more on the tailored daywear from that decade than its superb 'Greek' dresses. This may simply be because very few people could recreate the technique required, and manufacturers may be forgiven for avoiding the complex feats needed to create the impression of molten cloth.

In Venice from 1907 Mariano Fortuny y de Madrazo (1871–1949) produced unusual clothes based on classical originals. Often known simply as Fortuny, this Spanish-born designer used a process for pleating fabrics to resemble the fluted dress of antique statuary [47]. The process remained a secret, and its use was the dominant legacy of this designer, who combined it with specially dyed textiles often weighted in the antique manner by glass beads; the style was instantly recognizable as that of Fortuny, and could be bought from outlets opening in both Paris and London after the Great War. The clothes were expensive, with a rather artistic reputation; the styles, based on both classical and Renaissance sources, changed little, but Fortuny had a following for the entire period from 1907 until his death. He is best remembered for this contribution of distinctive designs of subtle colour and texture, redolent of the statues and paintings of antiquity and the Renaissance, in contrast to Vionnet or Grès, for example, who would use such sources as their starting point rather than their goal.

A taste for ancient Egypt had been manifest during Napoleon's Egyptian campaigns, within the frame-

47 *Left* Peach evening dress by Fortuny, *c.*1912. This master of the revived Greek style has himself enjoyed a revival in 1980.

48 *Right* A dress in silk crêpe from Liberty, 1915.

work of neo-classicism. During the nineteenth century there were examples of milliners and dressmakers using the names if not exact replicas of ancient Egyptian features, but the most outstanding revivals from this rich and plentiful source occurred just after the First World War. There were shorter-lived, more limited revivals later, stemming from the English film *Caesar and Cleopatra* which starred Vivien Leigh in 1945, and the American 1962 epic *Cleopatra* in which Elizabeth Taylor played the title role. Both films were lavish, well publicized events, respectively England's and the world's most costly films, and various fashions followed in their wake. After the 1962 film, cosmetics also had a 'Cleopatra' phase; however, neither of these films produced as much neo-Egyptian style as was seen after the First World War. It has been suggested that this earlier revival was sparked off solely by the dramatic revelation of the contents of the tomb of Tutankhamun (c.1361–1352 BC) in 1922,[10] but these breathtaking treasures gave a ready name to, and compounded what was already a fairly common inclination in, women's dress. The *Queen* magazine noted on 1 May 1920: 'The Egyptian influence is strong both in the design of frocks and the embroideries which adorn them.' In the same year Liberty's Egyptian dress was well advertised, and in April 1920, the *Queen* also commented on an attractive toque decorated with a turquoise scarab.

The name of Tutankhamun was unknown in fashion until the excitement of the November 1922 discoveries, but there had previously been plenty of re-use of other ancient Egyptian treasures in both dress and jewellery. Theda Bara had played Cleopatra in a film in 1917; she was the first screen actress to be called a 'vamp' and the fanciful tales of Cleopatra's life (69–30 BC) fitted well with Bara's popularization of a sultry, predatory feminity. Considerable information was brought to light from excavations in Egypt over many years. Howard Carter, partner of Lord Carnarvon in the Tutankhamun discovery had first dug in Egypt in 1892, and had begun the search for Tutankhamun before the First World War. In a more general sense, the dominant shape associated with ancient Egyptian female dress was usefully close to the shapes required in the years just after the war; for instance, in the spring of 1920 the House of Worth produced a crêpe georgette evening dress, with an 'Egyptian sash' knotted in front, and decorated with blue silk grapes. The wide sash helped to cover any indecision about the position of the waist: its lower edge encouraged a dropped place and the bold front knot and falling ends of the sash persuaded an increasingly straight and vertical silhouette into being. The wrapped, swathed look had

49 Antique Greek drapery reinterpreted in silver lamé, 1963.

previously been well established by the 1914 'knotted' dresses of *haute couture* and imitated elsewhere and had employed the bold jewelled clasps associated with wealthy ancient Egyptian dress. Designers at all levels of the market tend consciously or unconsciously to revive a past style when it offers features which will tide them over a period of transition or hesitancy; in that way the Egyptian sash helped in the change to leaner and lower waisted styles. After 1922 the general trend was established and 'Tutmania' was a decorative addition found from hats to shoes, from embroidery to bracelets. There was scarcely any aspect of female dress and adornment which was not touched at some point during the 1920s by the vogue.

By summer 1923, hardly more than six months after the famous tomb had been opened, the craze was beginning to pall, especially on fashion commentators whose pages needed some fresh ideas. 'Judging from the beautiful model dresses already being shown, there seems every likelihood that we shall grow more than a little tired of the over-popularity of the Egyptian influence . . . striking as such gowns are, they may well be regarded with some restraint,' warned *Queen* on 10 May 1923. The same writer suggested that one of the reasons for the enormous hold which the influence was enjoying was due to pressure from the French fabric manufacturers whose rich embroidered satins and brocades were used to such advantage during the craze and had been turned out in great quantity. It was only sound business to hope the Egyptian fashion would last until their stocks were cleared.

The two later films of Cleopatra (who lived more than a thousand years after Tutankhamun) encouraged new Egyptian revivals, and the hugely popular exhibition *Treasures of Tutankhamun* held in London in 1972 at the British Museum prompted yet more appearances of ancient Egyptian features in which distinctions between 1300 BC and 30 BC were not important, and in which hairstyles, sandals and jewellery played prominent parts. As a result of these several events and the subsequent profusion of reproduced images, ancient Egypt has become a readily accessible part of the vocabulary of fashion, to which manufacturers, dress and textile designers and jewellers can turn at will.

In post-war years a number of designers and manufacturers have used the classical idea in evening wear for women, and it looks set for a long life, especially as a Grecian style is often the choice of costume designers for cinema and TV science-fiction films. In addition to these by now traditional styles and variations, the Scottish London-based designer Jean Muir has provided a new focus to women's dress in the classical idiom, as fresh in its way as the earlier innovations of Madeleine Vionnet. Jean Muir, who first opened her own establishment in 1960, has added to the vocabulary of softly worked fabrics eased into comfortable shapes which enhance the body beneath without explicitly revealing it. Her clothes have a deserved reputation for achieving a lucidity which has rarely been equalled elsewhere in the market despite frequent commercial use of fluted draperies or other more obviously classical features [49, 51].

The battle fought by dress reformers in the last century was a more organized version of a confrontation which has always been present in English dress. The introduction of loosely draped clothes based on those of classical antiquity has had opponents who believed that firm sartorial structure was necessary for the maintenance of morality, but this traditional opposition is no longer an issue in the present century because the free movement and natural shape sought by 'classicists' have been achieved generally: these days we have come to expect comfort and economy in our dress as a right and not as a hard-won concession. Elasticated fabrics developed for sportswear are now in use for ordinary dress, shorts for both sexes come out with the sun every summer now on city streets, and there is a large market for health and slimming magazines to help us beautify our age of imitation nudity. All this leaves classical dress mostly as evening wear, though much loved, with a curiously formal look, in contrast to its previous brave and radical spirit.

50 The spirit of the antique past elegantly recaptured in 1930 by Cecil Beaton.

51 Elevated dressmaking. Carefully detailed construction underlying a perfect ease and fluidity which sculptors of the classical world would have admired. By Jean Muir.

PART II *Rural Revivals*

6 *Delectable Varietee*

THE SIXTEENTH CENTURY

. . . our Country habitacion is more godly, more honourable, more holesome, more quiet, more pleasant and profitable, then it can be in any Cittie or Burrough.

The English Courtier and the Cutrey-gentleman, 1586

At the start of this period, when the countryside was considerably wilder and more wooded than it later was, and before massive landscaping projects had romantically re-designed the land round great houses, the Elizabethans enjoyed the distinctive art form of the enclosed garden. Like an extension to the house, it was a protected box of cultivated beauty, sustained by the same sensibility which decorated dress with floral motifs.

Entering through a door in the wall of the garden at Kenilworth, exhausted after a round of elaborate festivities for the Queen's 1575 visit there, in summer heat, a visitor felt himself in paradise to 'smell such fragrancy of sweet odoourz, breathing from the plants, earbs and floours: to heer such naturall meloodious musik and tunez of the burds . . . all in such delectable varietee, order, dignitee.'[1] When a garden also functioned as a medicine cupboard there was additional reason to cultivate it with care and appreciation. Thomas Hill suggested in 1568 in *The Profitable Art of Gardening* that mazes and knots could be planted with savoury and thyme, to remain green all winter, and a visitor to Hampton Court in 1592 noticed gardens 'planted with nothing but rosemary; others laid out with various other plants, which are trained, intertwined, and trimmed in so wonderful a manner, and in such extraordinary shapes. . . .'[2]

52 This miniature by Isaac Oliver shows a melancholy young man, his back turned on society, seeking solace under the wild greenwood tree. *c.*1590.

Love of plants and flowers, and the merging where possible of indoors and outdoors, is strikingly evident in the second half of the sixteenth century. In 1555 the Earl of Rutland paid for bowls and pots 'to sett flowers in the galerre,'[3] and in 1559, in Greenwich Park, a temporary banqueting house was entirely covered with 'all manner of flowers, both of the field and garden, as roses, july flowers, lavender, marygolds. . . .'[4] A royal barge in 1557 was garlanded with artificial flowers, and a canopy 'wrought with branches of eglantine in embroidery; and powdered with blossoms of gold. . . .'[5] Plants gained an emblematic significance in addition to their association with healing and health. The eglantine came to be the flower of Queen Elizabeth herself, as did the ordinary rose, the lily and the pansy.

Between 1599 and 1605 Margaret Hoby kept a diary in which her garden is a constant presence; it is possible that she was working (sewing) flowers when she wrote, in July 1601: 'After privat praier, I walked into the Garden: after diner I wrought tell almost night, and then I went abroad with my Maides that were busie pullinge hempe.'[6] In the diary of Lady Anne Clifford her garden was an escape from a tense domestic life; a closed garden could be a particularly significant attachment to a house which contained a large number of servants, retainers and extended family, the very solitude it could offer was a moral danger in the eyes of Philip Stubbes, a place where 'they meeting their sweete heartes, receive their wished desires' behind the locked garden door.[7]

Making meaning of them, and highly attuned to them, the Elizabethans brought their gardens indoors, not only in pots, but woven and embroidered and appliquéed on hangings, furniture and clothes. Quite simply, without affectation, they wore their flowers and plants. Almost every visible part of a suit of clothes for a woman could be decorated in this way. Fine neck and wrist bands were sewn with the same intricate, interwoven patterns which were used in garden knots and mazes. The 1567 portrait of Mary Hill, Mrs Mackwilliam, by the artist known as The Master of the Countess of Warwick, shows an entire dress decorated in this style. The bands on the necks and cuffs of men's shirts could also display strapwork ornament, although the increased use of stiffened ruffs in the last two decades of the century tended to diminish this practice. Women's sleeves gave an obvious opportunity to display embroidery of various kinds; the fuller shapes of the 1580s allowed some virtuoso ornament; birds or insects or other natural and accurately observed creatures also appeared [53]. In the *c.*1600 picture of Queen Elizabeth, known as the Rainbow Portrait [122], delicate and humble garden flowers survive in delicious detail on the bodice and sleeves of a suit of clothes otherwise ablaze with exotic notions and emblems. George Clifford, Earl of Cumberland, and Queen's Champion at the Accession Day Tilts, had a suit of armour for these occasions decorated all over with roses and lovers' knots.

Part of a welcome arranged for the Queen by Lady Russell in 1591 had involved her two daughters in being dressed as shepherdesses and embroidering samplers, one with flowers, suggestive of the Queen herself,[8] and a joint floral sampler was expressive of the friendship between Hermia and Helena in *A Midsummer Night's Dream*, written 1595–6:

We, Hermia, like two artificial gods,
Have with our neelds created both one flower,
Both on one sampler, sitting on one cushion,
Both warbling of one song, both in one key

The offer made by Christopher Marlowe's Passionate Shepherd to his love included an entire set of clothes, not only embroidered but with a curious combination of rustic and exotic items:

And I will make thee beds of roses,
With a thousand fragrant poesies,
A cap of flowers, and a kirtle,
Imbroydred all with leaves of Mirtle.

53 Girl's sleeve magnificently embroidered with both flora *and* fauna, 1587. Thin over-sleeve, itself decorated with pale flowers, protected this painstaking decoration.

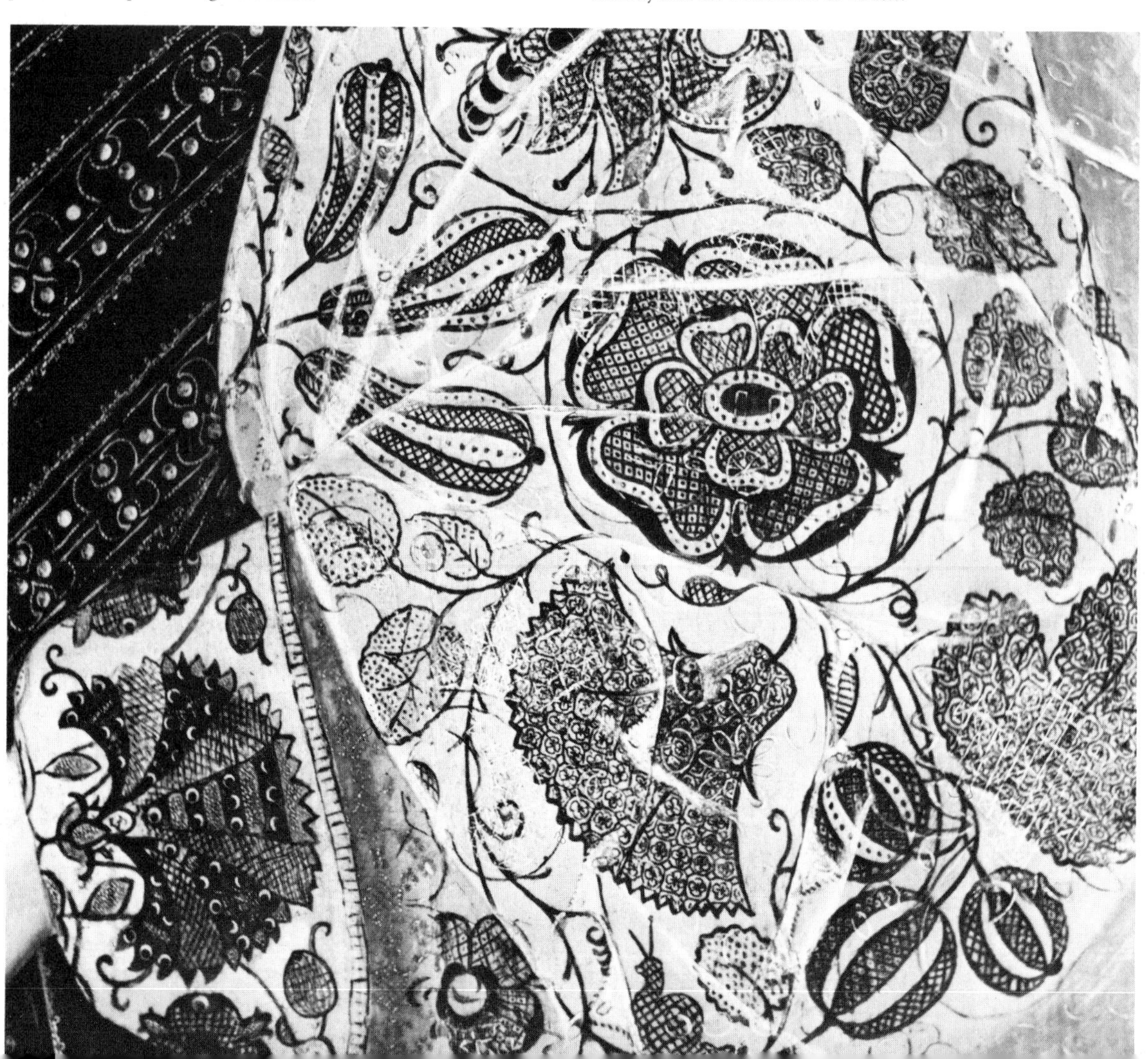

A gowne made of the finest wooll,
Which from our pretty lambes we pull;
Fayre lined slippers for the cold:
With buckles of the purest gold;

A belt of straw and ivie buds,
With corall clasps and amber studs. . . .

In his poem *Hero and Leander* Marlow recognized the beauty of the imitative decoration of the clothes of his generation when he dressed Hero in a 'vaile' of 'artificiall flowers and leaves' so lifelike that its 'workmanship both man and beast deceaves,' 'And there for honey, bees have sought in vaine.'

The Elizabethan appreciation of flowers to be worn, either real or imitation, was long lived and a significant part of the pastoral ideal of the time. The love, even apotheosis, of flowers can hardly be better demonstrated than by these lines by Edmund Spenser, from the April of his *Shephearde's Calender* (1579) in which Queen Elizabeth appears in Arcady, as Eliza Queen of the Shepherds; as the flower of the virgins, she is seated on the grass, in scarlet and white:

Upon her head a Cremosin coronet,
With Damaske roses and Daffadillies set:
Bay leaves betweene,
And Primroses greene
Embellish the sweete Violet

Shepherds' daughters were bidden to:

Bring hether the Pincke and purple Cullambine,
With gells floweres:

Strowe me the ground with Daffodowndillies,
And Cowslips, and Kingcups, and loved Lillies:

This magnificent spectacle of Eliza, crowned and strewn with quantities of fresh flowers, was an expression of the same taste which produced less prodigious, but equally loving details of flowers and plants on garments, and the specially attractive quality of this aspect of Elizabethan dress owes much to the fact that embroidery is a slow and idiosyncratic skill. Although some printed fabrics were available in the later sixteenth century, and woven pattern was common, these methods tended towards less individual detail and more repetition in their depiction of natural forms than needlework.

Wearing flowers, real or otherwise did not preclude the absorption into fashionable life of dress which was derived from that of country life. It is worth noting that although deep distinctions were felt between the court and the city on one hand and the country on the other, the court as a source of taste, elegance, novelty and foreign influences was frequently peripatetic, and in moving in 'progresses' about the Kingdom, particularly in the summer, its influence in these matters was spread beyond the confines of London.

Underpinning the fashionable response to clothes originating from ideas about the countryside was the debate about the disadvantages and advantages of city and country life itself which went on then as persistently as now. In 1586, for example, the book *The English Courtier and the Cutrey-gentleman* detailed the problems and the pleasures of both; in a debate the townsman argued that the wives of country gentlemen could not, by the nature of their work, be as elegant as a city gentlewoman. He indicated that fashion had no role, and no support, in the sort of lives they led. He gave no mention at all to the clothes of their servants or labourers; presumably these were beyond the bounds of the debate, since they were of an entirely different order:

. . . how uncumly a thing it is to see . . . a Gentlewoman walkinge in the pastures, among her Cowes and Calves, al to be dabled with dew

54 These intricate linear patterns echo the inter-linked hedges carefully trimmed around Elizabethan flowerbeds. There is a flower in each space. 1557. [See 52.]

and dyrte, and other whiles wandering in the hot sommer, a longe mile, to find out her heymakers, or corne reapers . . . she bee returned home to her husbands bord or bed . . . with myre in winter, and sweating in sommer, she is become a morsell more meete for a Mowre or a Mason, than a Gentleman or a Civill husbande.[9]

This picture allows for no attractions in countrywork, and highlights sad efforts to imitate fashion when outside the urban context. The separate vision of an Arcadian life possessed of its own style of dress is not present, and when the countryman made his reply in the debate, he argued not that pastoral simplicity was a good substitute, but that country gentlewomen were every bit as fashionable and stylish as their urban sisters; on holidays, or in fine company the country wife 'hath good garments, and can weare them well and courtly. So can also our Gentlemen of the Countrey, for though we walke at home plainely apparrelled: yet when we come to the Assizes, London, or any place of assembly, wee will put on Courtlike garments and . . . some of us weare them with good grace.'[10]

There were several books based on this debating topic, and they contain realistic accounts of the distinctions in the two lifestyles for that social class. What they describe was not at all attractive as a solution to the ache for Arcadia which fashionable people sought in their versions of pastoral dress. These urban and courtly versions were more to do with what the countryside should be like, or was imagined to have been like in the past. Social distinctions were maintained by revivals in dress, even reinforced, and it would have been unthinkable for an Elizabethan lady to assume the 'dabled' look for a gentlewoman of the country, or for a courtier to be mistaken for a real woodsman, but they could enjoy pastoral dress if they gave it a pseudo-historical slant. In appearing as pastoral figures they simultaneously advertised their erudite familiarity with these conventions, whilst relaxing in temporary exemption from normal dress.

It is almost certain that pastoral dress would not have been worn habitually by courtiers or well-to-do people, but it is fair to assume it was worn on regular occasions not only for masques, but for celebration dancing, or more informal revels involving perhaps a ride into the May woods. More research may reveal that some occasions for the use of pastoral clothes by people of rank may have had to do with local traditions and seasonal customs of a regional nature, but at present it seems probable that it was called for principally by events contained within their own rank, stemming from courtly duties or social activities.

There is no doubt that there was widespread familiarity with the desired appearance of pastoral types. In Spenser's *Faerie Queene*, a young boy of rank appeared dressed as a forester, and Spenser listed the details of his costume, suggesting a close knowledge, even a recent memory:

All in a woodman's jacket he was clad
Of Lincolne greene, belayd with silver lace;
And on his head a hood with aglets sprad . . .

Buskins he wore of costliest cordwayne,
Pinckt upon gold, and paled part per part,
As then the guize was for each gentle swayne.[11]

A huntress, again from *Faerie Queene*, also wore gilt buskins, or half-boots; hers were fastened by a rich jewel, suggesting they could be opened and closed for a snug fit.

Foresters and hunters appearing in a court masque in 1573 were issued with 'greene sattyn gaskon cotes';[12] as each masque or revel occured, the costumes no doubt tended to endorse themselves, so without reference to real hunters or woodsmen, their presence could be evoked by a costume seen at a previous event. The materials and ornament and accessories were of a calibre suitable to the rank of the wearer; the colours and the type of accessories and the cut could denote the pastoral occupation being assumed. Hunters might be in green, shepherds in grey or brown. The fair Pamela of Philip Sidney's *Arcadia* could not be confused with a real rustic for, although her costume was cut and coloured after a rustic mode, it was of fine materials; her costume 'was of russet velvet, cut after their [the shepherds'] fashion, with a straight body, open breasted, the nether part full of pleats, with wide open sleeves, hanging down very low; her hair at the full length, only wound about with gold lace.'[13] She also wore an elaborate jewel. Literary sources described these pastoral forms of fanciful dress with a confidence which underlines the likelihood that their authors had seen similar ones at various entertainments, and it is clear they enjoyed the sight and details of such clothes, responding to them as a welcome addition to the current canon of taste.

Another characteristic of pastoral style for women was long, loose hair. Pamela, in russet velvet, had 'her hair at the full length,' and another woman, also in *Arcadia* (Sidney's *Arcadia* was published in 1590 but begun in 1580) had loose hair: 'It hong down at the free liberty of his goodly length, but that sometimes falling before the clear stars of her sight, she was forced to put it behind her ears. . . .'[14] A number of portraits of women in what appears to be pastoral and fanciful dress, possibly from masques or perhaps individually prompted, have long hair flowing freely, not artificially curled or contained in wired head-dresses as would be expected in the normal formalities of everyday high-ranking fashion [55]. It is sometimes

55 A feather in Lady Elizabeth's cap. In melancholic mood, sheltered under the greenwood, this may be pastoral masque dress. Made of a 'pall' of silk, it glistens with pearl-embroidered leaves. Part of her hair is plaited, *c.*1615.

Eliz: wife to Sr Wm Pope
Sole Heir of Sr Tho: Watson
of Halstead in Kent.

quite surprising how closely one era's ideas of pastoral innocence and simplicity tally with those of another. When Spenser described an ideal country girl, his words conjure up an appearance with which we were familiar in the 1960s: a 'faire damzell, which did weare a crowne/Of sundry flowres, with silken ribbands tyde, Yclad in homemade greene that her own hands had dyde.'[15]

This raises a theme which was current for as long as shepherds and shepherdesses remained a romantic vision; not only did they live in pastoral simplicity, but they were also often imagined as wearing the unembellished cloth woven from the wool of their own sheep. Wool 'which from our pretty lambs we pull' as Marlowe wrote, garlands and coronets of flowers gathered from the fields to decorate their crooks and their hair, were elements emphasizing the virtues of the home-made and the hand-made simple artifacts. These remain virtues in the eyes of modern seekers of simplicity – hand-made pots, hand-woven sweaters, home-baked bread, farmhouse recipes in pine-clad kitchens, and so on. In 1583, Philip Stubbes made an early case for this now common link between simplicity and health, much as the 'Woolleners' and other nineteenth-century dress reformers did; Stubbes also set it in a vision of 'the good old days':

I have heard my father, with other wise sages, affirme that, in his time, within the compasse of fower or five score yeares, when men went clothed in black or white frize coates, in hosen of huswives carzie, of the same colour that the sheepe bare them . . . whereof some were streight to the thigh, other some little bigger; and when they ware shirtes of hemp or flaxe . . . men were stronger, healthfuller, fayrer complectioned, longer living, and finally, ten times harder than wee be now. . . .[16]

56 The vanity of fashionable velvet breeches paraded before honest plain cloth breeches. This is an image of the Elizabethan debate about city-versus-country life. 1592.

Stubbes felt the sixteenth-century use of rich cloth had not only softened people, it had also deprived wool makers of work and turned them into beggars. Modern fashionable men were more like 'rather nice dames and wanton girls, than puissant agentes or manly men, as our forefathers have bene. . . .'[17]

In calling for this revival of the simple and hardy life, Stubbes was not lobbying for the courtiers' idea of pastoral dress; he was in fact denigrating its luxury. Had he seen the pastoral revivals put up by some courtly events, he might have felt simplicity had gone dangerously far: ancient beings, on whom the court masque torch bearers of 1573 'attyred in Mosse and Ivye'[18] were probably based, came to have a place in pastoral evocations of various sorts. These wild men, dressed in skins or foliage were of shadowy origins, partly remembered as characters from pagan rites and partly revived by their connections with the Green Knight of Arthurian tales. Arthur's legends were much liked by the Elizabethans, and recreated to some extent by occasions such as the royal visit to Kenilworth in 1575: when finishing a hunt, the Queen and her party were met in the woods by a savage man all 'moss and ivy,' with a sapling in his hand; a pre-arranged scene was enacted there and then, the Queen narrowly missing a collision with the sapling. While it seems unlikely that these more precarious costumes would have had a direct influence on fashionable dress, especially the hairy version, they may have provided ideas for embroidery, and they certainly vividly recalled attention to the mysteries and legends of rural life, and reminded people of another Arthurian link.

In addition to wearing flowers and foliage as embroidered decoration and emblems, and appearing as idealized pastoral types on various occasions, the fashionable circle of the late sixteenth and early seventeenth centuries extended their ideas of rural life by a fashion for 'melancholic' dress. This stemmed from a phenomenon which was not directly connected with rural life, but which used it as a solace and an escape, and as a setting for a specific mental stance. Robert Burton published his diagnostic treatise, the famous *Anatomy of Melancholy*, in 1621, but it looked back on a condition to be found from the 1580s onwards.

Melancholy was a state of mind for which there was a vogue, so it was in that sense an affectation; weariness and contemplative introspection were characteristics. Burton, however, presumed it to be a serious though temporary, condition and in so doing was to describe moods of authentic depression, and to prescribe sensible treatments, such as a diet of oranges and pure wheat bread, with fresh air and clean water. Soothing exercises such as 'to take a Boat in a pleasant evening and with musicke to rowe upon the waters,' were commended. Burton saw the curative power of the countryside – to walk 'in a faire medowe, by a riverside, to disport in some pleasant plain or runne up a steep hill, or sit in a shady seat, must needs bee a delectable recreation.' These non-competitive delights featured as much as more muscular sports and games, and played a part in promoting new ways of regarding the countryside as enjoyable in its own right.

Melancholy, the condition for which Burton prescribed so much sense, was marked by a characteristic appearance:

His face being masked with his hat pull'd downe
And in french doublet without gowne or cloake,
His hose the largest ever came to towne,
And from his nostrels came much stinking smoake;
Garters would make two ensignes for a neede,
And shoe-ties that for circle did exceede.

His head hung downe, his armes were held acrosse,
And in his hat cole-blacke feather stucke,
His melancholy argued some great losse,
He stood so like the picture of ill lucke. . . .[19]

This melancholy knight revealed his nostalgia for the days of Arthurian legend; the modern world jaded him. A number of portraits were made depicting this fashionable stance; in addition to a sombre suit with no overgarment and a floppy hat, the arms were usually crossed, and the figure turned away from the world. Even the garden was too restricted a place for the melancholic spirit; he sought instead the greenwood tree [52]. There exist also paintings of women who appear to be following this vogue; partly rejecting tailored or formal clothes with decoration, they wear loose hair, and unstructured draperies, and either rest their head in their hands, or perhaps reach up into the trees they shelter by. Obviously a cultivated mood such as this, with its own sartorial terms, was dependent on the urban world of fashion for a contrasting backdrop, but it made the rural setting and the sylvan glade more modish, and prompted Burton's suggestions for making the most of the countryside in ways quite unconnected with agricultural life or labour.

Rustic settings also played a part in sophisticated events of an entirely different nature. These were the Accession Day Tilts, which had a central role in the courtly re-enactment and re-establishment of past and present virtues, and they had Arthurian overtones which dictated a pastoral setting, in portraiture if not always in actuality. The Accession Day Tilts usually took place in Whitehall, though other tilts, with equally romantic atmospheres, asserting a courtly sixteenth-century version of a chivalric code, took place elsewhere, for different occasions. Whatever their actual setting which was not always rural, and if attended by large crowds, which was usual, they needed complicated temporary structures and fences. These events were usually commemorated in portraiture in exclusively sylvan settings. To portray them in a cityscape would seem ridiculous, and a garden too cramping; in Spenser's *Faerie Queene* the knights roam so far and wide that they ride over the boundaries of history and geography altogether; they fight dragons and Amazons in romantic landscapes of great beauty. In similar vein, Elizabeth's courtier-knights were portrayed in woodland, or in settings almost devoid of any mundane detail of place. The Earl of Cumberland, for instance, has little but one tree and the sky for company [79]; and if Nicholas Hilliard's 'Young Man among Roses' has any connection with the pageantry of tilting, he is certainly deep in greenwood, so entwined by the eglantine that its flowers appear almost part of his clothes.

7 *More Gay than Foppery*

THE SEVENTEENTH CENTURY

I will the country see,
Where old simplicity,
Though hid in grey
Doth looke more gay
Than foppery in plush and scarlet cladd. . . .

Thomas Randolph (1605–35), *An Ode to Master Anthony Stafford to Hasten Him into the Country*

In February 1685, when Lady Walgrave and Lord Litchfield went to a great court ball as shepherds, they were enjoying an established bucolic tradition for members of their class.[1] The death of Elizabeth in 1603 had removed one purpose for pastoral settings in various media and events: Eliza Queen of the Shepherds had no equal and no successor. But for other reasons the pastoral mode in both court entertainment and portraiture, and in dress generally, remained a firmly settled convention for most of the seventeenth century.

It has been said that the vision of England's merry rural past had to wait for Joseph Strutt's book *Sports*

57 Pearl jewellery adorned this 'shepherdess' drawn by Sir Peter Lely in the 1660s. Her houlette was an alternative to the crook.

and Pastimes of the People of England (1801) to catch on as a version of history, but the seventeenth century had its own ideas of the evermerry rustic life so attractive to urban people. In 1618 Nicholas Breton drew a picture of rural labour mollified 'with delight and mirth,' and on holy days 'betweene our Lads and Wenches, such true mirth at honest meetings, such dauncing on the greene, in the market house, or about the May-poole, where the young folkes smiling kisse at every turning, and the old folkes checking with laughing at their children, when dauncing for the garland. . . .'[2] Breton also reaffirmed a rural life pleasantly and generously self-sufficient; in both physical and spirtual ways independent of the town: 'milke in the dairy, creame in the pot, butter in the dish, ale in the tub . . . hearbs in the garden, and water at our doores, whole clothes to our backes, and some money in our cophers, and having all this, if we serve God withall, what in Gods name can we desire to have more?'[3]

When the Worshipful Company of Drapers undertook the 1638 London Lord Mayor's pageant, called *Porta Pietatis* by Thomas Heywood, they condoned plenty of emphasis on sheep and shepherds. One shepherd, with his satchel, bottle, dog and hook, made a long and articulate rhyming speech in praise of sheep. Some decades earlier, shepherds were deemed the least dishonest class of workers, for there seemed little means, up in the hills far from company, that they could defraud their employer and this tradition remained. However, in contrast to a fond view of shepherds and the pleasures of their life, rustics in general were sometimes depicted as hopelessly boorish. In another pageant in 1660, in full view of the metropolitan crowds, actors as participating rustics were given lines to speak in a thick, almost incomprehensible dialect, anticipating the 'zider apple' accents now used to tease rusticity.

Richard Brathwait, in 1641, noted that too many women were putting wrong emphasis on ornate appearance, and he saw that this defect in pastoral dress was beginning to glint rather too attractively for his taste: 'Let Maygames and Morrices beautifie themselves with Anticke dressings, to captivate the vulgar eye; your breeding has beene better, your judgements clearer, your observations wiser, than to stoope to such base lures.'[4]

Brathwait was concerned to maintain traditional social and sartorial distinctions between the country, the city and court. Mopsa, a shepherdess in *The Winter's Tale* (1609–10) preferred perfumed gloves and 'tawdry lace' to her former work, and there were other indications that Arcadia was slipping away. What Brathwait and others of his time most wanted was a countryside populated with distinctive types who would be ornamental only in traditional ways, and thus contribute to the maintenance of the tripartite status quo. They would not ape the city folk who could then enjoy such picturesque sights as this shepherdess ready for a holiday celebration; the straw hat had become one of her signs:

I am readie, all is done,
From my heade unto my foote,
I am fitted each way to't;
  Buskins gay
  Gowne of gray,
Best that all our flocks do render,
  Hat of stroe,
  Platted through
Cherrie lip and middle slender.[5]

These versions of pastoral appearances were encouraged partly by a sense that urban fashion had got an increasing grip on men and women, and that life and dress were simpler in previous years. Perhaps pastoral dress could repair the sort of decline as sung in 1612:

Home-spun thread and household bread
Then held out all the yeare:
But th'attyres of women now
Weare out both house and land,
That the wyves in silkes may flow,
At ebbe the good-men stand[6]

In 1654 John Evelyn noted that women had begun to paint their faces, in a way which had previously been confined to prostitutes, and there was widespread censure of what was taken to be an unusual degree of change and vanity in dress. 'Your faces tricked and painted bee,/Your breasts all open bare' went one seventeenth century ballad, and 'Chamelion-like, themselves they change/To any colour seene;/How many severall fashions strange/Hath here observed beene.'[7] From a more sober quarter came Thomas Fuller's 1648 question: 'But what shall we say to the riot of our age, wherein, as peacocks are more gay than the eagle himself, subjects are grown braver than their sovereign?'[8]

Of all the supposed rural occupations, that which most caught the eye of the jaded city dwellers was that of the shepherdess, and in the seventeenth century the milkmaid joined her as an ideal figure. It was assumed that they were happy and guileless, and during the worldly revelries of the court of Charles I, and the dissolute life reported from the later circle of Charles II, the apparently simple life of these pastoral figures seemed a haven of ease, a release and an idyll. When Samuel Pepys was on Epsom Downs on one of his fairly rare, longer excursions into the countryside from London, in July 1667, he rapturously enjoyed the sight of an aged shepherd and his boy with their flock: 'it brought those thoughts of the old age of the world in my mind for two or three days after. . . .' Pepys noted the old shepherd's woollen stockings and iron-clad shoes and thought even they were 'mighty pretty.'[9]

Notably it was a boy and an old man minding this particular flock, not a shepherdess, and so it usually was in English pastures outside a village. Shepherdesses hardly existed in the sense the Arcadian-minded ladies of the court and the gentry might have had in mind when they sat for their shepherdess portraits. More likely the model for this enthusiastic imitation was a milkmaid, straw plaiter, swineherd and shepherdess rolled into one, and then only found near the farmhouse or village: she would usually not be found far from home.

A letter from Dorothy Osborne, in search of Arcadia, in May 1653 described a Bedfordshire scene where the women in charge of the sheep were on a common near her house:

a great many young wenches keep sheep and cows, and sit in the shade singing ballads. I go to them and compare their voices and beauties to some ancient shepherdesses that I have read of, and find a vast difference there; but, trust me, I think these are as innocent as those could be. I talk to them, and find they want nothing to make them the happiest people in the world but the knowledge that they are so. Most commonly, when we are in the midst of our discourse, one looks about her, and spies her cows going into the corn, and then away they all run as if they had wings at their heels. I, that am not so nimble, stay behind. . . .[10]

It was their cows they chased, not their sheep, and they probably acted as milkmaids also. It is interesting to note how literary sources helped to mould Dorothy Osborne's view of the scene.

Lacking perfumes and lotions or other artificial aids, the milkmaids could be seen as the ideal females for those who resented the 'prodigious transmutations' and 'phantastick innovations' of fashionable women described by the ballad. 'In milking a cow, and straining the teats through her fingers, it seemes that so sweet a milk-presse makes the milk whiter or sweeter, for never came almond glove or aromatique oyntment on her palme to taint it.'[11] Thrift, innocence, and artless beauty were some of the qualities attributed to these ideal figures, and fashionable women sought to acquire a little of this winsomeness for themselves. A comparison of two portraits of Catherine of Braganza (1638–1705) indicates the pastoral ideal aimed for, and its relation to other tastes in dress.

Catherine married Charles II (1630–85) in 1662. Two years later Samuel Pepys, looking at some paintings by Jacob Huysman, 'as good pictures, I think, as ever I saw,' singled out two of the new Queen. In one picture she was portrayed as St Catherine, a popular portrait guise. Pepys' own wife was painted thus in 1666. In the other picture the Queen appeared as a shepherdess; 'I was mightily pleased with this sight indeed,' Pepys added.[12] Only shortly before, on 25 May 1662, Pepys had observed the strange farthingales of the Portuguese ladies who accompanied the King's bride to London, a style of dress which John Evelyn, at the same time, considered to be monstrous, and he thought the Queen's hairstyle to be very strange.

In her national Portuguese dress the small Catherine was safe in the custody of a ponderous and lavishly embellished farthingale, her hair stiff and careful, conveying altogether an aloof, stately and even sad formality [58]. In the portrait seen and liked by Pepys, which Huysman had done in the shepherdess manner, Catherine had abandoned her farthingale, and her sleek, stiff hairstyle had come undone, to wander uncontained over her shoulders. In a magnificent and voluminous satin shift, draped with a rich sash of brocade, Catherine was *décolletée*, and voluptuous, all she was not in her earlier style of dress [59]. This portrait was similar in effect to many others of the later seventeenth century; using a pastoral manner and accessories, the painter and the sitter sought to convey a temporary Arcadian placement without entirely losing

58 Portrait of Catherine of Braganza as she appeared in her native Portuguese court dress on arrival in England for her marriage to Charles II. Evelyn thought her farthingale was monstrous. *c.*1660.

details of rank and wealth. By removing dominant features of more formal fashion, such as long-fronted stomachers, stiff stays or controlled ringlets at the side of the head, the portrait contrived to put the sitter in a timeless zone, with, so it seemed at the time, none of the features which would appear dated in a few years' time. However, no dream of membership of Arcadia, and no amount of cunning on the painter's part, can entirely remove the commanding taste of the day.

A characteristically fashionable item no 'shepherdess' could bring herself to part with was her set of pearls. Catherine retained a close necklace of fat ones when she sat to Huysman, sometime between 1662 and 1664; so too, for instance, did Dorothy Sidney when she sat as a shepherdess to Anthony van Dyck around 1640; she also framed her face with a large, soft, cartwheel hat with upturned brim, and kept pearls at her neck and ears. In the 1670s, Barbara Villiers, Duchess of Cleveland and mother to at least six of the King's children, was painted by Sir Peter Lely in fluttering 'undress,' carrying a houlette (a form of shepherd's crook) and wearing a necklace and large pendant earrings of pearl; so too the unknown lady drawn by the same artist in the 1660s [57] mixes jewellery and pastoral features. Given the beauty and bloom of pearls it is not surprising that they enjoyed a long vogue during the century, and that their owners wished to include them in portraits, despite the fact they contradicted other affected simplicity. An inventory of 1651 showed not only the quantities of pearls possessed by a wealthy family, but also the numbers strung into each piece: 'a necklace of seven and forty pearls; another necklace of seven strings made up of 2,735 pearls; two bracelets of 153 and 155 pearls respectively; three pendant pearls.'[13]

During this and other pastoral revivals, Arcadia had to accommodate the good life and conspicious consumption, as well as rank. In 1630 Sir Richard Fanshawe wrote an ode on Charles I's proclamation that gentry in the city must return to their country estates; he tried to reassure the ladies they would find 'more solid joys' there than in the town, but his endeavour to attract them back to real rather than idealized nature had a hollow ring, quite unlike similar Tudor expressions. No pearly shepherdess in a London park was going to take this idea seriously when he suggested that the flowers themselves contained as much gaiety and splendour as the court itself.

Like other revivals, the cultivation of a shepherdess-look sought to retain status and its necessities, whilst borrowing, by association, the better attributes of the original model. Although the imitation could not claim close similarities with a pastoral original, it was a vogue which did manage to promote a more relaxed and comfortable alternative to the stiffer formalities of other fashions. It was in this aspect affiliated to the concurrent taste for classical dress, and the modish adoption of loose 'undress.' Both of these, in addition to the shepherdess form, were actively abetted by portrait painters, to the extent that it is not always possible to know if the appearances they created preceded or succeeded the actual garments worn elsewhere; what is certain is that portrait painters in the seventeenth century had considerable influence in shaping taste in dress, arguably more than at any other period.

One of the most impressive seventeenth-century portrait painters was Sir Anthony van Dyck, whose influence in fashion lived on after his death into the eighteenth century. For the greater part of that century fashionable men and women turned to his paintings for favourite styles to copy in their clothes, and incidentally thereby perpetuated a sleek appearance partly created by van Dyck's original attempt to reduce dating details of dress; in employing rather busy and large areas of vibrant, reflective fabrics, often adding to

59 Catherine of Braganza after her marriage to Charles II, depicted as a shepherdess. Pastoral taste at court had transformed her earlier appearance. *c.*1662.

1 This Elizabethan girl subtly tempered her formal appearance by undersleeves embroidered with lovingly observed natural detail. 1587 (detail in Plate 53).

2 With flamboyant style, James II combined the grandeur of Roman armour and his own late seventeenth-century taste for exquisitely fashionable cane and periwig. c. 1672.

what was actually worn, van Dyck drew attention away from detail. He had a tendency to diminish visually the slashing on a sleeve, or the run of seams or the pull of the sitter's body inside the garments, and he concentrated instead on the fabric surface and its capacity to generate atmosphere, grace and movement [83]. Van Dyck had first come to England in 1620, leaving to return again in 1632 when he was honoured with a knighthood from the grateful Charles I, and with an annual pension and a house. He died in 1641, but in those few years he added immeasurably to the possibilities in English art, and his output of masterly portraits of the royal family, the courtiers, the aristocrats and wealthy gentry has left a full record of that generation, and played a considerable role then and later in creating ideals of personal beauty and dress. For instance, in the double female portrait from the National Gallery [18] van Dyck demonstrated that even stout stays confining the torso could be persuaded to look more relaxed and sensual by assymetric ornament and a loosely swathed scarf or shawl.

In women's dress during the seventeenth century, the waist, which had been high in the 1630s and forties, began to drop until it was significantly lower by the 1660s. Using this as a focus, it is possible to gauge from portraits that loose, pastoral dress still revealed the prevailing shape. The Huysman portrait of Catherine [59] signifies by the wrinkles in the satin a ghost waist somewhere near the upper edge of the sash draped over the knees. One of the early shepherdess portraits, that of Mrs Henslowe, done in 1635 by Cornelius Johnson, indicates a high waist, above the bend of the elbow. Later portraits of the 1660s and seventies show the same shepherdess features but worn with shifts whose configurations suggest, while not actually delineating, a longer, lower waist and bodice: Sir Peter Lely's portrait of Barbara Villiers, for example.

Shepherdess accessories added focus to a widespread taste for a vaguer form of undress which, although respectable, could also signify an inclination to renounce convention. The Duchess of Portsmouth, painted by Lely in about 1670 (the picture is now in the Paul Getty Museum), showed a long bodice, only just held together by jewelled clasps at the centre front and on the sleeves, through which gaps there drifts a wide-sleeved chemise; when John Evelyn saw the future Duchess at Euston Hall in October 1671 he noted she 'was for the most part in her undresse all day.' In this case what could often be an acceptable informal state was obviously not: 'and that there was fondnesse and toying with that young wanton,'[14] and Evelyn imputed extremely free behaviour to her. Undress could be as innocent as a shepherdess, or as *risqué* as a court beauty; when it was worn by Mrs Samuel Pepys the diary records no slight on its respectability.

There is evidence in the Pepys diary of an enthusiasm for rustic features on a less grand scale than that dealt with by Lely or van Dyck and their colleagues. In July 1667, Mr and Mrs Pepys enjoyed themselves out on Epsom Downs, and Pepys had his moving encounter with the old shepherd; in August they were off to Hatfield, and had 'great delight' and a walk in the park 'of as much pleasure as could be desired in the world for country pleasure and good air.' Pepys gave no indication of their clothes, except that they had a cold journey from London, so when his wife and Mrs Turner put on country hats, it was probably over their usual city clothes. 'Being come back [from the park], and weary with the walk, the women had pleasure in putting on some straw hats, which are much worn in this country, and did become them mightily, but especially my wife.'[15]

Straw hats gradually gained admirers outside their original rural locations, although Pepys hinted at their novelty for urban women even in 1667. Earlier, in 1608, when Thomas Coryat was travelling in Italy he found himself at one of the sources of fine straw hats which were later to make a considerable reputation in fashionable circles, and he too obviously regarded them as novel enough to deserve description. Coryat noticed that both men and women wore them, although the women's were more fully decorated, 'some of them having at the least an hundred seames made with silke, and some pretily woven in the seames with silver, and many flowers, borders, and branches very curiously wrought in them.'[16] A long tradition had bred great skills, both in Italy and also in Hertfordshire and Bedfordshire as Pepys saw, and it was only a matter of time before these were tapped by urban fashion. Coryat's description is very close to the spirit common to many modern straw hats, redolent of the pleasures of a summer's day [78].

The restful qualities associated with dress made to conjure up the countryside must have been welcome in busy urban lives. Pepys came home from business for a midday meal one August and enjoyed the company of one of their guests dressed 'in a *paysan* dress, that looks mighty pretty,'[17] but it must have seemed plain beside the court's idea of idyllic rural dress. In 1675, there was a performance at court of a masque called *Calisto* for which the participants had splendid costumes including pastoral dress. This masque was very elaborate, and apart from the fact it was enacted by the courtiers themselves as amateurs, it was closer to an opera or musical than the former style of masquing. Because its records and accounts survive it is possible to know in detail what the pastoral dress consisted of, and it was obviously based on imaginative sources rather than real ones: 'a shepherdesses habbit the gowne of sky coloured sattine the body of a cherry colloured sattin the pettycoate of silver tinsell with Bullions on it, the bace and sleeves of silver tinsell lined with a Cherry colloured sarsnet. . . .'[18] There was gold tinsel as well, and the wearer, a Mrs Butler, had six strings of pearls, pearl silk hose and a fine white straw hat lined with red silk and faced with cherry taffeta. She seems to have provided her own shoes, which were probably suitably elaborate: she also carried a crook, and there were several others equally richly dressed who shared between them a very substantial length of green taffeta ribbon, and who also wore silk-lined straw hats. The shepherds were not provided with straw hats, but were equally finely equipped with gold tinsel waistcoats and green taffeta breeches laced with gold and silver, and had pearl silk hose. Some had cherry and white feathers, and fourteen dozen cherry and silver roses found a use amongst them.

The large upturned hats seen in some portraits of ladies dressed as shepherdesses [59] may be of straw lined with silk or taffeta; it would be difficult to imagine how a purely cloth brim could hold up the shape, and a rich lining may have been thought necessary to beautify a rough, country straw hat enough for a lady of rank to wear, and to prevent it from snagging her hair.

8 *Houses in London, Homes in the Country*

THE EIGHTEENTH CENTURY

So manifold, all pleasing in their kind,
All healthfull, are th'employs of rural life,
Reiterated as the Wheel of time
Run round, still ending, and beginning still.

William Cowper, *The Garden*, 1785

In 1762 Johan Zoffany painted Mr and Mrs Garrick, with company, taking tea at an elegant table in their Hampton garden. David Garrick is seen handing a cup of tea to his brother, who is fishing in the nearby Thames. A delicate, newly planted willow tree adorns the lawn which slopes smoothly to the water's edge. More than three-quarters of this painting concentrates on landscape, and a view of landscape which epitomizes one of the dominant ways of seeing scenery during the eighteenth century; this is not a wild, unkempt view but an orderly and busy scene, with a barge on the river, seats under the trees and cows grazing across the water. The Garricks' garden was designed by Lancelot 'Capability' Brown (1716–83), and the lucky owners are seen taking their leisure amongst its careful forms, as trim and elegant as a drawing room.

If ever a century recorded itself as enjoying an elegant rustication, it was the eighteenth century. For example, enjoyment of such felicitously arranged vistas shows in W. Taylor's view of Stanway House taken in 1748; this time an entirely countrified setting provides a variety of quiet pursuits. Over twenty people are seen, some in a boat on a landscaped lake, others merely taking the air, and these two paintings are part of a large number of works commemorating such pastimes. In these modified vistas, sheltered from the extremes of nature, was an arena in which fashion and dress played an important part. In wilder landscapes imagined by painters and desired by travellers in search of a sublime experience, there was little place for nuances of fanciful dress, but within the mental frame of a re-designed parkscape, and tamed landscape, it was possible to see and want romantic dress to complement the evocative views. Familiarity with the pleasant modification of nature undertaken by painter and landscape gardeners was parallelled by an equally lyrical tendency in dress, either to wear within the real landscape, to complete the picture as it were, or to wear in town, to bring some rural delights into the vocabulary of fashion. In this atmosphere the dairy and the hayfield provided scenic backdrops for fashionable clothes, based on rural prototypes. In addition another phase of inventive and enthusiastic floral decoration arrived for both men and women. Unlike that of the sixteenth century, the eighteenth-century taste in this area was aided by the frequent addition of printed pattern to woven and embroidered ones.

Embroidered flowers and natural items gained from the vogue for hooped skirts to dresses; these, when opened at the front, revealed an expanse of petticoat offering a spacious display area for decorations. So too did the robings and facings of a gown, and the trains, extended behind for court wear, gave even more scope. These capacious settings for decoration allowed for the composition of themes, and ideas could be developed to help unify the ensemble; much ornament in the rural and natural idiom was used here and on the waistcoats of the men. In women's dress the expression of interest and pleasure in this idiom often came in for minute scrutiny, and it was no light undertaking to render large areas of a full-length garment decorative in an inventive and acceptable way, and to wear it well. These days such a daunting task is generally only undertaken for special dresses at state occasions, but for eighteenth-century women of fashion and taste, several ensembles were needed for a season, and to fail was to fail publicly and expensively: 'My Lady Scarborough was in violet-coloured satin, the petticoat embroidered with clumsy festoons of *nothing at all's supported by pillars* no better than posts, the gown covered with embroidery, a very unmeaning pattern, but altogether very fine.'[1]

Put to the test of surviving all manner of scrutiny and interpretations, these individual versions of rural and natural themes went the round of the busy urban season. Dresses, or gowns as they were then known, were especially elaborate for court occasions, and it is known that Queen Charlotte, for instance, passed comment on appearances. Charlotte married George III in 1761, and for the next forty years of his long reign, she maintained events which were an important part of the season, and an important contribution to the arena of display in dress. At her Drawing Rooms, for example, members of society would be introduced to various individuals of the royal family, and these crowded, formal occasions created difficulties of movement, as well as trials of taste and elegance. 'When her Majesty had done speaking to me unfortunately the flounce of my petticoat intangled with hers, and tho' I tore my own it was some little time before I could separate them. . . .'[2]

Of all the inventive and varied embroidery of decorative features of women's dress at glittering occasions in the eighteenth century, perhaps the most splendid 'landscape' recorded as worn on a petticoat and gown was that belonging to the Duchess of Queensberry in 1740. Although it was deep February in London, a place already known for smog, the Duchess brightened the proceedings by arriving with a sunny summer scene, a pastoral vision enlivened by artful details; there is every justification for this being one of the most quoted sartorial wonders of its day. The white satin gown and petticoat were embroidered as follows:

> . . . the bottom of the petticoat *brown hills* covered with all sorts of weeds, and every breadth had *an old stump of tree*, that ran up almost to the top of the petticoat, broken and ragged, and worked with brown chenille, round which twined nastersians, ivy, honeysuckles, periwinkles, convolvuleses and all sorts of twining flowers, which spread and covered the petticoat, vines with leaves variegated as you have seen them by the sun, all rather smaller than nature, which made them look very light; the robings and facings were little green banks with all sorts of weeds, and the sleeves and the rest of the gown loose twining branches of the same sort as those on the petticoat: many of the leaves were finished with gold and part of the stumps of the trees looked like the gilding of the sun. I never saw a piece of work so prettily fancied, and am quite angry with myself for not having the same thought, for it is infinitely handsomer than mine and could have *not* cost *much more*. . . .[3]

Men's clothes afforded less uninterrupted space on which to display such a quantity of embroidery, but their waistcoats were often decorated down the centre front, and on pockets. Depending on how much would show under the coat, and varied by the currently fashionable cut of the waistcoat, it was the focus of the wearer's display of taste and style; the ingenuity of the floral decoration and the colour and sheer magnificence have seldom been surpassed in male dress since. In the early and middle years of the century, waistcoats had long 'skirts,' and these, sometimes worn under whole suits patterned with matching embroidery, made a fine display. As the century went by the waistcoat became shorter and the male silhouettes paralleled the female's tendency to simplicity and slimness, but still the waistcoat carried the most careful decoration. Buttonholes, for practical purposes, benefit from embroidery, as do any seams which take strain, but it is not uncommon to find this grown into a wide band of flowers and vegetation rambling down from collar to hem. On the pocket flaps may be entire rustic scenes; even the hembands of knee breeches were to be seen with floral details. These patterns were often worked before the waistcoat was put together. Many examples survive in excellent condition to recall these flowery days in men's dress, as a long-lived taste which co-existed with plainer and more sobre suits, but which gradually declined in the early nineteenth century when the waistcoat itself shrank considerably. Men took to disliking pattern of most sorts, but particularly floral, and to mistrusting bright colour.

These years of magnificence are occasionally recalled by the appearance of what might be called today a 'fancy waistcoat', although only a vestige of its former self, but the waistcoat seems presently in danger of being discarded altogether, and without this smaller, and therefore more economical, parade-ground for embroidery men seem set for an era of plain suits, with stitched decoration shrunk to ties only or wholly relegated to informal wear.

Printed and woven materials also offered both men and women the opportunity to wear familiar floral and pastoral themes. Printed, fast-dyed textiles had been available from India from the early seventeenth century; indeed, their popularity was such that for most of the eighteenth century printed cottons, both imported

60 Embroidery in silk and metal thread on a lady's front skirt panel, showing cottages and trees by a fenced hill with abundant floral detail. *c.*1735.

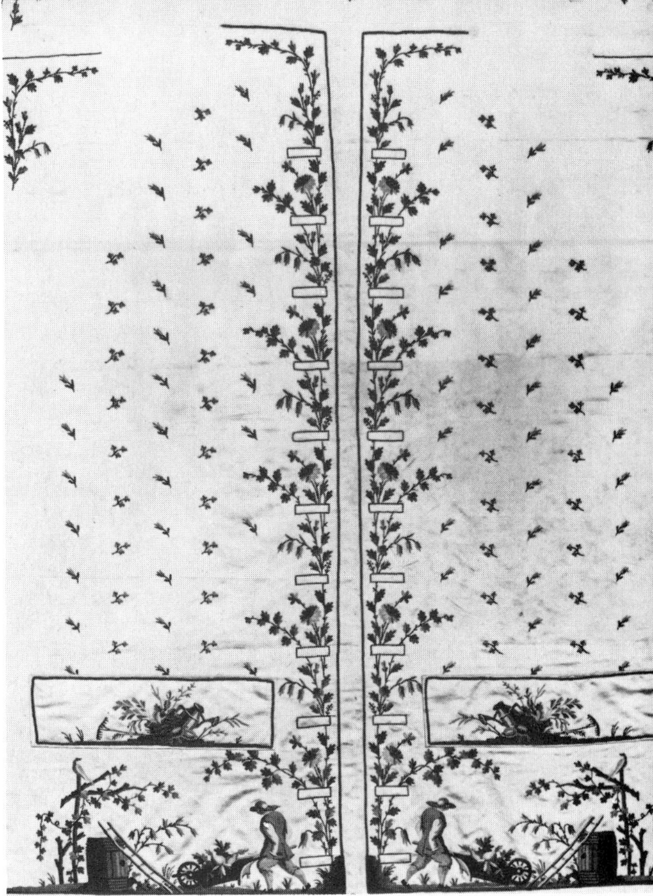

61 Carefully observed detail in silk embroidery to decorate a panel for a man's waistcoat. Pocket flaps show tools of the gardener. Late eighteenth century.

and home printed, had been banned for the sake of threatened wool and silk manufacturers. Nevertheless, printed cloths of other sorts were manufactured, and after 1774 the ban was lifted. In all its forms, printing on cloth produced a vast range of floral ideas, and whole pastoral scenes peopled with rustic characters, can be found.

The Duchess of Queensberry was an exponent of simplicity as well as magnificence in dress. Having displayed her embroidered rustic decoration so memorably in 1740, she was also known to demonstrate a shrewd, even humorous taste in dressing down, and discarding the usual trappings of her rank. Catherine Hyde until her marriage in 1720, she died in 1777, by which time she had amassed a reputation for arrogance and independence of behaviour. Protected by wealth and status, she indulged in episodes of unusually plain appearance, demonstrating in extreme the process by which this could, and still can, unsettle the regular pattern of rank and social division. For example, at the coronation of George II in 1727, at which occasion Queen Caroline was said to be wearing all the jewels she could find in London, the Duchess of Queensberry, in possession of many, wore none. She wore an apron at court in the full knowledge that they were proscribed; and on an occasion in 1743 she unexpectedly called on Mrs Mary Delany, conspicuously lacking a hoop or any ruffles. In these ways she flouted conventions for reasons probably known only to herself, but in the various recorded instances there was never any doubt about who she was; she was not disguised, only altered. Her plainness annoyed her contemporaries, because it was inappropriate and misplaced and so unsettled normal distinctions of rank. Plainness as an evocation of rusticity, however, was acceptable and fashionable; rank was not in doubt on such occasions, for the transformation was never entire, and the real rural communities knew their landowners and their own customary place well enough to maintain the normal patterns of life whenever wealthy, fashionable people temporarily took on their own version of a rural appearance. The Duchess of Queensberry, incidentally, had her portrait painted dressed as a milkmaid [62].

In 1764 Horace Walpole attended a haymaking party which was spoiled by the guests finding it too cold; in 1748 Mrs Delaney set down the pleasures: 'We sat an hour on the hay cocks, refreshed by the fragrancy

62 Many women of leisure enjoyed keeping a dairy at this time. Portrait of Duchess of Queensberry dressed as a milkmaid, *c.*1740. Simple, hoopless dress and an apron, and milkpail at the ready.

of the hay and the sweetness of the air, till the setting sun warned us to bend our footsteps home.'[4] Londoners would walk out on June evenings to enjoy the sight: 'after dinner walked with my father and sister to the fields between Paddington and Bayswater. The haymaking, a beautiful warm quiet evening; we sat for some time on the cocks of hay. . . .'[5] It was particularly inviting for the normally leisured classes because they had no need to travel from sight of home since parkland close to the house was cut for hay; haymaking was a job that was best done in fair weather, and could be begun and left at will since the real labourers would continue it to completion and would load the waggons and build the final rick. In using a wooden rake, delicate hands might occasionally get dusty or blistered, but it was generally the cleanest exercise offered to the gentry or aristocracy by their fields. Ploughing, shearing, sowing, weeding, scything – these tasks looked picturesque but were without the conveniences of haymaking, and were never taken up as fashionable pastimes.

Haymaking was a pursuit or a spectacle enjoyed by both those who remained in London and those who owned their own land and were able to spend time on it in the countryside. It encouraged simplified dress, and country straw hats, and brought the fashionable in contact with the unfashionable poor. The same month that Miss Berry went to see the hay near Bayswater she attended an evening masquerade party in Harley Street dressed as an old peasant woman.

A visitor to London in 1748 had noted the ordinary Londoner's habit of surrounding houses and yards with pots of trees and flowers: 'They thus sought to have some of the pleasant enjoyments of a country life in the midst of the hubbub of the town.'[6] Wealthier Londoners would go to considerable lengths to recreate or evoke this country life. As well as haymaking, the shepherdess continued to be popular in the eighteenth century. Regardless of the reality of her presence in agricultural life, she was so firmly implanted in the imagination, that she was almost a personification of Arcadia and innocence of rural pleasures. Out walking in 1745, Mrs Delaney carried a shepherdess's crook, and earlier *The Spectator* complained of the enthusiasm for masquerade dress.

It is interesting to speculate on the reasons why fashionable appearance was not sufficient, and why people needed the additional outlet of this sort of fanciful dress:

> . . . it is a kind of acting to go in Masquerade, and a Man should be able to say or do things proper for the Dress in which he appears. . . . People dress themselves in what they have a Mind to be, and not what they are fit for. There is not a Girl in the Town, but let her have her Will in going to a Masque, and she shall dress as a Shepherdess. But let me beg of them to read the *Arcadia*, or some other good Romance, before they appear in any such Character at my House. The last Day we presented, every Body was so rashly habited, that when they came to speak to each other, a Nymph with a Crook had not a Word to say but in the pert Stile of a Pit Bawdry. . . .[7]

It seemed that no amount of rustic appurtenances would produce the desired effect; the clothes could do no more than clad the figure, whilst, if the critics were right, the modern urban personality persisted. The intrepid 'rustics' and shepherdesses, together with their critics, succeeded in emphasizing the truism we know today: rural clothes cannot make their wearer rural, and rural life itself is perpetually changing, so that our vision of its qualities is often illusory, yet by pseudo-rustic dress we persist in vain attempts to recreate Arcadia.

> The High-crowned Hat, after having been confined to cots and villages for so long a time, is become the favourite mode of quality, and is the politest distinction of a fashionable undress. I quarrel with it only because it seems to be a kind of masquerade; it would insinuate an idea of innocence and rusticity, though the Park is not the likeliest place to be the scene of either: in short, if a woman is dressed like a Wood Nymph, I expect the simplicity of manners, and full force of rural nature, which is of a piece with the character; but I am generally most egregiously disappointed.[8]

The writer in 1731 goes on to suggest that in this case the revival was made in the hope that it would simultaneously revive the romantic adventures somebody

63 Haymaking became a social occasion in the eighteenth century. Here both gentry and labourers participate, near Newbury. 1744.

had read of in association with the rustic original. In 1754 Samuel Richardson in the novel *Sir Charles Grandison* dressed Harriet Byron for a masquerade, as an Arcadian princess, and she wore elaborately trimmed and glittering satin waistcoat and petticoat with a silk scarf, bracelets, and carried a large Indian fan. It was an exercise in imaginative splendour rather than an attempt to recreate pastoral simplicity, although Harriet noted: 'I am not to have a hoop that is perceivable. They wore no hoops in Arcadia.'[9]

Rural simplicity eluded fashionable people, who, although recreating what they thought was appropriate dress, were searching for something that others said no longer existed, either in dress or manners or occupation. If these observers were right there was very little in the countryside on which fashion could model itself: '. . . the dairymaids wear large hoops and velvet hoods instead of the round [i.e. closed] *tight petticoat* and *straw hat . . . the pure simplicity of ye country is quite lost!*'[10] This observer, Mrs Delany, in 1745, was probably being ironic, knowing that the countryside had never been so simple. A Scandinavian visitor in 1748, no doubt conscious of the English lack of regional dress, noted similarities between rural and urban dress, and was very surprised to find women confined to the houses whilst the men did the field work. In this picture of the English countryside there is no place for even a shepherdess, and Londoners would have searched in vain for a milkmaid:

I could not believe I saw aright, when I first came here, out in the country, and saw the farmers' houses full of young women, while the men, on the contrary, went out both morning and evening to where the cattle were, milk-pail in hand, sat down to milk, and afterwards carried the milk home.[11]

This referred only to eastern England, but his account of the dress of country women accords with a wider picture:

. . . they commonly wear a red cloak. They also wear *pattens* under their ordinary shoes when they go out, to prevent dirt on the roads and streets from soiling their ordinary shoes. All go laced, and use for everyday a sort of *Manteau*, made commonly of brownish *Camlot*. The same head-dress as in London. Here it is not unusual to see a farmer's or another small personage's wife clad on Sundays like a lady of 'quality' at other places in the world, and her every-day attire in proportion. 'Paniers' are seldom used in the country. When they go out they always wear straw hats, which they have made themselves from wheat-straw, and are pretty enough. On high days they have on ruffles. One hardly ever sees a woman here trouble herself in the least about outdoor duties, such as *tending*, in the arable and meadows. . . .[12]

Although women elsewhere did field work, and tended animals, including milk cows, it was by no means universal; there were considerable regional and seasonal differences in patterns of agricultural labour, and no easily identifiable uniform associated with particular occupations. Thus there was no simple or ready picture for an urban mode to imitate, and the urban shepherdesses or milkmaids, for example, were self-perpetuating figures more wishful than actual, copied from fanciful sources and presumably highly curious to the eyes of a country person. For example, in June 1791, at a public masquerade at Vauxhall Gardens, there was not one milkmaid, but a group, complete with a Jack in the Green and 'haymakers, shepherdesses, housemaids, etc. out of number.'[13]

For wealthier people the pursuit of Arcadia did not need to take place in such a bustling crowd; *fêtes champêtres* and rustic events were commonly arranged in private grounds or parks. One fete in 1774, near Epsom, had a singing shepherd and shepherdess to entertain the guests, who were dressed amongst other themes as peasants and gardeners, and invited to 'various country sports.'[14]

One of the events described by Horace Walpole in 1791 demonstrated the effort one fashionable lady was prepared to make to recreate the pastoral ideal in the 'hubbub' of the urban social season; it was an unusually cold June and Walpole had already suffered from a chilly excursion to look at his own haymakers: '. . . the contents of an English June are, hay and ice, orange-flowers and rheumatisms.' He was then attracted to Mrs Hobart's announcement of a rural breakfast at her house on Ham Common: 'It rained early in the morning; she dispatched post-boys – for want of cupids and zephyrs, to stop the nymphs and shepherds who tend their flocks in Pall Mall and St James Street, but half of them missed the couriers and arrived.'[15] What Walpole called 'the second edition' of this pastoral pastime also suffered from rain the following Saturday, but enough people attended to ensure its success. The *London Chronicle* reported:

The Hon. Mrs Hobart's rural breakfast, on Saturday last, . . . was numerously attended; almost every person of distinction who had not gone 'further-a-field' were present: the garden was formed to represent a French village, in which tables were placed under the trees decorated with flowers, at which the company breakfasted in the centre under a tree; on a tub a rustic was placed, who played during the repast on the pipe and tabor. The lawn was surrounded with trees, and under them a *traiteur & cabaret*, a village bake-house, a fruit shop, and cook-shop, from which the company refreshed themselves with wines, cakes, fruit and the most delicate viands. It was nearly six o'clock in the afternoon before the whole of company retired. . . .[16]

Not surprisingly when James Gillray caricatured Mrs Hobart in 1795, he drew her as an excessively fat milkmaid with a bunch of flowers in her straining stays, a 'Cowslip, with a bowl of Cream.' The good life was guaranteed; it was decorated rather than threatened by these rural evocations.

Less than two weeks after Mrs Hobart's rural fete, at the Grand Scottish Sheep Shearing festival, in July 1791, about a hundred and twenty people 'of rank and distinction' gathered to watch events promoted by the Society for the Improvement of British Wool. The shearing was accompanied by a musical band, and one might have imagined that real shepherds, shearing sheep with great skill and competence to the sound of music, would have satisfied any need for a picturesque pastoral scene. However, the spectators themselves fully entered into the spirit of the event; with no apparent sense of being *de trop*, the 'Ladies were in general dressed in white muslin, with flowers and various coloured ribbons; and each bore a Shepherdess's crook, decorated with taste and fancy. The day being favourable, the appearance on the green of so much beauty and elegance afforded a spectacle at once pleasing and interesting.' Evidently with no change of clothes, the 'shepherdesses' sat down to tea, and then ended the day with a fine ball which lasted until midnight.[17]

The straw hat was one article of country dress which was not the result of urban imaginations; but by the early part of the eighteenth century it had become so popular that it no longer made any suggestion that its wearer was either rustic or poor. Fashion embraced a taste for straw so thoroughly that even some shoes and bands of dress decoration came to be made of it. As the straw hat went up the social scale it became more elaborate and was no longer a home-made, or merely locally consumed, item, but was manufactured in quantity for a new market in other areas. It provides an instance of a rural item of dress absorbed by fashionable dress but remaining in production in its regional base. Bedfordshire, for example, being close to London, grew as a straw hat centre; Luton still remains so. For once it was provincial pockets which gained from the urban espousal of rural taste. If the following account from 1716 is accurate, the straw hat conquered the beau monde all of a sudden. This seems unlikely, nevertheless it catches the mechanism by which a fashion can be created:

64 Straw hat, basket of flowers and old-fashioned lacing for a lady of fashion whose pearls and satin indicate that she is a shepherdess for only a day.

The Prince and Princess admit everybody of any fashion, the meanest persons whatsoever, to come and see them at dinner. One day they interested themselves with seeing the country folks come in their straw hats and because one came without her straw hat the Princess sent her back again to fetch it. Upon this several of the gentry came in with straw hats very fine with footmen attending. . . .[18]

Young men of fashion engaged in a vogue for occupational and class disguise, which had partially rural overtones; in attempts to appear as unkempt and uncouth as possible they succeeded, on occasion, in being mistaken for their own stable boys. In some instances this seems to have been based on a desire to reject urban fashion and social rank, and to align themselves superficially, with rather vagrant occupations. In 1738, for instance, there appeared in the audience of a London theatre: 'a parcel of the strangest fellows that ever I saw in my life; some of them had those loose kind of great Coats on, which I have heard called *Wrap rascals*, with gold-laced Hats slouched, in humble imitation of Stage-coachmen: others aspired at being *Grooms*, and had dirty Boots and Spurs, with black Caps on, and long Whips in their hands. . . .'[19]

Whether or not this was the same deliberately unsettling activity as that undertaken by the Duchess of Queensberry in her plain dress is open to question, but the occasions were recorded fairly close to each other. Horace Walpole noticed that young men were still doing much the same thing some fifty years later, in 1791. With something of the septuagenarian's bemusement he recorded: 'I do not know the present generation by sight, for though I pass them in the streets, the hats with valances, the folds above the chin of the ladies, and the dirty shirts and shaggy hair of the young men, who have *levelled nobility* almost as much as the *mobility* in France have confounded all individuality.'[20]

A few years later, in 1807, a correspondent in the *Ladies Monthly Museum* expressed concern that all elegance and urbanity had gone, and blunders of identification were too common: '*Dukes* for *Grooms*, *Earls* for *Postillions*, and *Squires* for *Stableboys*. . . .'[21] Jockey waistcoats, slouched hats, cropped heads and unpowdered hair were all denounced as 'ruffian' fashions, and the days of Lord Chesterfield's notions of elegance were mourned. There is no certain evidence to suggest such confusion caused by these fashions was serious or widespread; all the commentators, whilst claiming confusion, were acknowledging a recognizable imitation rather than any fool-proof disguising, but they aired the long-felt view that fanciful dress was acceptable as long as it did not threaten to overturn social distinctions entirely.

It is worth quoting at length here what the American Ambassador observed about the English in 1818; it was characteristic of the eighteenth as well as the nineteenth century, and underpins any account of the taste for pastoral or occupational dress of the countryside. With a shrewd eye, Richard Rush observed the system he found:

The enthusiastic fondness of the English for the country, is the effect of their laws. Primogeniture is at the root of it. Scarcely any persons who hold a leading place in the circles of their society live in London. They have *houses* in London, in which they stay while Parliament sits, and occasionally visit at other seasons; but their *homes* are in the country. Their turreted mansions are there, with all that denotes perpetuity – heirlooms, family memorials, pictures, tombs. This spreads the ambition among other classes, and the taste for rural life, however diversified or graduated the scale, becomes widely diffused. . . . The permanent interests and affections of the most opulent classes centre almost universally in the country. Heads of families go there to resume their stand in the midst of these feelings; and all, to partake of the pastimes of the country life, where they flourish in pomp and joy.[22]

9 *To Gather Roses All Day Long*

THE NINETEENTH CENTURY

All English women think it necessary to profess loving the country, and to long to be in the country, altho' their minds are often neither sufficiently opened, nor their pursuits sufficiently interesting, to make such a taste rational.

Miss Berry, *Letter to a friend*, 1806

Changes had occurred in both male and female dress at the end of the eighteenth century which resulted in the slimming of the silhouettes of both: very high waisted, tubular dresses were established for women, and men wore close, cutaway suits, dispensing altogether with the wider shapes of coats and waistcoats which had previously been fashionable. The interest in classical, antique features was a major characteristic, but there was no lessening of the pastoral taste, which co-existed with it at the start of the nineteenth century.

An interesting pastoral detail in fashions for women was the so-called gipsy hat. To our eyes, accustomed to a decline in the wearing of hats by both sexes, they seem to have much ornamental impact, but at the time they were thought of as simple and ingenuous. In 1806 a morning dress was to be worn with a 'Nankeen Pelisse, border of white lace; Straw Gipsey Hat,

65 Poor children in mid-nineteenth-century school. These smocks and pinafores are the model for present-day pastoral fashions worn by the well-to-do.

ornamented with a Wreath of White flowers, and Bow of Ribbons on one side';[1] Ackermann's recommended in 1819 'a gypsy hat, composed of British *Leghorn*, and ornamented with full plume of ostrich feathers; the brim is turned up before and behind.' These popular hats were usually intended for wear with walking or morning dress, having an air of jaunty leisure rather than formality, and they extended the possibilities of the established vogue for a variety of straw types and styles in headwear. 'The Caledonian Gipsy, the Cottage and the Pomona hat, are the most admired; they are ornamented with autumnal flowers, or branches of vine, and have in general a half handkerchief of net, embroidered to correspond.'[2]

It is interesting that these fetching evocations of rural life could be admired at the same time as the gipsies themselves were subject to considerable prejudice: in Mary Russell Mitford's account of village life, which originally appeared in *The Ladies Magazine* between 1824 and 1832, gipsies were seen in a poetic light by the author, but in quite another by the villagers: 'The arrival of these vagabonds spread a general consternation through the village. Gamekeepers and housewives were in equal dismay. . . . "The gypsies!" was the answer general to every inquiry for things missing.'[3] Earlier, in 1748, Kalm had 'wondered highly that this useless folk could be tolerated in this country,'[4] but although gipsies have been mistrusted, they have also been envied for their nomadic life; 'gipsying' came to mean doing things out of doors, such as picnicking. (Londoners were shown gipsying in Epping Forest, in a painting by C.R. Leslie now in the Geffreye Museum.) The gipsy hat or bonnet, usually with a shallow crown and deep brim often folded down to the sides of the head, was a romantic idea; in fact gipsies themselves in Britain have not been known for a standardized form of dress, and have resembled any other poor group, making use of cast-offs. (The modern 'gipsy style' for women consisting of a deeply frilled skirt and low-cut blouse is in fact a romanticized version of Spanish dress.)

As 'gipsy,' applied to fashionable items, suggested times of sunny leisure, so the name of 'cottage' became loosely applied to dress meant for pastoral pastimes rather than real cottage life. Gentle pursuits in the garden or conservatory prompted fashion writers in early nineteenth-century periodicals to name suitable gowns or hats as 'cottage.' This did not conflict with the cheerful use of impractical colours and cloth, such as the peach and white satin used in the trimmings for the bombasine 'round' cottage gown [66] depicted in Ackermann's *Repository*; there, the peach-coloured handkerchief at the neck was described as being 'tied carelessly round the throat,' and the ribbons to tie the cottage bonnet were shown hanging casually over the shoulders. These features correspond with the relaxed sense of clothes inspired by an idealized view of country life. They gave no indication of the ceaseless activity which would have characterized real cottage life. The fashionable world saw such life as a hobby to be indulged in for holidays, and it is likely that reality did not impinge on the fantasy at all.

In the evening Lady Douglas proposed a walk, though all the colours of the prospect were buried in one twilight tint. When we came in sight of the cottage, the reason for our walk was cleared up – its little pediment was prettily lighted up with coloured lamps, amongst the fresh green fern-leaves with which the front of the pediment was tastefully covered . . . upon the table two large flower-pots, and the tea set out with the cottage tea-things. It was very pretty, and well suited to the place . . . for myself, I was as much pleased and surprised as any child could have been.[5]

Miss Berry, who enjoyed this cottage surprise in 1808, also enjoyed breakfast in tents especially erected in some woods by another of her hostesses, and went to a masquerade dressed as a peasant woman, '. . . a dress and a masque which I had possessed some time.'[6] This sort of pastoral enjoyment for the well-to-do was typical during the first and second decades of the nineteenth century, as it was in the eighteenth.

66 Bombasine 'cottage' dress, 1820, worn with a 'peasant' apron, as described by *Ackermann's Repository*.

Mary Russell Mitford described enthusiastic urban converts to rural life, who, as refugees from the city, wanted to bake their own bread and learn the self-sufficiency they associated with the country, and who even wished to look the part: two young women rented a hopelessly small villa called Rosedale, and the real villagers sat back to enjoy their folly: 'Laura was tall and lean and scraggy and yellow, dressing in an Arcadian sort of way, pretty much like an opera shepherdess without a crook, singing pastoral songs prodigiously out of tune. . . .'[7] She had never previously been out of the sound of Bow Bells and wished ardently 'that she might ruralize after the fashion of the poets, sit under trees and gather roses all day long.'[8] Her friend Barbara was well travelled, but only from city to city, yet 'she *yearned to keep cows*, fatten pigs, breed poultry, grow cabbages, make hay, brew and bake, and wash and churn. Visions of killing her own mutton flitted over her delighted fancy.'[9] Their idyll did not last, their animals soon returned to the care of more competent villagers, and Laura and Barbara forsook Arcadia for the city and other fashions again.

The same author also made a portrait of another duo, this time drawing attention to dress which was considered appropriate to a quiet country life at that time, regardless of the wearer's lack of participation in agriculture; mere residence in the country, with no role in its labour, ordained a certain style. As Mary and Hetta set off for Ascot Races from Miss Mitford's village, the censure is clear: 'Mary in a new dark gown, a handsome shawl, and a pretty straw hat, with a cloth cloak hanging on her arm; Hetta in a flutter of gauze and ribbons, pink and green, and yellow and blue, looking like a parrot tulip, or a milliner's doll, or a picture of the fashions in the *Lady's Magazine*, or like anything under the sun but an English country girl.'[10]

Both the yearning of country girls to be as modish as they thought city girls were, and the yearning of city girls to look as prettily pastoral as they thought country girls were, were promoted in part by the expansion of illustrated fashion periodicals. Nicholas von Heideloff started his *Gallery of Fashion* in London in 1794, and continued it until 1803. This was a costly publication, unlikely to be read by Miss Mitford's Hetta and her like, but *La Belle Assemblée* (1806–32, 1834–50) or Ackermann's *Repository of Arts, Literature, Commerce, Manufactures, Fashion and Politics* (1809–29), usually referred to simply as Ackermann's, or *The Ladies Monthly Museum* (1798–1832) or *The Ladies Magazine* (1800–1839) may have been more accessible to Hetta and such dress-loving girls and may have spurred them on to emulate the advice and illustrations they contained. The circulation of city-based periodicals helped to bring fashion more accurately and rapidly into the provinces, and made it an imitable commodity for anyone with an eye to the vogue, enough pin money and a good local draper. Fashion could be borrowed and copied in isolation from the grander and more adventurous urban social circles which created much of it; in reality far more people follow fashion than make it.

Despite the magazines and milliners' dolls, and the increasing human traffic into the cities in the nineteenth century, fashion-conscious people living in the country could worry about wearing what was right, and there was for them little question of emulating the appearance of the country people themselves: 'The simplicity of the peasantry is soon discovered to be tiresome ignorance; and their wisdom little better than cunning.'[11] Roundly complaining in this way, Nellie Weeton, who lived at the time in the Lake District near to the Wordsworths conveyed some of that gentrified provincial sense that fashion was always somewhere else, always elusive: '. . . I have no female acquaintance except a village surgeon's wife, and an acquaintance of hers, both of them plain in their dress, and knowing

67 Charming so-called Cheltenham dress. Rustic day dreams under the greenwood tree, with leafy straw hat, negligent shawl and plenty of imitation 'shepherdess' lacing.

as little about fashion as can be.'[12] Miss Weeton was a woman of small means, but when she wrote in 1810 asking for the rest of her clothes to be sent on to her, it is clear she possessed garments indicative of an active leisure in the countryside in the Lakes, as well as more sedentary, ladylike clothes.

Inclosed with this you will find the necessary keys for the three long drawers: in the bottom are a black Chambray gown, a silk petticoat, a cambric muslin petticoat and a blue flannel bathing dress; in the middle drawer is some black lace net, wrapped in a piece of black mode, and a black silk work bag with some crape and a blue duffil coat, which will be very useful when sailing. There are some patterns for fancy work. I am not quite sure whether they are in a work bag in the bottom, or middle drawer, or bound up with the last new Lady's Magazine in the top drawer; if they are, I shall be obliged to you to take them out and send them in the bundle.[13]

These clothes suggest a vigorous enjoyment of country pursuits, without any pseudo-cottage look, or incompetent self-sufficiency; like many women of her era, Miss Weeton was not overwhelmed by tender sensibilities: she strode off alone on holiday in the hills of the Isle of Man and walked twenty miles in one go, in raptures over the picturesque views. A provincial contemporary of hers echoed this robust approach to country life, and a rejection of poorer rural appearances, however picturesque: Elizabeth Ham walked alone through icebound lanes 'on Pattens without getting a fall,' but she was not at all inclined to dress 'native'; after a boating accident off the island of Herm, her own clothes were soaked and local assistance had to be sought: 'the only costume a short loose jacket and petticoat, white dimity for Sunday wear. The women of the Islands are very short in general. I pleaded strongly for the longest petticoat, yet still felt ashamed of its shortness. Mr Hulbert lent me a pair of pumps that he had in his pocket, which I tied on with pack thread.'[14]

If English peasant dress, as it was actually worn, did not appeal to fashionable or genteel provincial people, both they and the city set reached by fashion periodicals were treated to plenty of fashionable ideas based on European peasant clothes. Once able to travel freely again after the limitations caused by hostilities with Napoleonic France, English travellers set out in larger numbers and in the various surviving accounts of their journeys, their enthusiastic response to the appearance of peasants is characteristic, and quite in tune with the tone adopted by fashion periodicals. The Italian peasantry, for instance, seemed more attractive than the English; 'all the peasants dressed in their bright coloured cottons were continually passing and repassing either seated on well loaded asses or on foot. All appeared animated gay and romantic and formed exactly one of those views which are so often to be seen in Italian paintings.'[15]

Travellers who remarked on the striking regional differences in peasant dress so lacking in England were echoed by several commentators who wished to promote this picturesque rural attire as a more appropriate form of dress than the classical mode for adoption by those seeking reform in English dress. Charles Reade had praised the appearance of uncorseted and gaily dressed Scottish women in his novel *Christie Johnstone*, and in his later 1857 story, *The Bloomer*, European peasant dress was paraded as an example of graceful freedom in women's clothing, at a private pageant arranged to demonstrate the folly of inconvenient dress and the advantages and predecessors of the Bloomer suit:

Armenian, Polish and Sicilian Peasants were then introduced whose limbs were free enough goodness knows – they ranged themselves in a line opposite their stiff competitors [nineteenth, eighteenth and sixteenth century dress] – and a Bloomer took up the recitative,

All these unlike the Bloomer confine the limbs and make the ribs to crack.
All those like Bloomers free the mind, the body and the back,
So hail to great Amelia who takes a sex out of a sack.[16]

To some commentators concerned about the restrictions of contemporary dress for women, peasant dress of this sort represented a continuation of the antique mode, and a repository of natural beauty which high fashion could not match; Mrs Oliphant in her 1878 book, *Dress*, considered the Italian male peasant cloak to be a dignified descendant of the toga itself, and in 1854 Mrs Merrifield had written at length in her book, *Dress as a Fine Art*, on the advantages of modern Greek peasant dress, which she considered modest, dignified and graceful, and therefore very suitable for adoption into an English wardrobe of a lady of fashion.

There began in the nineteenth century a widespread copying of peasant styles, based on this frequently expressed admiration, but chiefly serving as decorative additions to, rather than a replacement or reform of, English high fashion; Swedish and Circassian caps were amongst the earliest examples; Garibaldi shirts; variations of the prevailing tightly fitted women's bodices of the 1860s were known as *le corsage Russe* or *les vestes grecques*; in 1885 'short vests in either the Zouave or Spanish styles are much worn. . . . They are made of rich materials, fastened at the throat, and fly open to display a lace, embroidered, or braided waistcoat.'[17] These were mostly decorative superimpositions on the main shape of the day and did not offer a substantially different construction method or garment type; they were enjoyed for the opportunity they provided for embroidery, or gold braid, or different fastenings, and European peasant dress has continued to the present day to make decorative additions to our dress.

People of fashion also took up what was perhaps the most distinctive and practical garment to emerge from

English rural life – the smock. It enjoyed an extensive revival in and after the 1870s, as part of the vogue for simpler, alternative clothes in artistic circles, and the smock and smocking played an important part in the styles for women and children made and sold by Liberty's costume department from 1884, for example. Previously smocks had been confined to men and boys [68] and were treasured additions to a labourer's wardrobe. Some smocks, for example, survive which were even decorated especially to commemorate Victoria's coronation in 1837. It seems likely they were not commonly marked with signs of their owner's occupation. They were a remarkable testimony to rural skills and they come into the fashionable consciousness partly through the influence of the illustrations by Kate Greenaway (1846–1901), who depicted the early nineteenth century dress when smocks were common, and whose work became an inspiring model in the 1880s and nineties to those involved in the movement to promote alternative, more picturesque styles.

Observers had noted that distinctive occupational dress was declining and that artisans' dress was then becoming merely a crude copy of gentlemen's dress. At the very point when the male smock was disappearing from the fields and reappearing in the wardrobes of fashionable women and children, Richard Jefferies remarked in 1883 that traditional features of rural dress at a hiring fair were becoming scarce:

> Formerly they came in smock-frocks and gaiters, the shepherds with their crooks, the carters with a zone of whipcord round their hats, thatchers with a straw tucked in the brim and so on. [Jefferies was describing special marks of identification for the purposes of a hiring fair.] Now, with the exception of the crook in the hands of an occasional old shepherd, there is no mark of speciality in the groups, who might be tailors or undertaker's men, for what they exhibit externally . . . the genuine white smock-frock of Russian duck and the whity-brown one of drabbet, are rarely seen now afield . . . often a group of these honest fellows on the arable has the aspect of a body of tramps up to some mischief in the field, rather than its natural tillers at their work.[18]

Jefferies also noted that the peculiarity of the English urban poor in their preference for the cast-off clothes of a class richer than their own had spread to agricultural workers, including women. 'Like the men, the women are, pictorially, less interesting than they used to be.'[19]

Back in fashionable circles, a number of articles and books at this time helped to revive the intricate art of smocking for the urban well-to-do who had no previous tradition of such a skill; it was transferred to finer fabrics such as silk, or light wool, Liberty's smocked and embroidered cashmere, for example. Some urban people sent to have their smocking done by villagers. (On the fine fabrics it was not so hard, but on thick unbleached calico which still remained in diminishing rural use it could be an arduous task: '. . . I

68 Countryman's smock drawn by James Ward (1769–1859). These useful work smocks were part of the rural scene from the mid-eighteenth century until the end of the nineteenth.

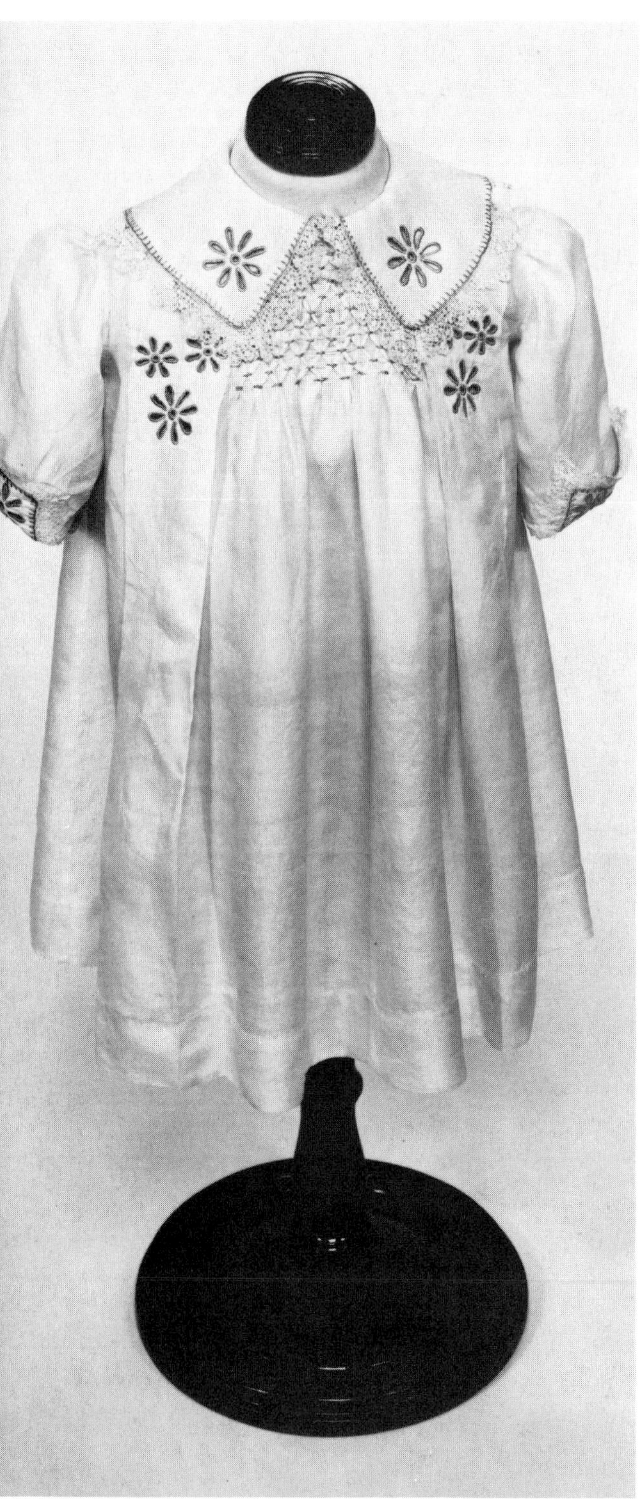

69 Child's fashionable silk smock, *c.*1918. Similar to earlier examples from the late nineteenth-century smock revival. Vanished from its original haunts, the smart revived smock remains a much-loved style.

as a child have seen, on a winter's day, some of the cottage wives with bandages on their fingers: they had been doing smocking with that stuff.'[20] Smocks and smocking have remained in the fashionable repertoire ever since, and until very recently their traditional male role was maintained by their use as 'dresses' for boy toddlers [69].

Hats and bonnets, as indispensable items of wear in the nineteenth century, accumulated a wide variety of shapes and degrees of formality. Straw hats continued to be popular and, for women, they maintained the rural overtones they had possessed for several generations since their initial revival. In the early part of 1835 the *Ladies Cabinet* summed up some of the styles and uses expected of these hats as they remained for most of the century: 'Split straw, mottled straw, and a very large coarse plait, are all expected to be fashionable – the two latter for the early morning walk, or for the country; the former for the public promenades, or morning exhibitions. Those that have already appeared in split straw are trimmed with spring flowers, and ribbons quadrilled alternately in satin and gauze. . . . Plain taffeta ribbons, or plain satin ones, are adopted for the other kinds of straw; they are trimmed in a simple style, without flowers.'[21]

Despite this particular style of pastoral hat which was to be worn without flowers, and would therefore have made a noticeably plain effect, the wearing of flowers, leaves and other such decorations continued to be a feature of fashionable attire as it had been at previous periods, but it was during the nineteenth century chiefly confined to the dress of women and girls. Men had mostly forfeited the decorated waistcoat by the early part of the century, and wore very little such decoration except for the occasional grand waistcoat, and the floral decoration, either woven or sewn, of a whole suit of clothes such as might have been seen in the eighteenth century would have been ludicrous to a Victorian man. Women, however, wore three-dimensional artificial flowers in abundance, and in a variety not seen before outside floral textiles.

For a ball or gala, coronets of flowers or leaves would be worn in the hair, in at least the same quantities that we are better accustomed to seeing at weddings nowadays, and often more. Some ladies chose to wear arrangements of real flowers in their hair or on their dresses, despite the inconvenience and possibly disappointing effects during a long evening of dancing. In 1864 the *Englishwoman's Domestic Magazine* reported seeing a young lady with real cherries in her hair, considered a poetical impersonation of summer itself. There was considerable invention employed to create new ideas in the wearing of ready-made flowers, and oak leaves, ivy, ears of wheat and other additions were made to help embellish skirts, corsages and heads;

a full ball ensemble could be laden with carefully matched combinations of flowers, and the very expensive crinolines of the 1860s required a dressmaker with a generous hand if they were to make an appropriate impact. This ensemble took the floral taste to its reasonable limit, entwining its wearer in summer blooms in a winter ballroom:

> The tulle skirt is composed of puffings arranged spirally, commencing from left to right, these puffings diminish in size towards the waist. A beautiful bouquet of convolvolus, or roses, is placed in front of the body, and a wreath of the same flowers is carried to the left shoulder, round the top of the body behind, to the right shoulder, whence it falls onto the hips at the left side. The wreath continues round and round the skirt, and finishes at the bottom by two large bouquets on the left side.

This spectacular idea was reported in the *Englishwoman's Domestic Magazine*, in Feburary 1861.

70 Carefully chosen flowers in abundance were fashionable for wear at balls and evening functions during the nineteenth century in any season. 1866.

In the same issue it was advising the making of head-dresses for balls to be made of violets and rosebuds, or tea-roses and heartsease or white chrysanthemums and white geraniums, with green leaves.

Wide crinolines called for quantities of decoration of this kind, but when the crinoline disappeared, and the straighter, asymmetric silhouettes of the later decades appeared, the use of artificial flowers was undiminished. It was supplemented by an increasing taste for birds and birds' wings or feathers, particularly for use on hats. Between 1870 and 1920 the United Kingdom imported 20,000 tons of ornamental plumage, excluding the immense quantities of ostrich material from South Africa.[22] Fashions for whole birds ranged from pigeons to seabirds, and popular parts were terns' and parrots' wings, and owls' heads were in vogue in the 1890s. The taste included corsage decorations, and spread to street hats, golfing and walking hats, as well as more lavish ones for grander occasions, and plumes were worn without hats in head-dresses for evening

wear; this vogue reached its peak in the early years of the twentieth century. Aspects of this insistence on the most extreme and greedy relationship with nature would be unlikely today, since a shift in taste has coincided with import controls aimed at aiding conservation; any one wearing the corsage decoration noted by the magazine *The Queen*, 1 January 1898, would be unlikely to win friends today: tiny live tortoises were encased in filigree gold with jewels and attached to the dress by a fine gold chain and pin. 'The little reptiles appeared in no way inconvenienced by their adornment.'

Fancy dress parties and balls were a popular part of genteel nineteenth century life and allowed scope for numerous inventive garments. Adern Holt who wrote for *The Queen* magazine put together a book on the subject of what to wear for fancy dress balls for Debenham and Freebody, specialists in designs for 'National, Historical and Fancy Costumes for Tableaux, Theatricals, and Fancy Balls.'[23] Anyone who wished to be pastoral, to any degree, would have found the book most useful. It told how to dress as a hornet, a magpie, a buttercup or a butterfly; there were instructions on how to resemble Irish potato-gatherers, Italian peasants, reapers or dairy maids, and there were variations on shepherdess attire, such as a fifteenth century shepherdess in blue and red especially suitable for stout ladies. Much shepherdess imagery, in this and other such books of guidance, was based on historical appearance, particularly from the paintings of Watteau. Holt suggested that gentlemen might go to the ball as gamekeepers or millers; it was assumed they would not wish to be seen as daisies or wasps. Holt admitted in the book's introduction that perfect accuracy was not the aim, and that no one would view the peasant dress which the book suggested with more curiosity than the peasants whose dress it was intended to imitate.

There was a relationship between fancy dress and fashionable dress; they were both subject to prevailing taste, and often borrowed from each other directly. 'Fancy dress contributes many ideas to current fashions. The Normandy peasants' cap has suggested some becoming headgear for children out of doors, and now I see designers have fallen back on the piquante Swedish cap. . . ', said *The Queen* on 8 January 1898. In addition fancy dress allowed a certain escape, if only for the occasional chaperoned evening. Who knows what dreams may have been enacted as a young lady took the floor as a dairy maid in the arms of a 'gamekeeper'?

It was customary for fashionable dress which was for everyday wear to be made in readily discernible 'types,' so that a wide choice existed between various revivals and influences. *The Englishwoman's Domestic Magazine* observed in March 1867 a tendency which prevailed for many years, indeed for as long as women had the leisure and the means to support extensive wardrobes: 'This last toilet seems like a costume for a *bal travesti*; but it is not so. It is the fashion of the day to copy more or less exactly the dress worn by celebrated women in another age, and our fashionable *couturiere* will ask you in what *style* you wish to dress.' The request had much significance when a dress occupied so much space, and covered the figure from neck to toes; a 'style,' as the magazine described it, would be a dominant spectacle. Pastoral styles were one of these options, and were necessarily historical, based on paintings and prints, mostly eighteenth century in origin. As early as 1849, an old shepherd commented that women were usually only ever in charge of a flock as a contingency, and even so he said 'I have not seen a woman with a flock for many years.'[24] Like so many pastoral images, the shepherdess at the fancy dress ball, or the slightly less ornate version at a tea party, were rooted in wishful imagination.

10 *Daisy Chains*

THE TWENTIETH CENTURY

Daisy chains are the sole trimming of many large white straw and leghorn hats of the shady garden shape. Wreaths of other wild flowers, poppies and wheat and big cabbage roses are also worn, and rustic ribbons dangle down the back. . . .

The Daily Mirror, June 1913

If a love of wearing flowers, feathers and other natural decoration about one's person says something about attitudes to nature or the countryside in modern times, the early part of this century produced plenty of material for such an interpretation. Apart from toques and turbans, most ladies' hats of the first decade were loaded with flowers and feathers; they gradually increased in size and elaboration until about 1910 when they began to subside. At the famous Black Ascot following the death of Edward VII, they made a memorable picture.

As far as the eye could see there were black dresses trimmed with long black fringes, black lace parasols and huge black hats, wider than they had ever been before. Fashions tend to extremes before being dropped, and the elaborate headgear had now become like the last spurt of a Catherine wheel. These vast picture hats, perhaps set on one side of the head and piled high with black ostrich feathers mixed with osprey or black paradise feathers combined with black tulle, were worn not only in mourning for a King but for a glory that had gone forever.[1]

The way of life which by 1910 was thought to be disappearing, and was to be finished off almost completely by the First World War, had supported a taste in women's dress in which fashionable toilette could require hours of preparation and decoration. Cecil Beaton recalled that his mother had at this time an entire drawerful of artificial flowers, including roses, Parma violets and lilies of the valley.[2] Fitted to dresses, hats and coiffures, artificial or real flowers were seen on numberless occasions. Continuing the trend of the 1890s, feathers and parts of birds also remained important in the trimming of hats, and ostrich and other feather boas were common. In 1909, for example, Selfridges store advertised:

71 Hats and trimmings for *c.*1911. Birds joined flowers as favourite hat ornament in the late nineteenth century, and continued into the early years of this century. The Society for the Protection of Birds was first formed in 1889.

Half a thousand smart wings, black and all colours, 6d. each. Also about a thousand pairs of Wings, black and white and colours, 1/-, 1/6, 2/-, 2/6, and 3/3 a pair. Special Values in Ostrich feathers, black and colours . . . – and these are not all. If flowers are preferred, we are providing the newest thing in Brocaded Roses, 9/9 each. New Tinsel flowers in different shadings, 3/- a cluster; also Tinsel Roses. . . . Silk and Velvet Roses with foliage in rich autumn tints. . . .[3]

Peacocks' breasts and heads were worn on hats, as well as the separate tail feathers; and fashion periodicals devoted a good deal of space to the description of such things; millinery was considered, at its best, as a minor art form, and the mixing and dying of hat decorations might move a fashion writer to compare the effects with paintings by Titian or van Dyck. The sheer size of the hats made their decoration critical in the overall effect of an ensemble. 'Trimming a hat is like putting up a building. . . .'[4] With so much attention and skill concentrated on millinery, the opening of a hat shop was recommended by *The Lady's Realm* in 1904 as a refined career for a suitably skilled woman, largely because it was considered artistic and delicate work, and because the choice of a new hat was thought to be the most important of all matters of dress. 'Wheat ears of a novel kind, formed with ostrich feather fronds, lie picturesquely around the brim, and are finished off with a posy of forget-me-nots and roses (59s 6d).'[5]

Finely wrought, delicately dyed artificial flowers are still attractive to us today, and are suggestive not only of long hours of intricate skill and workmanship but also of the cost to the purchaser. Plumes and ostrich feathers would be attractive to the modern eye, if they could ever be divorced from the question of conservation. Such feathers are supple and graceful, and an ostrich boa swathes its wearer in a soft cloud which ripples at the merest breath. More difficult for modern taste to understand are the whole stuffed birds, or their heads with glass eyes stiffly gazing over a hat brim: today they might be seen as amusing bad taste, which is currently a cultivated feature in some quarters, but in the heyday of the hat they were thought of as items of beauty and smartness. Whether or not they also represented a love of nature is open to question; on the contrary, it seems reasonable to see them as totems of a predatory nature, or as signs of the careless whims of women so sequestered that they had no notion of the traffic they were encouraging.[6] The fact that feathers and whole, halved or quartered birds remained popular for a substantial number of years, suggests more than a whim, and is of the same order as the non-utilitarian purpose in killing and wearing of animal skins. Fur obviously has utility value in human clothing, yet the head and paws left dangling from the end of a fox stole do not help keep their new owner warm.

In 1930 the Freudian psychologist, J.C. Flugel, tried

to explain the use of floral decoration: he described the 'primitive' tendency for men to wear skins and furs as an expression of their capacity to hunt, and for women to prefer floral decoration; Flugel claimed that this sex distinction remained true in the western world in 1930 and probably to some extent depended on the 'deep-lying psychological identification of flowers and womanhood.'[7] This was hardly a satisfactory explanation, since it was based on inaccurate generalizations and where the generalizations were accurate, they begged the question. An eighteenth century English gentleman in his floral embroidered waistcoat might have taken issue with Flugel's argument. Flugel added virtually nothing on the wearing of furs or feathers, and had nothing to venture about the role of any of these features in expressing a nostalgia for a pastoral or older way of life. Perhaps it is worth examining our own thoughts and motives next time we choose to wear flowers or floral textiles; why do some of us adamantly discard such things altogether, and what have men *really* got against wearing flowers? In 1929 *The Lady* observed in its fashion feature that flowers are always essential for women, regardless of their material, and leather and enamel flowers were described as being modish that September. Perhaps either sex could expand and improve on Flugel's suggestion next time there is a wedding to attend.

A gentler pastoral spirit was visible in the dress of art students, especially those from the Slade, where a number of girls evolved a style of dressing influenced by Augustus and Dorelia John, to some extent continuing the spirit of Aesthetic dress; Dorelia made many of her own clothes, and both Augustus and she preferred them long and flowing, often with a large floppy hat, or a gipsy headscarf; one of the children of the unconventional John household 'contracted a habit of inserting secretly after the Lord's Prayer a little clause to the effect that Dorelia might be brought by divine intervention to wear proper clothes.'[8] His prayer was not answered.

Not only did Dorelia help to popularize a homespun look, the Johns also became interested in Romany culture and took up life in gipsy caravans for a while. This was also done by others. For example, an ex-Slade painting student lived in a donkey cart travelling rural England during 1912 and 1913, and as part of her dissatisfaction with city life, she made her own clothes: '. . . a new dress, which she made herself out of sack canvas, and afterwards stretched on the ground and painted with bright blue dye.'[9] The colours of this particular back-to-nature fashion usually gave offence, being often too bright for 'good taste.' Zoe, an art student in Aldous Huxley's 1923 novel *Antic Hay* was described as looking like a picture by Augustus John and wearing, 'depressingly,' blue and orange.

72 Influenced by Romany life, Dorelia John in her much-copied 'John'-style clothes which became a hall-mark of artistic and bohemian women. *c.*1908.

These predecessors of the hippies and pseudo-gipsies of the 1960s were usually in or on the fringe of artistic activity: a girl in the Bloomsbury set was typical in that she wore a rather shapeless dress and had her hair cut so that 'it stood out like a solid, perfectly grown and clipped yew hedge. . . .'[10] Cecil Beaton regarded Dorelia as the creator of a timeless, Biblical style, contriving to maintain a distinctive appearance wholly outside the reach of *haute couture*-dominated fashion. Beaton had a sharp eye for those who led taste and the process by which they were imitated.

Young women 'interested in art' all wore their hair straight, cut sharp at the base of the neck with shears, the trilby jacket or sweater, the dark flowing skirts falling in the pleats of the dirndl, somewhere a bold touch of colour – blues, oranges and emerald greens – and sandals. These goddesses of King's Road, Chelsea, the students of the ballet in Italy, America, France and Germany, all with or without knowing it, tried to look as much as possible like Mrs Augustus John, for she it was who had invented the 'John' type . . . before her in this century no woman wore those clothes that are almost Indian and yet are entirely European, that are classical and yet have abstracted something from the gypsies.[11]

Until her death in 1970 Dorelia wore the same kind of clothes which have remained an option within women's dress, enjoying perhaps its most obvious renaissance during the 1960s. Although Dorelia sustained the 'John' image in person, John's role was crucial. He once bawled her out for wearing a modern short dress in the 1920s; he was an aggressive Pygmalion.

In the 1920s fashionable women sought a far sharper, sleeker silhouette than that created at the same time in bold colours by the intrepid girls of the Slade; emerging from a dove-grey limousine, Mrs Beste-Chetwynde epitomized the more expensive styles of 1928: 'two lizard-skin feet, silk legs, chinchilla body, a tight little black hat, pinned with platinum and diamonds. . . .'[12] Any reference to rural life was unlikely to survive within that demand for a neat and uncluttered effect unless it could be made to conform to it. One way in which the dominant fashion absorbed rural flavour was in the use of peasant embroidery; unlike the contemporaneous Slade and other 'gipsies,' these peasant features could be inserted into the prevailing shape, as panels on blouse or skirt fronts, or as collars and cuffs. This had been a vogue before the First World War; for example, in 1912 and 1913 Bulgarian embroidery had been used; the prelude to the war, and the war itself was to draw attention to those parts of Europe which were rich in traditional regional dress which featured colourful embroidery. Various adaptations have remained in the fashionable vocabulary for most of the present century [73].

In knitted garments various influences have been used which can be defined as primarily rural or peasant. Before the First World War, knitting became increasingly common in high fashion, and whole knitted coats or suits found their way into fashionable sporting or motoring wardrobes, or as recommended wear for a country weekend. Gordon Selfridge, for instance, aided the trend by arranging for a group of Shetland Islanders to make their first visit to the mainland for a spinning and knitting demonstration in his Oxford Street store in 1912, where they produced delicate shawls and spencers which greatly fascinated the visitors to whom Shetland wool and patterns were then still something of a novelty.

Since then several provincial knitting traditions have been thoroughly absorbed into mainstream dress; in the 1920s, the Prince of Wales popularized the Fair Isle sweater; Arran and Guernsey patterns came readily into English use, and the very word 'jersey' reminds us of the island roots of a craft associated with fishing and sailing communities. The range of peasant- or rural-based styles was extended by the introduction of South American artifacts, such as sweaters, socks, leggings and caps knitted with bright, simple decorative patterns, particularly popular since about 1970; first available in specialist shops, they were then copied by British manufacturers.

A minority taste for authentic Tibetan or other Himalayan clothing has paralleled this South American peasant vogue, and is often a manifestation of interest in the religion and philosophy of that region [142], but in most cases, mass-produced imitations are not concerned with exact regional origins, and instead concentrate on the utilitarian gains in borrowing from these various traditions skilled in keeping people warm cheaply at high altitudes and in inhospitable terrain. This robust practicality goes easily with the long-established English trust in knitted garments, and several new partnerships have emerged to help make up for our lack of native peasant costume [74].

Interest in embroidery or knitting from peasant sources is in part linked to the wish expressed by many people to escape what they see as an artificial environment. This often includes a preference for natural fibres in clothes. Man-made fibres have been improved and diversified out of all recognition since the early experiments at the start of the present century; first rayon, known initially as artificial silk, then synthetics, such as nylon, followed by the acrylic family and others, have provided attractive characteristics such as being machine washable, hardwearing and able to stretch without distortion, needing no ironing or pressing, and remaining relatively cheap. Nevertheless, until fairly recently they have only won grudging acceptance in *haute couture* and although they are in widespread use elsewhere, man-made fibres still seldom get a good fashion press in their own right. Natural fibres do. They are often important partners in pastoral dress; the last decade saw a popularization of tweeds and other heavy wools in natural colours as part of a countrified or 'county' look for men and women

73 Scarves and peasant embroidery, 1938.

which included copies of riding boots and hacking jackets for ordinary wear. A natural fabric seems to bring a happy glow to the fashion pages: 'Cottons are soft, thin, see-through, iridescent – fabrics that gather away to nothing . . . butter muslin dyed in dark juicy colours . . . spotted voiles in water-ice colours or printed with dark rich flowers. . . .'[13]

Undeterred by the decline of picturesque qualities in real rural dress, as noted at the end of the last century by Richard Jefferies and others, or perhaps actually because of it, the nostalgia for simple country life produced a resurrection of it in the 1960s through the clothes of

3 An Englishman in fine Turkish dress in 1798. Bought by travellers in Turkey for protective disguise and as souvenirs, dress such as this often appeared in England either for masquerade or as details absorbed into fashionable wear for both sexes.

4 Yves St Laurent's 1977 translation of traditional Turkish dress into a fashionable idiom for modern women.

Laura Ashley; significantly, the first shop opened by this company was in central London. The popularity of pure cotton is an important factor for devotees of the clothes of this company which was formed in 1954. There was a pressing demand for cotton or linen fabrics printed with patterns reminiscent of a country life, which sold also made up as simple items such as aprons and scarves. The first garment, marketed in 1961, was a smock intended for gardening, but used by customers for much else besides. The expressed design philosophy of the company takes for granted that most English people prefer country life to city life, and therefore tend to buy products which remind them of the country. Concentration on small motifs on the printed fabrics, for clothes or furnishing, is taken to express modesty and a lack of materialist concern; the company itself has a policy to place its factory facilities in the country, so as to aid the continuance of village life.

Although it has never been catered for quite so fully or so cheaply as now, the taste has seemingly existed throughout the present century. For example, in the First World War something of the same spirit pervades the caption to a fashion drawing: 'The woman gardener used to play at growing blushing rosebuds and tender violets. In these war times she raises the plebeian potato and the tedious turnip, and she does it in such practical costumes as this blue cotton smock over white cotton trousers. As for her hat, it's just an afterthought of white straw brim and blue cotton crown.'[14]

The rural overtones of the Laura Ashley clothes for women and children which characterized them from their beginning until the later 1970s (when plain bold colours were also introduced in more sporty shapes) are necessarily those of the past; for example, at the present time the once-picturesque farm workers present a different image. There are no more hiring fairs and if they dress in anything specifically occupational, it could well be a boiler suit, or hygenic white dairy overalls, or immense earmuffs to deaden the noise of the tractor they drive. When it comes to dress, the large modern farm takes more from industry than its own past. Other dress associated with country life has resurfaced fairly frequently in urban fashion since the Second World War; yet the special quality of the long cotton skirts, the smocks and the headscarves of Laura Ashley is that they are a reflection of the invisible; they are derived from an amalgam of pastoral pasts, reassuring because the styles are traditional with reserve enough for Nanny to have approved of, and the fabrics are reliable with a hint of Provence and summer in the prints. (The call of childhood is often

74 Authentic peasant knitting in bright colours imported from South America or the Himalayan regions encouraged retail manufacturers in the 1970s to produce garments in an anglicized fusion of peasant features.

75 Dresses and apron in hardwearing cottons evoke a bygone rural age.

WORKING DRESS.

These drawings will show the general construction of the proposed working dress. The girl reaching up to the orange blossom has drawn both sides of the dress into the loop on her left, and the sleeves are tucked up to the elbow. The one carrying hay wears the sleeves in the same way, but the two sides of the dress are drawn into the two different loops. The girl gathering violets wears the dress like the last, but the sleeves descend to the wrists.

These sketches were made from a lady wearing a rather stiff petticoat—a form which many might prefer—but more ideal lines might be obtained with a light and loose undergarment. Ladies will find that a scanty woollen petticoat over woollen combination is apt to

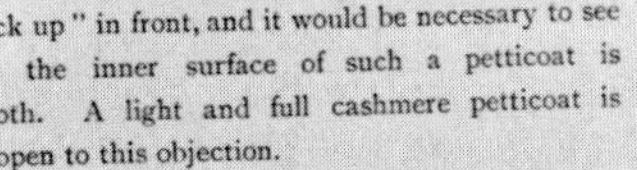

ıck up" in front, and it would be necessary to see t the inner surface of such a petticoat is ɔoth. A light and full cashmere petticoat is open to this objection.

Γhe design is offered merely as supplying a means :ontinuing the advantages of a short skirt with the .ce of a long one. It will be understood that en withdrawn from the loops, the skirt is an linary one of such length as the wearer likes to .ke it, and the whole dress can be modified to any :ent according to the taste of the wearer.

76 In 1893 idealized working dress had the same nostalgic echo as later versions.

heard in pastoral poetry; it probably is in pastoral dress too.) It is perhaps significant that so far Laura Ashley has not catered for menswear; and that the first garment shop achieved such success in 1968 just when dominant fashion was showing some post-mini-skirt uncertainty and fatigue.

When the whole history of twentieth century dress comes to be written there must certainly be a place reserved for this style, which has long been an option. Some of the garments have been in the same spirit as those promoted by the Healthy and Artistic Dress Union in the 1890s, for example [76]. This pastorale has altered a little at each modification undergone by the real countryside. In general, it is a mode of dressing to satisfy those who extend the old criticism of urban life to other features of modern existence, and who still feel deprived in the subtle way Margaret Hale did in 1855 as she left her village for the gloom of Darkshire: 'the air had a faint taste and smell of smoke; perhaps, after all, more a loss of the fragrance of grass and herbage than any positive taste or smell.'[15]

Men have not been wholly without the means of wearing any pastoral dreams they might harbour. Interestingly, they have often preferred contemporary country styles. For example, in the late 1940s the suits known as 'lounge suits,' which were then more formal than the word now implies, began to take on features taken from country hacking jackets; vents and ticket pockets appeared in city jackets where they had not been before, and later in the seventies exact replicas of various riding garments and boots were reanimated in fashionable outfits, and so was the Norfolk jacket, previously closely associated with knickerbockers and country pursuits. So too was the green Wellington boot with a buckle on the side which began to be seen for city wear by young men. Fishing bags and shooting jackets also became transformed for fashionable wear. Men evidently prefer to repossess for fashion the current or former styles of those who owned the land, unlike women who tend to revive the appearance of those who worked it.

The exception to this has been the affection for denim jeans, which began as a post-war importation from the United States, where jeans had become fashionable after generations of use as work clothing. Taken up by students and others as alternative dress, even as an anti-fashion, jeans eventually became worn so commonly that they lost most of their dissident reputation and achieved respectable conformity instead. The ready-to-wear market was so full of denim that by 1976 there was concern that its retailers were pushing up the rentals disproportionately in shopping areas such as Oxford Street, London, which consequently would suffer should denim suddenly lose favour. Denim was supporting London rentals for prime ground-floor trading space of over £70,000 per annum.[16] If fashionable Englishmen preferred to borrow only upper class dress from their own countryside, they were quite prepared to take on the appearance of the pioneers, hillbillys and cowboys of North America. The *Tailor and Cutter* called 1970 the year of the Cowpoke, and there were lumberjacks too joining in the general renaissance of the working dress from the North American frontiers.

James Laver observed that men's dress has had a tendency towards formalization; he noted that during the nineteenth century riding coats gradually turned into town wear and eventually into very formal tailcoats for evening wear. The informal country hat called a 'bowler' went the same way and is now considered very senior formal city wear. James Laver wrote in 1946 of the future of dress, and predicted very accurately the present trend in men's wear: informal or working garb creeps gradually up the social ladder. This has happened to denim jeans and jackets, to cowboy shirts, to dungarees and will be the fate of boiler suits before very long. Addressing a girl who would be twenty in 1956, Laver wrote:

> Another thing which may help to release men's clothes from their shackles and allow us to blossom out into something at least of the splendour of the primitive male, is the fact that social security (which we have agreed is what women seek, or used to seek, in men) is now spelt with capital letters. Social Security is an affair of the State not of the individual, and the prospective husband of *your* time may not need to look as if he could support a family. The family itself may have vanished.[17]

77 Once for work clothes only, blue denim came to dominate leisure wear for young people.

78 *Overleaf* Pastoral, 1977. Nostalgic cream voile and lace dress by Chloé.

PART III *Historical Revivals*

11 *In the Bravery of their Liveries*

THE SIXTEENTH CENTURY

for some be of the new fashion, some of the olde, some of thys fashion, and some of that. . . .

Philip Stubbes, *The Anatomie of Abuses*, 1585

The accession of Elizabeth I took place on 17 November 1558. The anniversary of this event became an occasion for widespread celebrations. Local festivities such as bell ringing or dancing, or special sermons marked the day, and the court itself established annual events known as the Accession Day Tournaments which gave rise to a variety of fanciful archaisms in dress. These illuminate the Elizabethan imagination at work, for the courtier-knights evoked their own vision of the past, and of the ideal. The significance of the tournaments lay in their role in celebrating the reign of Elizabeth as a reassertion of former glories; the reign was associated with the revival of a golden age, and the tournaments provided images and enactments of this. Elizabeth was also astute enough to realize the benefits of allowing her aristocrats to express energetically their prowess and their competitiveness in an organized way, under her eye at Whitehall, rather than having them do so more dangerously elsewhere:

. . . the use and cultivation of the imagery and motifs of legends of chivalry formed an integral part of the official 'image' projected by sixteenth-century monarchs. Through them they were able to surround the actualities of present-day politics with the sanctions of historical myth and legend. In a century of violent political and religious upheaval, of cosmic proportions to those who lived through it, this was of immense importance in preserving an illusion of continuity.[1]

These anniversary tournaments were elaborate affairs, and perhaps more than other aspects of courtly life of the time they provided an opportunity for romantic and quixotic dress, not just for the courtiers at the centre of the events, but for all their supporting retinues. To these people of humbler origins, the tournaments must have seemed visions of an almost fabulous world, and also to the crowds and the visiting dignitaries who watched from the stands, or the streets.

The field with listes was all about enclos'd,
To barre the prease of people farre away;
And at th'one side sixe judges were dispos'd,
To view and deeme the deedes of armes that day;
And on the other side in fresh aray,
Fayre *Canacee* upon a stately stage
Was set, to see the fortune of that fray,
And to be seene, as his most worthie wage,
That could her purchase with his lives adventur'd gage.[2]

Francis Bacon called such events 'toys,' but also saw that the events preceding the tilting were important, and captured for us something of the excitement and the central role they played in the imagination of the time: 'for justs, and towneys, and barriers; the glories of them are chiefly in the chariots, wherein the challengers make their entry; especially if they be drawn with strange beasts: as lions, bears, camels, and the like; or in the bravery of their liveries; or in the goodly furniture of their horses and armour.'[3]

A number of paintings survive to tell us what the courtier-knights looked like as they challenged and performed on the Accession Day Tournaments. A painting exists of Sir James Scudamore, done in the 1590s by an unknown artist, showing him full-length before a sylvan setting. His magnificently plumed helmet lies with his gauntlets on the ground. The armour he wears is otherwise complete to the knees, and over it he wears a bases, a wrapped skirt to mid-thigh, decorated with a fringe and overlaid with strips of braid which imitate the heavily quilted pleats or the plates of real military skirts of cloth or metal which had been used earlier when full armour was a military commonplace. By the later sixteenth century, armour for soldiering was more optional [80], and Scudamore and others wore romantic suits of armour as much for decoration as for protection during tournaments, suits which they would almost certainly not have worn had they engaged in real battle. The suits became highly ornamental; Scudamore wears not only an ornamental bases, of no protective use, but also an orange sash across his breast, tied in a knot at the shoulder, no doubt part of some dramatic design in which he and his retinue appeared, or a favour. Robert Devereux, Earl of Essex, painted in miniature by Nicholas Hilliard[4] in a tournament scene of the 1590s, wears a fringed sash in a bow on his right arm; also in this miniature his groom appears in a curiously striped knee-length garb of some theatricality, indicating something of the ingenuity shown in the processions and entries of the knights at Accession Day Tournaments.

Pure romance too, is the view of George, Earl of Cumberland, who became Queen's Champion in 1590, and was portrayed in his armour, blue as the sky and decorated with stars [79]. His gauntlets are thrown to the ground, and he stands, horseless, depicted perhaps as he appeared at the moment of challenge, before he mounted for the tilt. Beneath the armour is a shirt with a delicate neckband. This magnificent knight

Hasta

was not dressed for military efficiency; he was seeking in a picturesque effect to evoke romance and chivalry. His intricate blue surcoat twinkles with jewels and its impractically wide sleeves spill down to reveal linings of fine emblematic embroidery, made to match the equally splendid high crowned hat, which adds more than a head to his height. Viewed across a tournament yard this must have made a dazzling spectacle, 'In brave aray and goodly amenance, With scutchins gilt and banners broad displayd.'[5]

The wit, invention and splendour of these fanciful tournament costumes show what the Elizabethan Philip Stubbes sourly described in another context as a 'mingle mangle' of styles; but with hindsight, this is their magic. At modern reconstructed tournaments careful efforts are made to get historical detail as accurate as possible, as the twentieth-century weekend knights entertain Bank Holiday crowds, but at Elizabethan tournaments, particularly those of the Accession Day series, there was no attempt to fossilize the dress, and every attempt to interpret fresh features for the courtier-knights sought to express current issues in images which, as they conjured up a heroic age, both stimulated and entertained; a scene of mourning for the death of Sir Philip Sidney came into the 1586 events. It has been suggested that 'the tilts may have become a kind of yearly review of the Elizabethan world. . . .'[6]

The fanciful, often thematic, dress of the courtier-knights and their retinues were significant additions to an already expansive range of dress outside the limitations of mainstream fashion available to their social class during Elizabeth's reign. The Accession Day tilts put those clothes into an important annual arena which was more than the mere display of martial arts; the tilts fused several art forms and were interwoven with the dynamics of court life and politics, and as such should be distinguished from later neo-mediaeval tournaments which were usually reconstructions concentrating on the armour and the sport, with less reference to the entries, or themes, which characterize the sixteenth-century version of chivalric events, focusing on Elizabeth and her reign. (The Eglinton Tournament of 1839 is an example of a revival taking place outside any such cohesive context.)

One indirect cause of this romantic dress may have been widespread dissatisfaction with what appeared to many Elizabethans to be a breakdown of traditional distinctions in dress. By assuming an esoteric and nostalgic guise which could only be achieved through education and courtly experience, the courtiers at the tilts were putting themselves beyond the reach of mere sumptuousness or parvenu expenditure; romance needs leisure to sustain it, as well as a sense of the past, and in dress is a means of eluding those who wish to imitate the appearance of mere wealth.

79 Miniature by Hilliard, *c.*1590, depicts the Earl of Cumberland as Queen's Champion, magnificent for an Accession Day Tournament. The Queen's glove in his plumed hat. These annual events gave full scope to Elizabethan sartorial imagination.

80 English troops, 1581. The variety of practical armour worn in the field contrasted with the splendid imaginative displays for the Accession Day Tournaments.

> Those which are neither of the nobilitie, gentilitie, nor yeomanrie, no, nor yet any magistrate or officer in the common wealthe, go daiely in silkes, velvettes, satens, damaskes, taffaties, and such like; notwithstanding that they be bothe base by birthe, meane by estate, and servile by callyng. And this I compte a greate confusion, and a generall disorder in a Christian Commonwealth.[7]

Revived and romantic styles of dress have always played an important role for the elite; when the 'base by birthe' start to don the trappings of rank, those of rank can side-step their imitators by wearing clothes of historical or erudite allusions, or by actually imitating, with more expensive materials, the work-a-day dress of the 'base' and 'meane' themselves.

There was perhaps an element of this in 1575, when, as part of the bevy of spectacles arranged for the Queen's visit to Kenilworth, a comic rural wedding in a 'right merry mood' was staged, and no *nouveau-riche* man of fashion would have wished to forsake his newly gained ruff and up-to-the-minute suit of clothes for this or some Arthurian guise. At Kenilworth the Queen listened to verses read by a poet dressed with care to evoke an old-fashioned, unworldly atmosphere; he wore 'a long ceruleoous garment, with a side and wide sleeves Venecian wize drawen up to his elboz, his dooblett sleevez under that Crimzen, nothing but Silke, a Bay garland on hiz head. . . .'[8] 'The Lady of the Lake (famous in King Arthurz book) with too Nymphes waiting upon her, arrayed all in sylks,' appeared before the Queen on the same visit;[9] one account suggested that the step back into time past was entire 'so that the Castle of Kenelworth should seeme still to be kept by Arthur's heires and their servants.'[10]

This was an expedient and selective evocation of past appearances, by a group of people normally dressed in other clothes, but who temporarily sought to express what could not be expressed by their main fashionable dress. Antiquated dress had a role in another area of Elizabethan life, as it does today, in the manifestation of authority and institutionalized power. The archaic dress we see today of lawyers, academics, clergy and various officials of state refers us to the learning and high-minded functions they represent, and shares with similar Elizabethan dress the need to avoid fashion altogether in order that, by means of a timeless or time-honoured appearance, the individual demonstrates his sense of duty and willingness to conform rather than any inclination to frivolity.

The problem of sustaining social rank as well as the credibility of court functionaries, clerics and others was a real one in the later sixteenth century; this was still an age which believed in sumptuary regulations. Elizabeth I put her signature to several attempts at confining certain clothes to certain ranks, including one in 1597 which wished to limit silk embroidery and velvet in outergarments, for example, to women who ranked as the wives of knights or above. A knight's eldest son's wife would not even have been able to wear velvet in kirtles or petticoats, unless attending at court or serving ladies of higher rank.

There is no reason to suppose sumptuary regulations worked effectively but their presence signifies the concern felt for maintaining visible distinctions of rank. Philip Stubbes was very anxious that these distinctions should be clearly asserted in dress. In his 1583 book, *The Anatomie of Abuses*, he expressed the fear that 'pride of apparell,' more than any other pride, 'induceth the whole man to wickednesse and sinne,' and contributed to the breakdown of the vital social divisions. This 'arsnecke of pride,' however, had to be carefully balanced against the continuing need to signify social ranks in dress, and thus he concluded that rich fabrics could, or even should, be worn by high officials 'to strike a terror and feare into the hartes of the people to offend against their office and authority.' He must have approved of the sombre, but expensively long, garb of academics and others, in that they thus escaped from the 'confuse mingle mangle of apparell' into the dignity of archaism and a simpler, less decorated style.

Stubbes feared for the future, resented the present and longed for the past, and after citing the seamless robe of Christ as an ideal form of dress, he went on to complain:

> We lothe this simplicitie of Christ, and abhorring the Christian povertie and godly mediocritie of our fore fathers in apparell, are never content except wee have sundrie suites of apparell, one divers from an other, so as our presses cracke withall, our coffers burst, and our backs sweat with the cariage thereof; we must have one suite for the forenoone, an other for the after noone, one for the daie, an other for the night, one for the work daie, an other for the holidaie, one for sommer, an other for winter, one of the new fashion, an other of the old, one of this colour, an other of that. . . .[11]

The so-called godly middle way of the previous generation was an aim Stubbes felt to be a proper one in dress; those in high office should wear grand dress to help reinforce their status, but on lesser people he felt that soft clothes induced soft minds. In the past it seemed to Stubbes that even kings had been content with simpler dress:

> In tymes past, Kynges (as old historiographers in theyr bookes, yet extant, doe recorde) woulde not disdayne to weare a payre of hosen of a noble, ten shillinges, or a marke price, with all the rest of their apparell after the same rate; but now it is a small matter to bestowe twenty nobles, tenne pounde, forty pounde, yea a hundred pounde, on one payre of breeches (God be mercifull unto us!) and yet is this thought no abuse neither.[12]

Given his fond view of the past, Stubbes rather surprisingly objected to the fact that old-fashioned clothes formed part of a fashionable wardrobe. He implied they were somehow fashionable *because* they were out of date: '. . . as these gownes be of divers and sondry colours, so they are divers fashions, changing with the moone – for some be of the new fashion, some of the olde, some of thys fashion, and some of that. . . .'[13]

Clothes made in the substantial manner of the finest sixteenth-century dress for men and women, often fortified with copious embroidery, could last longer than their owners; they were made over into other things, or they were bequeathed to other people in

81 Unknown lady, *c.*1600, in superb lined and dagged hanging archaic sleeves of the International Gothic style of *c.*1400. Loose flowing hair. This may be a glimpse of masque appearance.

wills; it would not have been difficult to know about the dress of the recent past. In addition, aristocrats and others with power and success at court found paintings of living and dead relatives welcome evidence of their lineage and wealth; a long gallery of such portraits could contain a great deal of information about past fashions over a considerable span of time; any householder with enough money and space for portraits could register his loyalty by hanging a portrait of Elizabeth, and there was a vogue for whole series of portraits of the English monarchs: one such at Hardwick showed them all back to Edward II. Many houses displayed entire family histories on their gallery walls; at Theobalds, a country seat, Lord Burleigh had a series showing the principal European monarchs.

The use of historical features in dress found a place in the Accession Day Tournaments, and it was claimed as a right by aspects of officialdom. The Order of the Garter was also an important part of the Elizabethan sense of the past; it was believed by some in the sixteenth century to have Arthurian origins, and its chivalry to have links with knights throughout history.

82 International Gothic dress, early fifteenth century. Hanging sleeves lined with fur. Their dagged edges sometimes copied in Elizabethan dress nearly two hundred years later.

12 *An Higher Orb*

THE SEVENTEENTH CENTURY

Ancient stories have been best;
Fashions, that are now call'd new,
Have been worn by more than you;
Elder times have us'd the same,
Though these new ones get the name:
So in story what now told
That takes not part with days of old?
Then to approve times mutual glory,
Join new time's love to old time's story.

Thomas Middleton, *The Mayor of Quinborough,* 1661

In 1622 Henry Peacham published the first edition of his popular book, *The Compleat Gentleman*; he made references to both the exemplary and the foolish dress of the past, in an attempt to provide a framework of taste within which a young man of the early seventeenth century could properly acquit himself. Peacham (1576?–1643?), like other commentators of the age, had a strong sense of the past and he admired 'venerable antiquities' for their educational value; he felt that the attitudes of most of his contemporaries towards dress and fashion was lamentably less sensible than those of previous generations, although, like many who feel nostalgic about the dress of the past, he deeply disliked the dress of the generation immediately before him. He also wrote *The Truth of our Times* in 1638 and in referring to what must have been the fashions of his parents' lifetime, and of his own youth, Peacham scoffed at 'great-bellied doublets' and 'huge ruffes that stood like Cartwheeles about their neckes, and round breeches not much unlike Saint Omers onions. . . .'[1] He was writing at a time when both men's and women's dress was deflating, and a slimmer, longer outline was being established, and the dress of the previous forty years or so must have seemed most distasteful and extreme.

Peacham, however, had an eye for the inner process of fashion, as well as its manifestations; he called it 'an epidemical disease, first infecting the court, then the city, after the country.' He also observed that it had a tendency to be cyclical, so that elements would recur at intervals, which he seems to have thought of as a sign of a want of inventiveness, as if when the longed-for dress of the past did reappear it was not as simple and sensible as he had nostalgically thought, and was therefore disappointing. 'The fashion, like an higher orb, hath the revolution commonly every hundred year, when the same comes into request again; which I saw once in Antwerp handsomely described by an he- and she-fool turning a wheel about, with hats, hose, and doublets in the fashion fastened round about it, which, when they were below, began to mount up again, as we see them.'[2] This must have been a fascinating commentary on fashion; it would be interesting to know if English clowns ever used such a device.

Like other commentators on dress, Peacham quit his analysis of its history to concentrate on decrying his contemporaries; 'I have much wondered why our English above other nations should so much dote upon new fashions, but more I wonder at our want of wit that we cannot invent them ourselves, but, when one is grown stale, run presently over into France to seek a new, making that noble and flourishing Kingdom the magazine of our fooleries.' Forgetting his observations about the wheel of recurring fashion, Peacham fell back on nostalgia again; the past was better, whilst the dress of the present was spoiled 'with a thousand such fooleries unknown to our manly forefathers.' Those with really serious intentions, he thought, such as scholars or statesmen, did not bother with their appearance. 'They love their old clothes better than new; they care not for curious setting their ruffe, wearing cuffes etc.'[3]

Whilst Peacham thought being old-fashioned might indicate a properly serious, perhaps absent-minded scholar, there was criticism heard in the seventeenth century that even this area of life, which should eschew fashion and instead assert dignity through traditional historical dress, was being infected with frivolous novelties and vanity. Academic dress continued to demonstrate an aspect of the need for archaic styles, and amongst a chorus of complaints about the levity of the age, were complaints that the universities were lowering their sartorial standards. It was felt that being in fashion was not an appropriate concern for their members, and that historical dress invested them and their universities with more dignity. It was even said that 'Before the warr' scholars were more thorough, but that after the Civil War they did only what was necessary to pass exams, that they were no longer 'grave in the apparell,' that they were seen 'to swash it in apparell, to weare long periwigs etc. and the theologists to ride abroad in grey coats with swords by their sides.'[4] In the event, the university in question did seek to regulate the dress of its members, and to fortify the old method of manifesting rank in dress (aristocrats could wear coloured robes, for example). In short, there was in the seventeenth century a continuing need for historical styles in such areas as academic or clerical life, the academic example offering perhaps the more interesting chances to observe Gown reacting to the temptations of Town, to observe past styles responding to current ones.

A similar need to assert continuity of appearance in an age of shifting values and political upheavals can be seen in the efforts to design appropriate dress for the coronation of James II in 1685. (Charles II and James II were the first monarchs to be crowned without St Edward's relics which had disappeared after the execution of Charles I.) A detailed account written at the

83 Van Dyck's portrait of the Earl of Warwick, *c.*1630, shows deep collar of rich lace and arrival of longer, sleeker outline for men in fashion at that date.

time by the Lancaster Herald, Francis Sandford, described the 'Pomp, the Dignity and the many Glorious Circumstances which Accompany this Matter and Occasion,' and illustrated the monarch's robes devised to replace the ancient ones, the new ones being consciously based on archaic models. Sandford acknowledged, in his address to the King, that 'a Man cannot do Right to the Soleminity that is here in Question, without carrying his Thoughts back at the same time into the Boundless Antiquity of Your Imperial Descent through so many Ages. . .', and to reinforce these visible reminders of ancient authority, there was 'All that *Art*, *Ornament*, and *Expence* could do to the making of the *Spectacle*, *Dazling* and *Stupendious*. . . .'[5]

At the earlier coronation of Charles II, in 1661, Samuel Pepys had observed the procession on the day before, from a window in Cornhill, and had been conscious of the great impact of such pageantry and pomp '. . . it is impossible to relate the glory of this day, expressed in the clothes of them that rode. . . .'[6]

As in the previous century, chivalry was linked with historical dress; for example, Charles II revived the Order of the Garter whose ceremonies had been dormant since before the Civil War, and elaborate costume was designed for the knights to wear under the grand robe; this costume remained in use until the twentieth century. It would not be appropriate to discuss here all the historical dress which has remained in use for ceremonial, and which has taken on the dignity of antiquity; we are accustomed to many modern examples, such as the state robes of the Speaker of the House of Commons, consisting of an eighteenth-century style suit under a long gown of mediaeval origins, topped by a full-bottomed wig of seventeenth-century style. To modern eyes, these various items have merged into an impressive sight, a sign of the long tradition of the House. The need for such archaic elements is not new, and suffice it to say here that the seventeenth century saw this same process at work in the dress of various official and elevated ceremonials, and the series of drawings of figures from the procession of the Order of the Garter, done by Peter Lely in the 1660s is one of the best examples of the period's capacity to enjoy and exploit styles redolent of the past.

In court life under James I and Charles I the masque continued to be an occasion on which ingenious and fanciful dress found a special place. After 1605 when Ben Jonson (1572–1637) began his masque writing and when he combined with Inigo Jones (1573–1652) these events became especially spectacular. Jones had been to Italy and had found new sources and influences there which can be seen in his scene and costume designs for the masques. These drawings, often in a lively, impatient hand, give a vivid impression of the appearance of both men and women who took part. As in the Elizabethan masque, the seventeenth-century version involved dancing and Jonson introduced the anti-masque, a unique opportunity for inventive dress outside the main story, and the members of the royal family themselves would take part. In this way whatever costumes Jones or others might dream up they remained within the prevailing manners and protocol, but whilst this might seem a restriction, the designs reveal imaginative and novel features which indicate the court's preference for pleasurable fantasy rather than overmuch stuffiness. The character of masquing was not to survive the later changes, and the Jones designs show a side to English sartorial sensitivity which was to lose an important vehicle by the Restoration; Enid Welsford suggested it had been lost before, and that during the Caroline period there 'was an unpleasant mingling of pompous deities and realistic contemporary types. . . . Gradually the spirit of the dance faded out of the English masque, and when this happened the day of the masque was over, for in spite of all the efforts of the dramatists it was never really turned into art; it was always a form of amusement and revelling, closely bound up with the social system, and therefore unable to survive the social revolution of the Puritans.'[7]

Sir William d'Avenant (1606–68), who wrote masques for Charles I, had his *Britannia Triumphans* published with the open acknowledgment, in 1638, that a masque was to gratify tired monarchs' need for entertainment 'to recreate their spirits wasted in grave affairs of State, and for the entertainment of their nobility, ladies and courts.' This he expanded the following year with the suggestion that Charles had a political purpose, to seek 'by all means to reduce tempestuous and turbulent natures into a sweet calm of civil concord.'[8]

In the earlier 1638 masque there appeared four 'old-fashioned Parasitical Courtiers,' who were seen with others whose clothes showed their 'base professions,' including 'the master of two baboons and an ape.' These courtiers were seen in dramatic contrast to the other masquers who came with clothes 'beautiful, rich, and light for dancing. . . .'[9] The old-fashioned quartet must have resembled Inigo Jones's original designs [85]; this page of sketches is an interesting example of an artist in the 1630s achieving an out-of-date look by using an analgam of previous styles. Each of the four courtiers has an element of dress which is characteristic of Elizabethan high fashion, but none can be exactly placed in time, chiefly because the artist was obviously uncertain about where to place the waists. In each figure the depth of the doublet's skirt and the position of the top of the trunk hose are made ambiguous by

84 Continental costume book illustrates English dress, 1581. Used with others by Inigo Jones as a source for masque costume designs in the next century.

nervous lines repeated several times, yet the short cloak, the tall befeathered hat and the cartwheel ruff are all boldly sixteenth century in spirit, quite unlike the garments worn by Inigo Jones and his contemporaries.

Van Dyck's portrait of the Earl of Warwick [83] shows how men's dress had abandoned these more extreme silhouettes for a narrower, smoother outline; breeches had by then replaced the earlier trunk hose, and the ruff was almost wholly displaced by deep collars of falling lace. It is interesting that Inigo Jones seemed to dwell on the intricate folds of the ruff; whether in fascination or frustration is not clear, but ruffs were a central feature of fashion during his childhood and youth, so he may only have been refreshing his memory. Any protrusion at the neck would have been thoroughly distasteful in 1638, when men sought an even, uninterrupted line down their long hair, over sloping shoulders, to their smooth long sleeves. In the sketches there is clearly an element of parody.

Inigo Jones could draw on personal memory and perhaps actual surviving garments for mdoels in this particular project. He could also have used portraits, and it seems possible that the central top figure at least may have been borrowed from Abraham de Bruyn's 1581 costume book (see note 14 of Introduction), which contained several illustrations of English dress, and from which Jones is thought to have taken ideas more exotic dress for a 1631 masque. If he owned a copy then, or had access to one, it seems possible that he would have turned to it when refreshing his memory in 1638 about Elizabethan dress. (On the whole, the seventeenth century used historical references and revivals more sparingly than later periods, and confined more spectacular cases to the sort of events already mentioned.) Inigo Jones would have been much more accustomed to conjuring up ancient history and mythology but in the same masque, *Britannia Triumphans*, a girl in a 'mock Romanza' appeared in dress which was perhaps fifteenth or fourteenth century in style, and therefore more dignified to seventeenth-century eyes than the parasitical courtiers in sixteenth-century dress: 'the damsel in a

85 Masque designs for Elizabethan courtiers, 1638. Inigo Jones noted the complexities of ruffs.

straight bodied gown and wide sleeves of changeable, with a safeguard of silver stuff, and a past and partlet like a moral figure in old paintings.'[10]

Interestingly female dress from the more recent past seemed to come more easily to Inigo Jones than its male equivalent. In 1639, at a swansong for the court masque, Jones thought out the dress for *Salmacida Spolia*, a masque by William d'Avenant, in which the King and Queen took part. In the anti-masque, an 'old fashioned' Englishwoman appeared, about whose dress Inigo Jones had no hesitancy. By cutting away the upper front of the Elizabethan gown, he transformed its otherwise stiff and stately appearance into something revealing such as any court 'Nymph' or 'goddess' might have worn in other more ethereal events. His sketch created a torso stemming from a pointed waist; it is both broader and more curvaceous than it would have been in the sixteenth century.

Another continuation of the Elizabethan use of fanciful historical attire was in the dress made for tournaments; in the Jacobean period this form of courtly event remained central. Considerable sums were expended on dress not only for the participating knights but also for the retinues, and all the paraphernalia of pageantry. In 1616, for tilting, the Earl of Rutland paid out £53 15s 4d for silver and gold fringe lace 'and other things,' £19 for feathers and plumes for himself and his pages, and a further £29 on their special clothes. Even if a well-fitted suit of armour could do service for a man's entire tournament career, each 'tilting' called for fresh surcoats and retinue apparel or decorations, including 'shelde' and 'embleance' and presentation books (13s 6d in the Earl of Rutland's case) in which were recorded the details of the proceedings.[11] The evocative romance of tournaments continued to be enjoyed and promoted by men such as the Earl, who was also prepared to pay £60 to Edward Morris, the embroiderer, in 1613 for a 'masking suyte' for himself.[12] Henry, Prince of Wales, had been an enthusiastic supporter of the arts, and martial skills; Ben Jonson and Inigo Jones had worked together for the 1610 *Prince Henry's Barriers*. His death in 1612, at a young age, deprived this sort of event of a great patron, but tournaments returned in the later eighteenth and early nineteenth centuries in yet another phase of neo-mediaevalism.

On a more public scale, the seventeenth century enjoyed annual spectacles in London known collectively as the Lord Mayor's Pageants. It would have been hard to ignore or be indifferent to the resourceful costumes which offered lavish alternatives or additions to current modes, such as those made for *The Feild of Happines*, paid for by the Worshipfull Society of Ironmongers in 1629, or the *Port of Piety* paid for by the Drapers in 1638. These public shows of highly imaginative dress often used historical appearances, especially for figures personifying abstract virtues. Concord, in the 1678 *Triumphs of London* was 'a fair virgin in a Scarlet-colour'd robe, a sky-colour and gold scarf, a fair bright hair, and about her head a garland of white and red roses; intimating the concord of York and Lancaster; white buskins, laced with watchet and gold ribon; in her left hand a shield, charged with a bower of mirtles. . . . .[13] These were occasions of great splendour, although in 1663, Samuel Pepys thought the shows 'were very silly.' He had bothered to watch as much of the day's proceedings as possible, and being aware of the likely press of people, he decided not to wear his new velvet cloak: 'I thought it better to go without it because of the crowd, and so I did not wear it.'[14] The following year, his 'boy and three maids' were allowed out for the pageantry.[15] For people such as Pepys' servants, these must have been the most inventive and bizarre clothes they could see; in 1678, there was not only Concord, but Fidelity and Loyalty in a fortress, with Justice and Religion and others, all in suitably impressive garb.

'What a simple, honest Rusticity our Ancestors reteined in their weare,' when there was 'distinction in our attires, differences of ranks and qualities, a civill observance of decent habits. . . .' This nostalgic comment was made in 1641 in a book called *The English Gentlewoman* by Richard Brathwait, a commentator who felt that his own era was imperilled by its failure to observe social distinctions in historical dress; he saw other abuses in terms of foreign fashions, and 'superfluity of apparel,' by which he meant not only the failure to give clothes away to the poor, but also excessive length and yardage in individual garments. He wrote of 'great sleeves, mishapen Elephantine bodies, traines sweeping the earth, with huge poakes to shroud their phantastike heads,' and said that fashion in the 1640s was quite unlike the better dress of the past, '. . . within this 30, or 40, or 60 yeares never saw such cutting, carving, nor indenting as they now see. . . .' He was concerned that 'Soft Cloathes introduce soft mindes,' and that women especially had 'made a firme Contract with vanity. . . .' Like others before and since, Brathwait complained that the English were the vainest nation of all, and unlike other nations, would not take notice of past dress, nor let antiquity be their tutor in the question of appropriate appearance.

It is interesting that his picture of large sleeves and long trains on elephantine bodies as an abuse in modern dress is closely reminiscent of a figure called Folly, who was shown on the 1631 title page of *The Needles Excellency* [86]. This is a much humbler scene than those employing historical fashion in masques and other events: the book sets out useful needlework patterns, and its title page, based on an earlier German illustration, sets out to demonstrate the appearance of Folly, Industry and Wisdom; Folly making a show of herself, with a voluminous overskirt, forming a 'sweeping' train, 'great sleeves,' and a 'phantastike' head, such as Brathwait complained of; Industry busily sewing in a plain, warm dress and sensible hat, looking like any ordinary gentlewoman of the period, in a style

86 Three degrees of female dress in 1631.

87 Fashion *c.*1640 in the provinces. Open sleeve seams, bows, lace cuffs were all to be revived a hundred years later.

which avoided the extremes of fashion and could have been worn over a long period of time, with a ruff which was going out of date; Wisdom, bookish and dignified, wearing a drum-shaped skirt with hiprolls and formal collar and head-dress more suggestive of Good Queen Bess than the 1630s. (Queen Elizabeth's needlework was praised in the book.) This figure suggested virtue by means of dress already historical in appearance, and the book pressed this further by providing a concise, if erratic, history of needlework, to encourage its practice by modern ladies:

The use of Sewing is exceeding old,
As in the sacred Text it is enrold:
Our Parents first in Paradice began. . .

Commentators contradicted themselves, and each other, by complaining of revivals as a sign of dullness, whilst longing nostalgically for the dress of the past to be returned in order to redeem modern weaknesses.

However wistfully they spoke of the past, it seems that fashion in the seventeenth century, generally, did not concentrate on historical revivals to the extent of later periods; although it saw many events and expressions exploiting historical themes, these were not in such everyday use as those of, for example, the nineteenth century. This is not to say that there was a lack of imagination or any complacency about contemporary dress. On the contrary, amidst a good deal of complaining and moralizing about current style by the anti-fashion school of thought, people of fashion sought escapist and fanciful styles in the revival of other themes; much of the spirit of sartorial ingenuity for men and women was channelled and expressed in various versions of the dress of classical antiquity.

13 *All Kinds of Old Pictures*

THE EIGHTEENTH CENTURY

An affection to old habits and customs I take to be the predominant disposition of the mind, and novelty comes as an exception.

Sir Joshua Reynolds, *Eighth Discourse*, 10 December 1776

Horace Walpole went to a masquerade ball in February 1742 and met Henry VIII and Jane Seymour and 'dozens of ugly Queens of Scots.'[1] Mary Delany went to a *fête champêtre* in June 1774: 'The master of the entertainment [Lord Stanley] was dressed liked Rubens, and Lady Betty Hamilton [for whom the feast was made], like Ruben's wife.'[2] The range of masquerade, fanciful and escapist clothes created during the eighteenth century was rich and eclectic, with a particular inclination to styles inspired by Old Master paintings. These clothes were not limited to the court or the aristocracy; they were revivals which could reach as far as fashion could reach. During this period several factors helped to create a fresh blossoming of romantic historical revivals, and to democratize the past; the public masquerade and private events of an equally fanciful nature co-existed with increasingly available knowledge about the past and an antiquarian phase which produced serious publications and popular history paintings. Given the noticeable eagerness to dress up, or down, the range of sources to imitate and the settings in which to display them, the eighteenth century populace exhibited an understandably vivid delight in the dress of the past. As Horace Walpole suggested, five hundred people, each bent on looking like somebody else, was a remarkable sight: 'It was an assemblage of all ages and nations; and would have looked like the day of judgement, if tradition did not persuade us that we are all to meet naked, and if something else did not tell us, that we shall not meet then with quite so much indifference, nor thinking quite so much of the *becoming*.'[3]

Masquerades were an arena for the display of dress and invention; they varied in size, and the participants varied in social background. The one Walpole attended in 1742 was grand, given by the Duchess of Norfolk in honour of a nephew of the King of Denmark (he attended in armour). There were five hundred guests, in 'all the jewels of London – and London has some!'[4] Members of the royal family attended, including the Princess of Wales who was said to be covered in diamonds, thus easily recognizable although she did not remove her mask. Walpole did not get home until five in the morning. At this kind of occasion the rich and the powerful could show off well-educated or witty evocations of the past, and not only maintain their rank, but even, temporarily, surpass it: it was the Duke of Richmond who chose to go as Henry VIII.

At public events, the top people could still be seen, but the sheer size of some masquerades made them very different affairs; in 1791 one was attended by nearly three thousand people, at Vauxhall. The newspapers and periodicals had by then taken to reviewing goings-on, and their readers could dwell on the details at leisure. Going to Vauxhall or Ranelagh was not a prohibitively expensive outing; in 1748 for example, entrance cost a shilling to Vauxhall, and for that, without a masquerade, people could watch the fashionable world go by: 'those who have come out there either promenade, in the garden, or sit down at one of the many tables there are, and have brought to them various foods and drinks, wines, confitures, punch, meat, apples, fruits; etc. . . .' Having paid the fee, 'anyone is free to buy anything or not. One can in the meantime listen to the music, walk about, see and be seen, without further cost.'[5]

Vauxhall had been a prominent pleasure ground since about 1660 (Pepys enjoyed going there) but Ranelagh, in Chelsea, had opened in 1742. Its huge wooden rotunda was distinctive [seen in the background of 92]. *The Times* reported on 23 May 1791 a masquerade there:

88 Wife of a York Alderman in 1752. She has copied a dress from a hundred years before (see plate 87).

There certainly was a drawback of company, by the Pantheon Masquerade happening the night before, and by one being advertised for Vauxhall, at so short a distance of time to come . . . there was a good Lady Pentweazle, and not a bad Pantomimick clown – and Mr Petit's shoemaker had some humour in it. . . . One heavy-heeled Harlequin convinced us that the patched coat was ill bestowed on his abilities. There was neither invention in his head, or agility in his feet, and with an unmagical sword, he stalked the night away – Sailors and Romps, with a couple of watchmen and a Quack Doctor, were all that are worth mentioning.

It is possible that all or some of these clothes may have been hired from Ranelagh House; tickets had cost a guinea, for this festivity had followed a 'Magnificent firework,' and was in honour of the Queen's birthday, under the patronage of the Prince of Wales. The Prince, later George IV, loved dressing up in adult life; two portraits can testify to his early experience. Johan Zoffany painted him and his brother, together with their mother, in 1764. The Prince of Wales, at the age of two, was dressed as Telemachus, and Frederick as a Turk. In 1770 he, his parents and their other children were painted by the same artist as a group dressed in pseudo-seventeenth century clothes, known widely for obvious reasons as 'van Dyck' dress.

The degree of escapism or fantasy open to those inclined to follow it was arguably greater than it had previously ever been; royalty and the court had always had routes to evoke the past, or whatever their fancy suggested, but in the eighteenth century it was a popular possibility. At the theatre or in the street young men could pose as grooms, and in 1778 there was a chance for young women to dress as men: 'in Men's Dominos our Hair immensely well dressed, smart Bags, Fierce Hats and Feathers, etc., and we made two smart Beaux. . . .'[6] A play produced in 1780, which put an eighteenth-century face on the Shakespearian ploy of disguise, based part of its plot on the muddle made possible by similar costumes at a masquerade, but more seriously the epilogue raised the possibility that widespread dressing-up had more significance off-stage than on:

'Tis plain, in real life, from youth to age,
All wear their masks. Here only on the stage,
You see us as we are; here trust your eyes,
Our wish to please cannot be mere disguise[7]

In urban life, when populations were not so huge as now and therefore could not offer such spontaneous anonymity in sheer size as they now can, masquerades and associated events were a means to that end within a smaller population and a smaller elite.

Knowing about clothes of the past, and so having some selection and inspiration for fanciful dress was easier for the growth in antiquarian studies. There were also numerous depictions of historical figures in paintings exhibited at the Royal Academy, founded in 1768; for instance, between then and 1800 there were eleven modern pictures recreating scenes from the life of Edward III, six of Henry VIII, fourteen of the Anglo-Saxons; Mary Queen of Scots was most popular with twenty paintings, five shown in the same exhibition. Alongside these glimpses of the past, the eighteenth century produced publications which could be said to mark the beginning of the history of costume as we understand it today.

For example, in 1757, Thomas Jefferys published his massive four-volume book usually known, for convenience as *A Collection of the Dresses of Different Nations*, but its full title continues, by way of explanation, as follows: *Antient and Modern, particularly Old English Dresses, after the designs of Holbein, Vandyke, Hollar and others, with an account of the authorities from which the figures are taken.* Jefferys drew on a range of secondary and primary sources, including the 1581 costume book by Boissard, and Ferriol's book too, *Receuil de Cent Estampes representant differentes Nations du Levant* (Paris, 1714), and provided full captions to the illustrations with a variety of information or anecdotes quoted from his secondary sources. It pro-

89 A page from Joseph Strutt's important costume history book, 1796. Strutt showed the English their own past.

vided more than a pattern book for masquerade; it was an attempt to compile an entertaining history of costume which referred the reader back to historical sources, and as such must have been of general educational value, as well as of potential use to history painters. Jefferys introduced the work with a serious essay in which the seventeenth-century origin of dress such as wigs or breeches was described, and he also attempted a theory of the function of dress.

Attention to purely English history was a feature of the work of the tireless antiquarian Joseph Strutt. Jefferys' book in a sense anticipated Strutt's work, but could never seriously compete with it. The years 1796–9 saw *A Complete View of the Dress and Habits of the People of England.* Obviously this book was to have its impact on romantic, fashionable interpretations of the past in the following century, when people searched it for models, but it was the product of eighteenth-century concerns for accuracy and accessible information. This book, in addition to painstaking textual research, used visual sources not published before, and in Strutt's own words, he aimed to enliven the illustrations (engravings) 'by grouping them as pleasingly as the nature of the subject would admit,' whilst they were 'faithfully copied from the originals, without an additional fold being made to the draperies or the least deviation from the form of the garments.'[9] He was alert to the difficulties of copying, a refreshing virtue which his followers, such as F.W.

90 Portraits of ancestors help revivals of historical dress in the pre-photographic age. In 1764 these children play beneath those painted by van Dyck in the 1630s. Van Dyck dress revivals were very tenacious in the eighteenth century.

Fairholt, would have done well to imitate. Thomas Hope, for example, concerned for accuracy in the question of classical dress, simply gave up on a wholly faithful representation of 'that prodigious diversity in the texture of the stuffs and in the forms of the folds,' with the result that his 1809 *Costume of the Ancients* over-simplified its originals.[10] This tendency has no doubt helped new interpretations and departures from the original wherever engraved or line drawings have been used as models for recreated historical dress, although our present access to colour photography or film does not make us see the past they portray any less selectively than our predecessors saw their past.

Strutt's laudable aim to combine authenticity and animation made his book a prop for the work of Planché and Fairholt and other nineteenth-century dress historians. It contained information about the dress of all walks of life, with careful illustrations [89]. Strutt also produced another important book, in 1801, called by the informative title *The Sports and Pastimes of the People of England (Including the Rural and Domestic Recreations, May Games, Mummeries, Shows, Processions, Pageants, and Pompous Spectacles from the Earliest Period to the Present Time)*. This account of English life, ranging from chivalry to gambling, from military games to needlework, afforded English people for the first time a comprehensive and easily digested account of how their ancestors lived. It showed the other side of history's coin, and its influence was even greater for the presence of nearly 150 illustrations from original sources. This last of Strutt's books fed nineteenth-century nostalgia for old England and was the final contribution of the previous century's social history research, but Strutt's first book had been published in 1773 (*The Regal and Ecclesiastical Antiquities of England*). For thirty years, Strutt had set an example of antiquarian zest, which was an eye-opener for anyone interested in the dress of the past.

Books and public exhibitions of paintings recreated the past, but many English families would have to do no more than raise their eyes from the breakfast table to meet the gaze of their ancestoral portraits: 'Two double half-lengths of Ladies by Vandyck, the first Duchess by Sir Godfrey Kneller. The Duke's entry at Venice, by Canaletti's master: good.' Walpole's visit to country houses revealed the extent of the private collections, this small extract being from a long list of paintings seen at Kimbolton Castle in May 1763. Due perhaps to one or several of the circumstances mentioned, English fashionable circles were so captivated by van Dyck's portraits that for more than half the century, dress worn imitated the dress seen in them. In so popular a vogue, hardly more than a tiny percentage of the enthusiasts could have possessed their own van Dyck; of those who had actually seen one, most were outclassed looking at portrayals of the wealthy and the aristocratic; and the court itself. It is almost certainly the case that a gentlewoman or her husband looking rather like a van Dyck *felt* like a van Dyck: glamorous, sleek, confident and, above all, rich. It is useful to concentrate on the details of one seventeenth-century portrait which won the hearts of the eighteenth century, for it demonstrates similarities of taste which endorse the other attractions of its era.

The portrait in question was not actually by van Dyck, although initially it was considered so; it was Peter Paul Rubens's portrait of his wife Hélène [91]. Jefferys named it correctly in his 1757 book; by the 1740s it had established itself as a model for a style in women's dress which continued until the 1770s. Some features of it survived separately for longer, and there are isolated instances appearing in nineteenth-century portraits. There are a number of coincidences in taste between the portrait and the eighteenth century; the long, seventeenth-century feather fan was imitated without change; it was another novelty to add to the established range of fans; the bunched-up sides to the skirt echoed the fullness so sought after with the use of hoops; Hélène's deportment and carefully displayed hands and wrists complied closely with eighteenth-century ideals. 'A lady should carry the head erect, the shoulders low, and the arms bent and held backwards close to the body, while the hands should be in front, one over the other, clasping a fan. But remember, above all, no affectation.'[11] This advice would help to achieve elegant movement within a bulky dress and petticoat; the long feather fan added grace and softness to an otherwise rather stiff ensemble. Hélène's chains, looped asymmetrically across her bodice, were copied too, and her feather hat. (Hogarth observed in the

91 The portrait of Rubens's wife. Hélène inspired many imitations a century later.

Analysis of Beauty, 1753, that asymmetry seemed a natural inclination in women's dress.) The full soft sleeves of the chemise and falling lace wrist bands in the portrait were equally enthusiastically copied, with ribbons and rosettes. No doubt Rubens's portrait also appealed in a general way by its rich combination of stateliness and vivacity, and Hélène's convincing vibrant presence. Sometimes only a selected combination of some of its features was used, but there was sufficient familiarity with them for Rubens's wife to be conjured up very easily. The low stomacher might be omitted altogether, or echoed in a decorative rather than a functional way [92]. Usually the skirt was raised to show ankles above pretty buckled shoes, not a feature of the original. The low squared-off bodice and falling ruff also presented problems of taste and were altered accordingly.

In identifying and then modifying a style of a previous era, the fashion for Rubens's dress was true to the general pattern of dress revivals, but for sheer tenacity and duration and stylistic sympathy it must be one of the most remarkable cases in English dress history. It is interesting to search for any equivalent in modern experience; it may be that even such a vigorous portrait as the Rubens is no longer open to direct imitation; our attitude to portraiture has changed, and cinema and the machinery of stardom, may have helped to alter the process of emulation.

After the zealous pursuit of Rubens's wife for thirty or so years after the 1740s, separate features of her dress had so merged with ordinary dress that their pedigree was forgotten and the fusion makes it pointless to label this revival as 'fancy' dress or purely masquerade dress; it was both of these, but it was also part of the mainstream fashion vocabulary. Walpole saw at the 1742 masquerade that there 'were quantities of pretty Vandykes, and all kinds of old pictures, walked out of their frame.' Copying old portraits had become part of the fashion process.

The van Dyck revivals, as long lived as the Rubens one, were less exactly based; some of the surviving portraits of neo-van Dyck dress do not indicate any particular source picture, and some were obviously using the looser 'undress' of the seventeenth century which could equally easily have been taken from pictures by Peter Lely or Godfrey Kneller. The 1770 family portrait by Zoffany of the King and Queen and six of their children all in van Dyck dress had exploited the large areas of lustrous satin in rich colours, whilst Queen Charlotte's dress, for instance, did not closely follow a seventeenth-century pattern.

Thomas Hudson, Joseph van Aken the drapery painter, Joseph Wright of Derby, Francis Cotes and Allan Ramsey – versions of seventeenth-century dress appeared with frequency in the portraits of such

92 So-called 'Rubens's wife,' actually the Duchess of Ancaster at Ranelagh Gardens in 1757.

painters. Sometimes the dress was obviously imaginary, and superficial, but as often as not it was substantially and accurately painted, as worn by the sitters both male and female. However, in either case, it served to reinforce the fashion. Painters certainly encouraged this style of dress; in 1776, in one of his lectures to the students of the Royal Academy, Sir Joshua Reynolds summed up the advantages of this style of dress to the portrait painter, 'who in his practice

93 Dress taken in 1767 from seventeenth-century portraits complemented an artistic taste (compare with Plates 18, 83 and Plate 94).

. . . wishes to dignify his subject, which we will suppose to be a lady, will not paint her in the modern dress, the familiarity of which alone is sufficient to destroy all dignity. He takes care that his work shall correspond to those ideas and that imagination which he knows will regulate the judgement of others; and therefore dresses his figure something with the general air of the antique for the sake of dignity, and preserves something of the modern for the sake of likeness.' Apart from these aims, Reynolds observed others in the practice of portrait painters; because England had no 'ancient portraits,' English artists, in their wish for a venerable tradition, emulated van Dyck, and by extension, the dress of his lifetime, and so: 'By this means it must be acknowledged very ordinary pictures acquired something of the air and effect of the works of Vandyck, and appeared therefore at first sight to be better pictures than they really were.'

A much sought-after feature of seventeenth-century dress was lace, which appeared to advantage in such van Dyck portraits as of Robert Rich, Earl of Warwick [83], or the royal portrait of Henrietta Maria and the three views of Charles I. Although van Dyck's contemporaries such as Cornelius Johnson or Daniel Muytens portrayed the same feature of dress, it is with his name that it became associated by the eighteenth century; in a popular poem, later sold as a song to the tune of *Derry Down*, the fashionable taste of 1753 was described:

Your neck and your shoulders both naked should be,
Was it not for Vandyke, blown with chevaux-de-frize,
Let your gown be a *sacque*, blew, yellow, or green

94 Fashionable clothes of about 1769 without seventeenth-century overtones. The younger children's simplicity points to future developments in women's dress.

And frizzle your elbows with ruffles sixteen;
Furl off your lawn apron, with flounces in rows,
Puff, and pucker up knots on your arms and your toes.[12]

Another verse of the 1750s linked sixteenth- and seventeenth-century dress:

Circling round her ivory neck
Frizzle out the smart Vandike;
Like the ruff that heretofore
Good Queen Bess's maidens wore.[13]

Eventually 'vandyke,' in any one of its numerous spellings, came to mean any surface trimmed with cut edges, whether of lace or not; it could be used synonymously with 'scallop'; it even turned into a verb. After the end of the century it was in frequent use in contexts quite unconnected with the original revival: 'a chemisette vandyked round the Throat,' 1808, or a 'Double *pelerine* or cape deeply *vandyked*, and edged with very narrow chinchilla fur,' 1826, 'trimmed with a narrow vandyke edging of dark brown silk', 1865. 'Little boys and girls wear the high boot vandyked at the top,' 1865. So thoroughly has the seventeenth-century painter's name become associated with an incised decorative edging that even cooks are advised to 'snip away the fins and trim the tail into a "vandyke". . . .'

14 *Olde Englande*

THE NINETEENTH CENTURY

In the eighteenth century the foundations of a more accessible history of English costume had been laid by Joseph Strutt, and during the nineteenth century others continued to popularize this aspect of the past. 'The taste for a correct conception of the arms and habits of our ancestors has of late years rapidly diffused itself throughout Europe.'[1] Because of history painting's central place in the canon of nineteenth-century art, a wide audience saw historical characters and events come alive; archaic clothes and rooms were familiar, painted with the belief that details mattered and that accuracy was a principal of the genre. For example, between 1860 and 1870, at least nine new paintings appeared at the Royal Academy showing scenes from the life and death of Lady Jane Grey, and a total of twenty-five during the century; Charles II appeared nearly thirty times, and scenes from the Civil Wars almost sixty times in the hundred years from 1800 to 1900; in addition, Oliver Cromwell was depicted in over thirty paintings. Mary Queen of Scots was the most popular single historical figure at the Academy exhibitions, with over fifty appearances. Edward III and the Black Prince, the Wars of the Roses, the ancient Britons, the Anglo-Saxons and Bonnie Prince Charlie:[2] the past was abundantly visible and if the Royal Academy attendances indicate the degree of interest in paintings, then it was considerable: in 1875 more than 333,000 people visited the summer exhibition, which included two pictures of Mary Queen of Scots and one of Margaret of Anjou, as well as a Civil War scene and one of fugitives from Culloden.

For all this recreation of the past, the artists needed information on historical details, and the costume and armour historians had risen to the need, thereby supplying illustrated books not only for artists' reference, but for any other interested reader. They were feeding a growing appetite, whose links with fashion were strong. Fashion periodicals took up the subject,

95 Longevity of 'Rubens's wife' style (see Plate 91) assisted by its similarity to the 1870s post-crinoline silhouette. Seventeenth-century dress for the boy too.

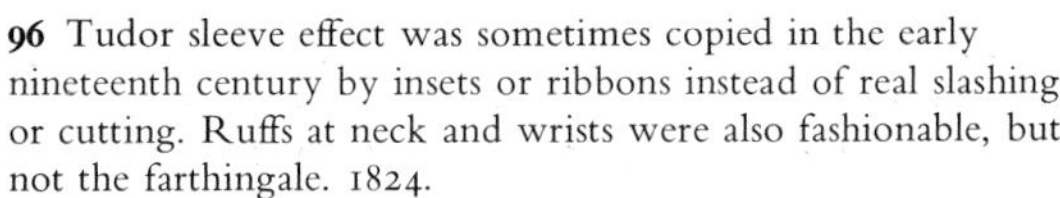

96 Tudor sleeve effect was sometimes copied in the early nineteenth century by insets or ribbons instead of real slashing or cutting. Ruffs at neck and wrists were also fashionable, but not the farthingale. 1824.

and amongst features on embroidery or serialized fiction came biographies of famous historical figures, and essays on historical dress; in December 1852, *The New Monthly Belle Assemblée* had a serious, four thousand word essay on the history of chains and bracelets, and 'we might go on adding link to link to our subject without exhausting it.' Books of advice on taste and dress often included historical examples; Mrs Haweis's *The Art of Beauty* in 1878 used more than three-quarters of its ninety or so illustrations for costume and jewellery of the past; the book was compiled from a series of articles which had previously also been seen in the *St Paul's Magazine*. Jaded milliners and dressmakers could rifle the past for ideas, and so could the journalists; in the periodicals of the nineteenth century there were countless allusions in dress to this or that historical era or person, many not more than a passing reference. However, some like the love of styles taken from original and modern portraits of Mary Queen of Scots, were a long-lived and significant taste, not confined to fashion commentaries only. *The Englishwoman's Domestic Magazine* noted in 1867: '. . . from Queen Berengaria, who wore her girdle midway down her skirt, to the Empress Josephine, whose skirts were as scant as the sheath of an umbrella, we imitate, as far as dress goes, an incredible number of fair and noble ladies who, in their day, were courted and admired, and whose taste for a time did rule. . . .'

Both the fashion industry and the painters owed a debt to two followers of Strutt's costume history researches, whose books tell us something of the way in which the dress of the past was then considered. J.R. Planché and F.W. Fairholt, both consciously aimed their books at the history painters, 'so no painter should falsify history by delineating the characters on his canvas in habits not known until many years after their death.'[3] Planché played an important role as an arbitrator on matters of historical dress, and made his intention to be rigorous and uncompromising quite plain in his 1837 book called *History of British Costume from the Earliest Period to the Close of the Eighteenth Century*. His reason was: '. . . the works of the indefatigable Strutt have . . . misled perhaps more than they have enlightened,' due to lack of proper chronological treatment. His little illustrated 'pocket volume' corrected this fault and went into its third edition in 1874; to anyone interested in the origins of costume history its bibliography reads like a roll call: Boissard, Vecellio, Hollar, Jefferys, Strutt, Meyrick, Stothard, and others. Planché acknowledged Strutt's authority, but in addition to regularizing the arrangement of the material, Planché brought vivid enthusiasm to the subject and, like the painters, brought the past into the present. In describing Queen Elizabeth's dress he admitted his task was superflous: 'Her great ruff rises up indignantly at the bare idea of being unknown or forgotten. Her jewelled stomacher is piqued to the extreme. . . .'[4] Planché's history did not treat the dress of the poor, except in a few instances, and he did not spare the reader his own judgements, calling, for example, full-bottomed wigs 'odious articles.' Nor could he avoid one of the perennial problems of describing dress: relative terms such as 'wide' or 'narrow' are made meaningless with the passing of time unless linked to informative illustrations; sentences such as the following did not help to inform readers, but almost certainly helped to reinforce nineteenth-century tastes about certain aspects of past dress: the waistcoat 'was soon made as ridiculously short as it had previously been unnecessarily long.'[5]

Despite teething troubles, interest was growing to such an extent and Planché's authority with it, that in his official commentary on Queen Victoria's great Bal Costumé at Buckingham Palace in May 1842, he treated the honoured guests to a history examination; the Duchess of Roxburghe, as Joan, Queen of Scotland, 1357, passed his scrutiny. 'It would have been impossible for the most rigid antiquary to have found a fault in her Grace's truly regal and imposing costume.' However, the Duke of Devonshire, as an Elizabethan courtier, made a mistake over his Star of the Order of the Garter, but was forgiven: 'the exceeding splendour of the ornament was held a sufficient excuse for the anachronism, particularly, as in this instance, no actually historical personage was represented.'[6]

F.W. Fairholt joined Planché in the footsteps of Strutt, with his book on English costume history which came out in 1846, based on costume articles previously published in the *Art-Union*; it was called *Costume in England: a History of Dress from the Earliest Period till the Close of the Eighteenth Century* and dedicated to Joseph Strutt. It was illustrated and had a glossary of terms, from 'ackerton' to 'worstead,' and again, whilst depicting past dress in clearer, larger format than Planché's first book, Fairholt's was also very much of its time; his taste, and that of his contemporaries, showed through both in the text and in the illustrations. Line drawings copied from originals or other copies almost without exception will bear the stamp of the copyist's unconscious bias. This can be seen in plate 98, where the seventeenth-century shape has been smoothed out to approximate more closely the shape of the 1840s, and as a result has lost important construction details; for instance, the long fallen collar is almost impossible to interpret as such. Fairholt included a line drawing of fourteenth-century dress (Mrs Haweis repeated the female figure in her 1879 *The Art of Dress*); it showed a style of male and female dress which seemed to the Victorians to be equal to Greek dress in its grace and simplicity: it was for many

97 Victoria and Albert looked convincingly at home in fourteenth-century dress, 1842. They gave three grand historical balls.

98 Fairholt's redrawing of seventeenth-century dress gives it an 1840s outline and makes the bodies (*right*) impossible to interpret.

99 This style of dressing copied from Edward III's tomb in Westminster Abbey was much admired by Fairholt and others later in the nineteenth century.

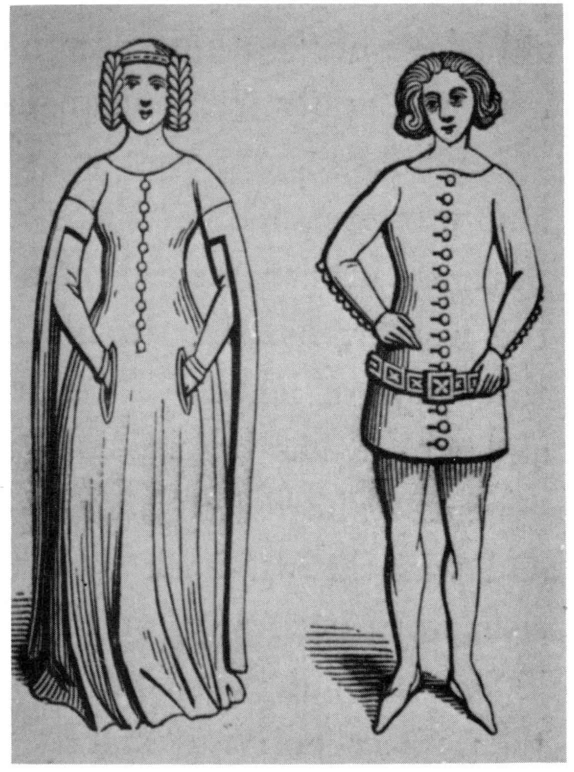

reformers a suitable model and aim [99], and Fairholt's comment exemplifies the modifications the taste of one era makes on that of another: 'The male figure is exceedingly simple, extravagant in nought but buttons. Indeed, that this is the most beautiful of the various dresses worn in England has long been my opinion; and if we omit the ugly streamer from the lady's costume, it must be granted that both figures, for elegant simplicity, could not be exceeded by any thing of classic times.'[7]

Eighteenth century dress had certain features which were to appeal to later nineteenth-century tastes, and to appear in fashion from the 1860s until the end of the century; but in 1846, Fairholt expressed complete distaste, particularly for the female dress of the 1780s and nineties: 'It is not easy to conceive anything more unbecoming, and it excites surprise how any invention with so little to recommend it could be universally adopted. The entire dress is ungraceful: the full buffont, the little frilled jacket, the tight sleeves, are all unpicturesque, and are only so many instances of the utter want of taste in dress exhibited at this period. . . .'[8]

Fairholt's book, like other costume histories of the period, and the fashion periodicals' potted histories, all help us to piece together the shifting views of past dress; some such as that of the fourteenth and very late eighteenth centuries were much liked and emulated in the nineteenth century although some writers rejected neo-classical dress entirely, and other periods, such as the second and third quarters of the eighteenth century or the reigns of Henry V to Richard III (1413–85), provided, according to Fairholt and others, quite unparalleled ugliness in male and female dress. There is not room here to present a comprehensive list of the nineteenth-century's voguish cultivation of various segments of English costume history. Suffice it to say that what was worn by both sexes and promoted by fashion periodicals during the century was often closely mixed up with this increasing availability of historical evidence. Much of it was described in biased language, and illustrated by line drawings, the very nature of which was to emphasize the similarities, whilst erasing the features not matching current taste.

Amongst the cluster of historical copies so characteristic of the nineteenth century, that of the dress associated with Mary Queen of Scots stands out as particularly heartfelt and enduring, although the phenomenon had begun in the previous century as we have seen. Mary's appearance was familiar from a few contemporary paintings, and from the fairly frequent appearance of spurious or copied ones, in addition to the generous number of modern recreations supplied by the history painters [8]. Both the eighteenth- and the nineteenth- century revivals made use of her cap or bonnet, being eras in which copies of the slightly raised and delicate shape made useful additions to the range of indoor head-dresses which were widely used. 'The bonnets are universally made in the Queen of Scots shape, either of crape or sarsnet,'[9] and in 1808 a straw version also appeared. The cap was sometimes exchanged for a hood, a feature also associated with Mary; black was often the colour used for these revivals as the surviving portraits principally depicted her in mourning: '. . . the upper part of the hood is made of black velvet, the rest of the garment of black silk. The trimming consists of black lace insertion and steel beads, and of velvet bows on the sleeves and upon the basque at the back.' This interesting effect coincided with the spread of seaside holidays; it was 'fashionable for wearing in a carriage by the seaside, where hoods are pleasanter to wear on windy days than hats.'[10]

Mary Queen of Scots' life was fully treated by George Chalmers's biography of 1822, and others followed, beginning to establish her as a model of piety living in an unscrupulous age. Walter Scott also played a role in her popularization. In his novels the past seemed to live again; Mary was not a distant figure from dusty history books, she was a vivid recreation, and imitations of her appearance must be set alongside scenes such as this, when, for instance, the tragic Mary herself came through the door, '. . . advancing with an air of peculiar grace and majesty.' Scott animated the portraits: 'Her dress was a robe of black velvet; a small ruff, open in front, gave a full view of her beautifully formed chin and neck, but veiled the bosom. On her head she wore a small cap of lace, and a transparent white veil hung from her shoulders over the long black robe, in large loose folds, so that it could be drawn at pleasure over the face and person. She wore a cross of gold around her neck, and had her rosary of gold and ebony hanging from her girdle.'[11] Alive again in fiction, Mary was depicted as beautiful, gentle and good; noble, but helpless against a ruthless Elizabeth, she become the heroine and the martyr; she suffered and wept. 'Yet the langour of her looks was so far from impairing her beauty, that it only substituted the frail delicacy of the lovely woman for the majestic grace of the Queen.'[12] Since the 1770s, in the hands of history painters, Mary had been blossoming into a heroine before Scott, anticipating Victorian sensibility, completed her new role. This viewpoint awarded nineteenth-century virtues of femininity to someone who was later, in twentieth-century eyes, seen as strong and masterful.

A painting of about 1810 [jacket and frontispiece] indicates how well her sixteenth-century clothes could be transmuted by nineteenth-century taste, and historical reference and nostalgia be balanced by elegant notes of modern fashion. Louisa O'Callaghan, whose husband, William Cavendish, was painted in fine 'van Dyck' dress at about the same time by George Sanders, kept a fashionably high bust line under an otherwise loose-fitting over-garment, and a carefully exposed area of pale lustrous satin hinted at the leg beneath just as any early nineteenth-century lady of fashion would wish. Folds in the satin of the sleeves provided the ghost shapes of contemporary nineteenth-century sleeve features, and the high roll of hair at the back of her head, and small side curls lost no modernity at all as they joined with the carefully observed head-dress of more than a hint of archaism. (The interesting head-dress is the least 'Scots' item of the portrait.) Louisa held a red book, her place marked by her left forefinger in a gesture imitating that of Mary Queen of Scots in the Blair College, Aberdeen, 'Memorial Portrait' (this portrait, done some time after Mary's death in 1587, also dressed Mary in turned-back lace wrist cuffs, instead of the ruffles found in other portraits). The O'Callaghan Mary Queen of Scots dress was an amalgam of several versions, with all the essential ingredients: the black of mourning, the gold chain or rosary, the book, the ruff and the cap, and all worn by a young woman who had married only a few years before into the Cavendish family, whose painting collection included a famous picture of Mary, inherited directly from Bess of Hardwick (whose daughter had married Mary's brother-in-law), and in whose property Mary had once been imprisoned. This particularly personal recreation of the appearance of a nineteenth-century heroine of more than two hundred years before, demonstrates perfectly that within the general framework of any widespread revival, there is generous scope for individual expression and invention.

Presumably the same personalization occurred to many of the recommended images contained in fashion periodicals; a long necklace like Louisa O'Callaghan's, shown in April 1812 in *The Ladies Monthly Museum*, was worn in conjunction with a head-dress *à la* Diana, and a similar chain shown in the same periodical in December 1811 was combined with a head-dress 'in the eastern style, composed of the hair in curls and ringlets, confined in a caul of silver net, fastened with a Chinese pin at the back of the head and in front with a knot of brilliants.' This was to be worn with a gown with long sleeves of white cuffs of Paris net, resembling Louisa O'Callaghan's in several ways. It was perfectly possible to be modish whilst cultivating a style two hundred years old, indeed of course the two were often, in fashionable circles, interdependent, and anything went: 'A Scot's bonnet of white satin, with a wreath of flowers.'[13] Mary Queen of Scots returned to haunt fashion for most of the century, and also had a steady vogue in the many fancy dress balls then so popular.

There were three coronations in the nineteenth century, of George IV in 1821, of William IV in 1831, and of Victoria in 1838. Each in their way displayed ceremonial dress based on the historical models thought most suitable and dignified, and reflected to some extent the circumstances and the personality of each new monarch. George IV, long an addict of dressing up and fancy dress, contrived an exceptionally inventive sartorial show, which fitted the antiquarian mood of the times and the details of which the former Regent had had plenty of time to ponder. The resulting processional costumes were perilously close to masquerade dress. They tended towards a theatrical past which is invariably less dignified than something more archaic. The dominant impression was Elizabethan [100]. For example, the attendants of the Earl Marshal wore dark suits with white sashes, 'stockings, shoes with large rosettes, and Queen Elizabeth ruffs.' George seemed to have been less than perfectly fit, and disguised his shortcomings by borrowing archaic grandeur. He was 'habited in robes of enormous size and richness, wearing a black hat with a monstrous plume of ostrich feathers, out of the midst of which rose a black heron's plume. His Majesty seemed very much oppressed with the weight of his robes. The train was of enormous length and breadth. . . .'[14] One wonders if he was also oppressed with concern lest poor Caroline of Brunswick should succeed in gate-crashing what could also have been her own coronation, but she failed to do so. The neo-mediaeval spirit of the age was well satisfied by the traditional challenge made by the King's champion after the religious ceremony. Riding into the banquet, fully armoured on horseback, the champion's duty was to fight anyone who opposed the new monarch. 'Nothing could exceed the impression produced by the approach of the champion and his loyal array. Every fair bosom felt an indescribable sensation of mingled surprise, pleasure and apprehension.' They clearly would have been prepared to believe that it was not an empty challenge, and have thrilled to see mediaeval chivalry come to life again.

William IV, sometimes known as 'Silly Billy,' had a consort present, Queen Adelaide. Neither felt under the same pressure to match the tremendous splendour of Napoleon's imperial coronation which had previously goaded George into his special efforts. Adelaide wore a gown with mediaeval features such as hanging sleeves and an open front. Being a consort and not a reigning queen, she had no need to change her robes during the service, but Victoria in 1838, like all reigning monarchs, had to disrobe for the anointing

100 George IV and nine trainbearers wearing revived Elizabethan dress which was in vogue at the time of his 1821 coronation, but became disliked later. Flowers were traditionally strewn in the monarch's path at coronations.

ceremony. Victoria's gown, like Adelaide's, was pseudo-mediaeval in appearance, but not in construction. The seemingly long open front was sewn together onto the under-dress, and its occupant disrobed from the rear. Victoria was accused of a penny-pinching attitude to her coronation, and making up for the lamented absence of the traditional armoured champion on horseback was one of the reasons for holding the Eglinton Tournament the following year. (Robes and other paraphernalia from these and later coronations are housed at the Museum of London, including George IV's suit and Victoria's splendid scarlet 'mediaeval' gown.)

The nineteenth century had room for many more revivals of English historical dress; any style that could be called mediaeval was sure of a welcome, and chivalry took on new guises. 'During this summer [1839] I used frequently to go to St John's Wood, where, in an enclosure, those who were to take part in the Eglinton Tournament, used to practise tilting, etc., to fit themselves for their *roles* as knights and esquires.'[15] The Eglinton Tournament was an inspired and inspiring occasion, and a reminder to us of how vivid and keen was the nineteenth century regard for 'Olde Englande.' '. . . None who were present at the most remarkable spectacle which modern eyes have witnessed, can regret the hours spent amidst the woods of Eglinton, in gazing on the achievements of the gallant knights of the nineteenth century.'[16] The tournament took place in August 1839, at Eglinton Park in Ayrshire, and attracted, according to an eye witness, 80,000 people. Young Lord Eglinton incurred its vast expense, aided in its organization by a group of friends, keen neo-mediaevalists who took part in the joust, and the tournament was a revival in toto: the clothes, the armour, the challenges in the lists, and the tents. Even the spectators were asked to come in period dress. It has already been pointed out that this spectacular revival was in part prompted by disappointment at the diminished pomp and ceremony of Victoria's economical 'penny' coronation the previous year.[17]

Interest in armour and mediaeval martial sports had earlier resulted in the publication of Francis Grose's *Treatise on Ancient Armour and Weapons* in 1786, and of the better *A Critical Inquiry into Ancient Armour* by Samuel Rush Meyrick in 1824. Meyrick had brought about a reorganization of the Tower Armoury; the armour was properly displayed, the entrance fee reduced, and crowds arriving in Victoria's coronation year visited the display in enormous numbers. In addition, anyone rich and interested enough could, by that time, buy whole suits of authentic armour and weapons, from the London premises of Samuel Pratt, a dealer who furnished a good deal of the tournament equipment.

101 Nineteenth-century neo-mediaevalism. Painstaking evocation of fifteenth-century garb worn in 1837. Such enthusiasms produced the Eglinton Tournament in 1839. Lady Syke's dress close in spirit to Queen Victoria's coronation robe, which had boning sewn into its bodice.

By and large, Eglinton, since it could not reasonably involve the more dangerous aspects of earlier mediaeval tournament activity, was a sixteenth-century event in spirit, but the costumes were much more various and eclectic. Not only did the event characterize the cult of revived mediaevalism, it also had its own internal drama. After elaborate and very costly preparations, rehearsals, disappointments and high expectations, the proceedings were to open with the arrival in the Lists of the nineteen knights and the Queen of Beauty, Lady Seymour, all with their resplendent retinues. 'The Queen of the festivities wore a rich antique dress, and was attended by her maids of honour and body guard of ladies, equipped as archers, in elegant and appropriate costume. The pavilion which was ornamented with Gothic architecture, and tastefully hung with drapery studded with cloth of gold, was crowded with a dazzling display of the beauty, rank, and wealth of the Kingdom. . . .' At the moment this procession commenced, so too did a dreadful rainstorm. Although 'in about a quarter of an hour the rain abated, and showed to advantage, in the arena, noble knights, with their plumage waving, glistening helmets, suits of bright armour, and gallant steeds in rich trappings, impatient for the onset,'[18] the storm in fact had dampened what was already an equivocal enterprise. The crowds were expectant but chilled and unfamiliar with the rules and scoring system of the challenges, and the small group of inexperienced 'knights,' had no grasp of the demands of the proceedings, except for a handful of them; it was an elaborate lesson in the difficulties of reconstructing history. 'The light and fantastic costumes were completely soaked, the representatives of the fourteenth and fifteenth centuries marched homewards under the cover of unromantic modern umbrellas; men and women, horses, coaches, and omnibuses, hurried helter-skelter through the avenues, now trodden and drenched into mire; and the railway station was beseiged by a host of applicants for seats to Ayr. . . .'[19]

Just as interesting as the efforts at reconstruction and re-enactment were the meanings which commentators read into them at the time. Reconstituted chivalry could be a means of improving wider ills: '. . . is not the utilitarian age grovelling, mean, and sordid, and does it not require some counteracting influence – some elevating and inspiring sentiment to redeem its character from the debasing bondage of that material "philosophy" under which the manly virtues, and all those generous energies that exalt and adorn humanity, are fast perishing from the soil of England, where they once flourished in such vigorous luxuriance?'[20] A tournament watched over by a queen of beauty elevated useful sport by the 'virtuous influence of women'; they could not be present in this way at other sports, and so a tournament was seen as a way of emphasizing the high moral role of women, and stabilizing the behaviour of young men; if you regretted the passing of a heroic aristocracy, and overmuch attention paid to continental pleasures, a 'mediaeval' tournament was also thought to encourage a more noble and patriotic stance in its participants. Indeed, it seemed as if tournaments and their revived pageantry and costumes were set to have a new lease of life, as a ready vehicle back to the good old days, and a solution to complaints about the behaviour of the young, and the idle beau monde generally. Revived costume could not only recall the past, but promote higher aims, reminding both the wearer and the onlooker of the possibility of an individual's betterment within the general belief that life was worthier in the 'olden times.' Tinges of mediaeval features at a ball or in day dress, or on a cap could all gather meaning from nostalgia for England's past, and help dispel this sort of frequently expressed concern:

> Were it permitted our ancestors to revisit the earth, great indeed would be their astonishment, at seeing their sons and daughters. . . . With difficulty would they be persuaded that this was the same country for which they bled and fought; that the weak effeminate creatures of the present age were their progeny. . . . The present age is certainly more enlightened, and far excels that of three centuries ago, in point of refinement. But, in the nobler traits of character, in hardiness, spirit, and magnanimity, it must be acknowledged that, with some exceptions, the present race has degenerated. . . .[21]

Mediaevelism and other historical revivals could, by the power of association, evoke in varying degrees chivalry, patriotism and heroism, and men seemed particularly romantic in these revivals because their usual dress was settling into a uniform tabular dullness during the nineteenth century; their chances of fantasy diminished whilst women's dress flourished. Men's dress, of course, continued to display rank, wealth and the authority of action, but by and large in middle and upper class life, the men left the women to demonstrate the leisure bought for them by male work and power. Turning back the pages of costume history allowed men, on occasion, to forsake the dress of activity for the dress of spectacular inactivity, as well as affording them the opportunity temporarily to change identity or status. The costume ball came to replace what had previously been called 'masquerade'; the nineteenth-century ball was usually not masked, but was certainly as elaborately inventive and nostalgic. Victoria, probably under Albert's influence, gave a conscience to dressing up; her 1851 costume ball at Buckingham Palace was 'to give an impetus to the trade of the metropolis.' On this occasion the gentlemen recaptured old splendours of Restoration dress; the 'brilliant effect of the costumes of the gentlemen was remarked on all sides. The waving feather, the gay colours, the flowing curls, and the splendid embroidery, the slashed sleeves and ruffles, the flattering streamers of ribbon, and the highly-picturesque baldrics, gave a colour and variety to the scene, strongly in contrast with the usual sombre effect produced by the universal black costume usually worn by gentlemen at balls.'[22]

Previously, in 1842, and shortly after their marriage, Victoria and Albert's first major costume ball had been set in the fourteenth century; their second, in 1845, had used a mid-eighteenth century theme. The costume

102 Photograph, *c.*1861, shows dress of revived eighteenth-century style. Note false lacing and sleeves. Crinoline adds fuller shape to looped skirt than would have been fashionable in the eighteenth century.

balls of the nineteenth century reflect the periods of history which were in favour in dress circles at that time; there was an Ivanhoe Ball in the 1820s, and Scott's influence continued with a Waverley Ball in 1871. During the 1890s *The Queen* reported fancy dress news at length, alongside its normal fashion items which in turn were very dependent on terms, and features, from costume history, and noted that fancy dress contributed many ideas to current fashions.

Historical allusions in dress were often referred to as 'picturesque,' also a favourite word to describe dress at late nineteenth-century society weddings: during the last two decades of the century there was a rapidly spreading vogue for wearing archaic dress, which included any attendant children; the seventeenth century provided many ideas for dress at weddings, and so too did some Tudor styles. The groom usually remained in standard formal dress. The custom has remained with us; at almost any wedding involving special dress, so-called 'traditional' or archaic styles will predominate for the bride and her attendants, and if the groom is in a morning suit, the picture from the past is complete.

High fashion of the last two decades of the nineteenth century was already finding styles of fifty years before not to its liking; there was a preference instead for eighteenth-century dress, particularly the Watteau taste, which took the loose-backed gown of Watteau's paintings as a starting point for modern needs. A Watteau jacket of the 1890s for instance, was hip length, and very full in both front and back; teagowns often used the same cut. Teagowns held a special place in a fashionable wardrobe: 'Ours is a luxurious age, and most women came in from their afternoon walk or drive and discard stiff bodices, to fall back on the ease and comfort of a loose gown. For this sort of thing there is nothing prettier than cream and almond cloth, made with a Watteau back, and a large frill cape, edged with lace, a cascade of lace down the front and round the edge of the sleeves. . . .'[23] The Watteau shape, also called the sacque shape, could mix in full dress with other styles very happily, including Restoration; as *The Queen* reported the week before its advice on Watteau teagowns: 'We have much to be thankful for, inasmuch as our fashions are culled from all periods in the history of dress when women looked their best, a remark which could hardly apply to the early Victorian era.'[24]

Dress in Watteau's paintings provided useful models for loosening the dress of the 1880s and nineties which had come to constrict the legs as well as the torso; it was also a useful model during the 1860s, not as encouragement to free the legs which were already unrestricted inside the bell of the crinoline, but as a source of ideas to decorate the expanse of the wide skirts over the crinoline. Festooning and draping became an intricate minor art form for dressmakers bent on diversifying the skirt ornamentation, and they gladly utilized the experience of dressmakers in the 1770s and eighties who used internal tapes to pull up the gown skirts into the large side puffs called a 'polonaise.' This same system could be used over a bell crinoline hidden beneath an underskirt [70]. It was used in conjunction with other features which hinted at the eighteenth century, and was known by various names, including 'Pompadour.' The same effect could be achieved by superimposing festoons of fabric caught by ribbons or flowers, but it was obviously an economical need which prompted the use of *porte-jupes* for this purpose: a 'Watteau' look could be attained by wearing over the skirt an extra waistband with a pendant loop on each side, through which the skirt was pulled, and because the *porte-jupe* in this style could be seen, it was decoratively made. *The Englishwoman's Domestic Magazine* in 1863 made a point of encouraging home dressmaking, and suggested that this device was so simple that any lady could manufacture one herself. So, at will, a skirt could be raised up into an eighteenth-century style, or lowered back into the present. (A 'Pompadour' *porte-jupe* worked on the wrong side of the skirt and pulled it up into smaller festoons all round the base.) This was not the same exploitation of eighteenth century style as the sack-backed gown modified and worn by Jane Morris [39] at the same period, and later taken up by the Aesthetic groups as an alternative to the straighter, and limper mediaeval styles. (Two such dresses appeared in 1881, in modified eighteenth-century style with 'Long polonaise with gauged neck+pli Watteau, sleeves with shoulder +elbow, puffs, +gathers in between, lace collar, cuffs. . . .'[25]

As well as appearing in many forms in everyday high fashion, and at costume balls and weddings, historical allusions also had a central role in Aesthetic taste. For those of Aesthetic inclinations, there developed the chance of expression of sensitivity and artistic feeling, outside the mainstream styles dictated by those they saw as the 'philistines.' Colours were chosen similar to those in darkly varnished Old Master paintings, and the bright new chemical dyes were considered garish. Some people at the time, the 1870s and eighties, called Aesthetic dress 'Pre-Raphaelite' dress because of its connections with the painting circle of that name whose work was first seen in 1849. (Part of the Pre-Raphaelite Brotherhood's aim had been to regenerate art by using very exact studies of nature, and to return to elevating historical subjects; the paintings provided details of mediaeval life, for example, which they keenly sought to make as accurate as possible. They made extensive use of Camille Bonnard's *Costumes*, a costume source book published in 1829–30 illustrating the thirteenth, fourteenth and fifteenth centuries.) One of the original painters of the Pre-Raphaelite Brotherhood was John Everett Millais, who was seen at a ball in London in the 1840s dressed, significantly, in seventeenth century dress: 'I can recall Millais looking as if he had stepped out of a picture by Van Dyck. He wore a long silk coat and breeches, lace cravat, and silk stockings, which suited him to perfection.'[26] (In his own later paintings, Millais made careful use of dress of the seventeenth and eighteenth centuries.)

From the Brotherhood of the 1840s, the love of old, rich fabrics and fresh but nostalgic ways of draping the body spread to the dress of their families and social circle, and became a means of expressing an individual and non-materialist stance in the midst of what was seen as widespread dullness and unsatisfactory dress. In Vernon Lee's novel *Miss Brown*, published in 1884, Hamlin mused on his undergraduate days when his taste seemed less shoddy than it later became; the group of friends at Oxford 'had welcomed young Hamlin, with his girlish beauty and pre-Raphaelite verses, as a

103 Aesthetic dress recalled past styles in inventive ways but was ridiculed by the 'Philistines' for its limp appearance due to lack of corsets and bustles.

sort of mixture of Apollo and Eros, sitting at the head of the supper-table dressed in green silk, with rose garlands on his head, while Perry led a chorus of praise, dressed in indigo velveteen, with peacocks' feathers in his button-hole, and silver-gilt grasshoppers in his hair.'[27] Perry was to marry a wife who had a 'Sapphic leer and limp dresses,' and it is just such later manifestations of Aesthetic taste which earned it attacks in du Maurier's cartoons in *Punch*; so accurate were these that they have become a widely used source of information about Aesthetic appearance [103].

The cartoons emphasized the lank bodies unsupported by the stays and furbelows of other fashions; but much as they were criticized, the attempts to re-establish more satisfactory historical styles and to evade the tyranny of the corset refreshed English dress considerably; it had begun in the 1850s and sixties, but reached a peak of Aesthetic taste in the 1870s and eighties. The colours, such as sage-green, terracotta, old gold and lavender, the amber beads and the flowers gave a new, softer palatte to dress, and provided a happy alternative to those women whose figures or budgets would not tolerate the harsh colours and complicated dresses of less 'artistic' styles. Men had an opportunity to discard their dull uniforms so suggestive of commerce and authority, and regain a little poetry in their lives:

> youngish men, with manners at once exotically courteous, and curiously free and easy, in velveteen coats and mustard-coloured shooting-jackets or elegiac-looking dress-coats, all rising in poetry, or art, or criticism; young ladies, varying from sixteen to six-and-thirty, with hair cut like medieval pages, or tousled like moenads, or tucked away under caps like eighteenth-century housekeepers, habited in limp and stayless garments, picturesque and economical, with Japanese chintzes for brocade, and flannel instead of stamped velvets – most of which young ladies appeared at one period, past, present, or future, to own a connection with the Slade school, and all of whom, when not poets or painters themselves, were the belongings of some such. . . .[28]

Undoubtedly the Aesthetic taste occasionally harboured pretentious and silly aims, but more often it made serious and inventive use of historical features in dress: the very soft lines of semi-fitted, fourteenth-century gowns, gigot sleeves with a sort of Tudor slashing, or loose sack-backed dresses copied from the eighteenth century. Simpler, less structured bodies to gowns meant that an 'artistic' woman had to make a decision about tight lacing. 'The waist of a "Prae-Raphaelite" is rather short, where a waist ought to be, in fact, between the hips and the last rib. Her skirt is cut full or scanty, as she chooses, but is never tied to her legs with strings and elastics. She can, therefore, stoop

104 Silk dress in historical spirit designed by H. Thorneycroft for his wife, *c.*1881. Note smocking on bodice and sleeves. This couple were founders of Healthy and Artistic Dress Union in 1893.

without gasping or cracking her corset-bone, and can sit down or walk upstairs at will, unlike some votaries of present fashions.'[29] The plainer lines of the dresses probably encouraged concentration on the sleeves, which were often the most elaborate part of the ensemble: 'Many very rich and complicated sleeves may be adopted from old pictures by Rubens, Rembrandt, and others. . . . Nothing is so ugly, or so spoils the appearance of a dress, as a poor, weak sleeve.'[30] Mrs Haweis advocated ways of copying graceful examples from the past, and thought that dresses which were longer than those generally worn in the later nineteenth century would add height and movement to the figure. She reproduced an illustration from F.W. Fairholt's costume book [99] to show the advantages of fourteenth-century dress. (Interestingly this 1879 redrawing of the 1846 line drawing contrived to make the skirt both narrower and longer; each were made in accordance with the dominant shapes of the day whilst being promoted nevertheless as authentic reproductions of fourteenth-century appearance.)

The year 1884 was important for those of Aesthetic taste; it was then that Arthur Liberty opened a costume department in his shop in Regent Street. Since opening in 1875, Liberty had quickly gained a reputation as a supplier of fine goods from the East, and these included shawls and fabrics, and other items of dress. They had provided colours in fine weaves which exactly suited Aesthetic taste: 'French and English mustards, sage-greens, greens that look like curry, and greens that are remarkable on lichen-coloured walls, and also among marshy vegetation – all of which will be warmly welcomed by those who indulge in artistic dress or in decorative revivals.'[31] Mrs Haweis was advising her readers, if they saw such artistic colour, to 'grapple it to your soul with hooks of steel.'[32] From 1884 the costume department of Liberty enjoyed success because it did not compete for sales in any other fashions. It adhered to its own style, using Liberty's own fine fabrics, and so established a 'look' which was to prevail until the 1920s: a dress without extremes, based on past styles, and, according to Liberty's own catalogues, never out of date. This department was to play a major role in spreading the taste which had grown up in the Aesthetic circles; in the public's mind, Liberty designs were synonymous with artistic appearance. In 1893 the company published a book called *Evolution in Costume* which showed their self-professed 'modifications' alongside the historical originals. A member of their staff recalled this as the characteristic behind the success: 'our designers have taken their models from historical costumes, modifying them for our own times and conditions, but always retaining something of the characteristic of the original. The designs for children's dresses, as shown in the books of Kate Greenaway, had already to some extent prepared the way; and soon it became very much the *mode* among artistic people and their imitators to wear a 'Liberty' gown at any special function. . . .'[33]

Children were treated, sometimes unwillingly, to many of these historical fancies; their dress has often, at different periods, been the vehicle for adult fancies, but in the last three decades of the nineteenth century, and in the first years of the twentieth, they found themselves subject to an unusually vigorous phase of invention. Kate Greenaway's best-selling books [46] helped to popularize the early nineteenth-century styles, and others were also produced for them. 'Antique styles, adapted to the young, are frequently delicious. Pictures by Velasquez, Vandyke, and earlier masters, offer fruitful hints: the little old aprons, poke bonnets, quaint sleeves, sacques and caps, gaberdines &c, may be daintily reproduced, and prove economical.'[34] Not all children liked to be quaint or dainty, and artistic historical dress made at home could make a child feel conspicious at parties: 'Elsie would have liked a dress with a sailor collar and pleated skirt like the others.'[35]

105 Greek and mediaeval dress were equally admired by reformers for their draped effects. Sixteenth- and seventeenth-century dress was strongly disliked, but later seventeenth-century dress enjoyed revival in early twentieth century.

15 *The Past All Over Again*

THE TWENTIETH CENTURY

What the next development will be even the experts hesitate to predict. Only one thing is certain. The future of fashion will be its past all over again.

Fashion and the Woman, Marshall and Snelgrove, 1930

The booklet published by the department store Marshall and Snelgrove in 1930 appeared just at the onset of the decade most characterized by romantic nostalgia; during the 1930s, it seemed, there was not a designer or a magazine who let a season go without some echo of past fashions, and the booklet, observing the start of this development, thought it was caused by a strong reaction in women's dress against the 'mannish' fashions of the First World War and the following decade. It noted that by 1929, in evening wear at least, there was 'a return to the long skirt, complete with train, and all the billowing draperies of that age of femininity before the war.'

This was certaintly the case, but it was over-simple to suggest that all or even most dress during the war or after was 'mannish'; in fact the First World War encouraged an overt nostalgia and pleasureable impracticality in modish evening dress, as a welcome alternative to the serviceable serge suits, uniforms or overalls of daywear. Too simple too was the suggestion that fashion's future was to be its past *all* over again. Amidst the wealth of historical borrowings enjoyed by men and women in the twentieth century, there has been a fastidious selection of *some* of the past, and a complete rejection of the rest: crinolines returned in the late 1930s but not for daywear; men revived Regency shapes in shirts and coats in the 1960s, but they wore them with trousers, preferring to leave breeches and stockings to history or to official ceremonial wear. But, as Marshall and Snelgrove's unknown author said in 1930, at no stage in the procession of fashions and revivals would it be safe to make predictions.

The century had opened with a bevy of historical styles thought to be both quaint and charming for young children, a continuation of the trend begun in the 1880s, and much promoted by those of artistic

106 Artistic and historical styles were specialities at Liberty. One of their velvet 'late mediaeval' dresses with front embroidered piece evoking Gothic belts (see Plate 82).

taste. *The Daily Mirror* was a newspaper partial to observing the goings-on of Society people in those days and in 1912 it reported on trends in children's dress, in conversation with the head of the juvenile department at Selfridges. This large department store had opened with much publicity only two years before, in 1909, and continued to remain in the public eye, with a happy knack of providing a wide range of goods in an exciting milieu. Just to visit the building in Oxford Street without purchasing anything could be an enjoyable event, and Mr Selfridge well knew how to use the press to his advantage. His 'juvenile' manager noted that little boys could be a fashionable accessory for their mothers:

> ... No longer is he merely a little boy in knickers and a tunic, just like every other little boy wears, but he must be 'perfectly sweet' in some suit that is 'perfectly quaint', and the colours of his little clothes must harmonise with his mother's. . . . We are always puzzling our brains for new ideas for little boy fashions. Suits of silk and velvet which have been copied from Cruickshank's pictures of Oliver Twist, Little Dombey and Nicholas Nickleby are having a great sale. We commissioned a lady artist who is well known for her quaintly garbed little people in the children's books she illustrates to design three new suits.[1]

These succeeded at once and others followed. The following year, for example, Selfridges were also advertising boy's washable suits in picturesque styles, such as the Gainsborough Suit at 17/6d and the Romney Suit at 12/6d. This was obviously following in the footsteps of Liberty who, since the 1880s, had been in part influenced by the children's illustrator Kate Greenaway; she had died in 1903, and Arthur Liberty had been the Honorary Treasurer of her memorial fund. It would be interesting to know which lady illustrator Gordon Selfridge had so directly utilized. That an illustrator of nostalgic images should transfer from books to clothes was a successful formula giving literal meaning to picturesque dress.

Liberty and Company continued to provide 'costumes never out of fashion,' including seventeenth- and eighteenth-century styles, mediaeval and one rather vaguely named Old English. The most popular of this range, which had for many years been a regular feature of the Liberty costume department, were to continue well into the 1920s. In a major promotion of their belief in this aspect of dress, Liberty published a lavish catalogue in 1905 which, besides illustrating the models for that year, set out to explain how such 'never out of fashion' clothes could exist; they must, it said, be 'based upon a close and intimate study of the history of costume and a definite knowledge of modern requirements.'[2]

Liberty's understanding of modern needs included probably an unspoken ability to adapt these otherwise 'unchanging' styles by subtle shifts of proportion and cut; for instance, the waistlines of the Stuart or Old England dresses dropped by gradual degrees from the fashionably high position of the first years of the century to the much lower fashionable place of the mid-1920s, yet both dresses retained their familiar features such as the 'Stuart's lacing across the bodice front. In 1905 the catalogue was continuing the serious tone of the original dress reformers, whose converts had turned to Mr Liberty *for* liberty: 'All that is good in current art is the outcome of the experiments and efforts of past centuries, there is nothing that is absolutely new, it is all a matter of evolution . . . the artists of Greece, of the Italian Renaissance and of eighteenth century France can all claim a share in the moulding of art as it is today.'[3] On the basis that in this continual process is an 'artistic truth,' the argument was continued that costume could have a share of it: 'It is never old, never out of date. Classic, Renaissance, and Empire styles, developed during long intervening years: absorbed into each other, reincarnated, but never lost, because they were good and true in

107 Nostalgic dress for children at Lincolnshire wedding in 1950. Page boy in eighteenth-century 'skeleton suit' with 'Kate Greenaway' bridesmaids (see Plate 46).

principle. And so today their appeal is as strong as ever.'[4]

This was the serious level at which it was then possible to discuss models in an 'artistic' dress catalogue. Unbeknown in 1905, the same process was to come to the fore again when Liberty and Company 'reincarnated' their own designs after the Second World War; that time, the object of interest was their textiles rather than made-up garments.

Before the 1914–18 war many features reminiscent of the eighteenth century, taken from both English and French portraits, were welcomed back into women's fashion and not just in self-consciously artistic circles; 'picture' hat came to mean a hat with a wide brim such as that seen, for example, in Thomas Gainsborough's 1785 portrait of Mr and Mrs William Hallett, known as 'The Morning Walk' and seen again revived in John Singer Sargent's 1902 portrait of the Acheson sisters. Picture dresses showed equally romanticized historical styles: 'It is impossible, in talking of picture frocks, to say which period predominates. We have seen an illustration of the Greek idea, and then we have beautiful copies of the old Gainsborough and Romney pictures as well as of Louis costumes, the last-named being well represented in Pompadour silk, and the painted buttons and wonderful buckles, clasps, and Pompadour floral trimmings which are all suggestive of the period.'[5]

The evocative 'picture frocks' continued to be so designated until well after the Second World War; in the meantime, a 1937 taffeta picture frock in Marshall and Snelgrove's winter sale, reduced to 69/6, had all the features associated with the name. It had a floor-length full skirt, the back being box pleated, a generous sash at the waist and a prettily ruched bodice; it could be bought in several colours including fuschsia, jade, framboise or 'patou blue'. A couple of years later the same company offered a picture hat in wide-brimmed pedal straw, with jersey swathing and a cascade of realistic flowers. This was expensive at 79/6, and was pitched forward high over an elaborately curled coiffure. It was described as part of a trend towards daring hats, accompanied by romantic gowns; the small waists were said to be inspired by tiny nineteenth century waistlines, and fashion frequently was observed to be turning back the pages of history. A hat

108 Two fashionable reanimations of the nineteenth century, drawn by Cecil Beaton.

109 The First World War helped to end clothes such as these, 1902, but they were recalled after the Second World War.

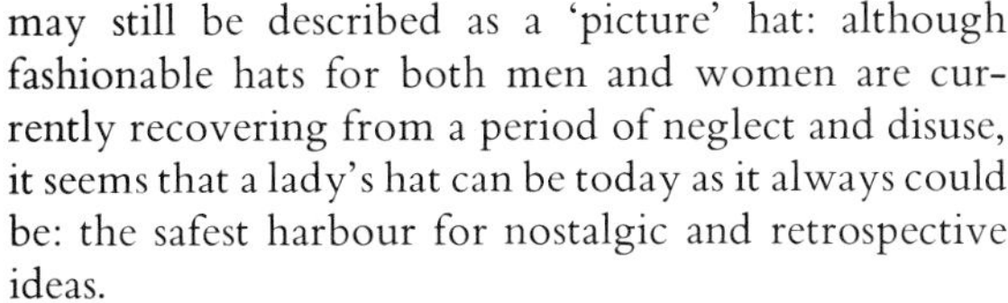

may still be described as a 'picture' hat: although fashionable hats for both men and women are currently recovering from a period of neglect and disuse, it seems that a lady's hat can be today as it always could be: the safest harbour for nostalgic and retrospective ideas.

The renaissance of certain eighteenth century features was to become almost a stock feature in evening wear for women, always certain to be likeable, but the early Victorian period was one part of fashion's past not so generally acceptable. In 1898 *The Queen* magazine had curtly dismissed the era as quite unwelcome, and favoured revivals of the seventeenth century instead. When people spoke of the mannish dress of the First World War and the subsequent decade they overlooked the fact that early Victorian styles did return to enjoy a revival at that time, succeeding that of the pre-Victorian Regency which enjoyed considerable vogue before the war. In 1915, for example, one lady of fashion on a tight budget had a black evening dress restyled, 'made fashionable, tully and sticky-out. The clothes have undergone enormous changes since the war and have become practically early Victorian with real full skirts. I thought the war would produce reactions to womanliness.' The same diary explained one of fashion's roles in war: 'I feel a peculiar appetite for buying clothes just now. So far from not wanting them in wartime, I think they are the one thing to distract one, and I long for lovely ones.'[6]

This was a natural response to a war which was taking place over the Channel; there were shortages, Zeppelins and personal tragedies to be endured but in the 1914–18 war the civilian population were not to be as personally endangered as they were by the 1939–45 war in the air; in this sense London particularly became a place of recreation and enjoyment for those on leave from the front, and as London *Vogue* saw things by December 1918, 'It is not for the kind of woman who wears ugly lingerie that a man fights.' The magazine expanded its viewpoint in the same issue, as it did on every opportunity. It was a woman's duty to be cheerful, attractive and alluringly feminine, in spite of her new wartime duties: 'In these days one must have freedom of movement, as never before, but we will

110 Revival of Edwardian taste, 1979, this time at an economic price and minus corsets.

not help the war by sacrificing our figures,' and 'When we are no longer feminine, when there is no more of lace and frills and loveliness, then indeed the world will be a sad place.' In the case of the historical revivals which took place in the days just before the First World War, the earlier style was probably no more restrictive or cumbersome than the modern shape onto which it was to be grafted. Today's attitudes would be unlikely to tolerate a superimposition of Elizabethan features, for instance, as happened briefly as the result of the Elizabethan Triumph at the 'Merry England of Yesterday and Today' held at Earl's Court in July 1912; dresses with long pointed stomachers, ruffles and bejewelled collars subsequently made several appearances. It is an interesting commentary on designers' inspirational techniques at this period to note that the copy of the lavishly illustrated 1842 *Souvenir of the Bal Costumé*, held at Buckingham Palace, which is now housed in the Bath Costume and Fashion Research Library, was previously in the possession of the House of Paquin, date stamped '4 Avr. 1901.' Queen Victoria's ball was set in the fourteenth century [97].

We may think of suffragettes as embodying the new modern spirit, but their struggles were carried on in restrictive clothes, at one stage partaking of the eighteenth-century revival, so swapping old for old, not old for new: 'Shoes were pointed, trimmed with huge buckles, and laced with silk ribbon. Suffragettes tying themselves to the railings of Buckingham Palace now wore Dolly Varden shepherdess hats tipped up at the back, with a bunch of ribbons under the rear of the brim,' wrote Cecil Beaton in his survey of the century, *The Glass of Fashion*. But the war changed circumstances, and helped to create less heavily cluttered clothes, which no doubt has also scuttled the chances of some historical eras ever again finding themselves resurrected.

Hereafter romantic nostalgia in women's dress could find itself in opposition to the more practical considerations engendered by the changing and widening options in women's lives. *Vogue* was fond of reminding its readers of the traditional association between soft, fulsome or frilly clothes and feminity itself, and this was challenged, and also confirmed in some minds, by the shorter, sharper lines to be found in the wardrobes of active and working women: '. . . there is an incompatibility between the motor-car and the sylph-like robe; a discord clangs when the woman hastens to a business occupation clothed as Lucretia or Portia might have clothed herself in the dim shadows of her secluded parlour. . . .'[7] The future of fashion's own past, as Marshall and Snelgrove put it, was dependent on these new possibilities; it is too simple to suggest that there were only two sides to take, the old-fashioned or the modern, but consciousness of these two moods in dress, and their significance, has been characteristic of much of women's dress this century. It was possible to talk of short hair on women, cropped '*à la* club-head' as unfeminine even by 1915, although this was an attitude largely gone by the next decade: 'I think it always looks a little uncanny or unpleasant – suggestive of prison, illness or suffragettes.'[8]

Conversely the modern appearance demanded more flexible clothes able to accommodate new activities; for example in 1914 only 300 women in Britain worked for bus companies, but by 1918 4300 did so, in banking the number jumped from 1500 in 1914 to 37,600 in 1918; many women left jobs after the war, but the trend was towards more varied activities rather than less; in 1914 there were 33,000 nurses, and by 1931 there were 118,909; and while there were 477 female doctors and surgeons in 1911, there were 2810 by 1931.[9] The modern options in dress began to echo these changes: 'Every wardrobe should contain at least one tailor-made costume of cloth made after the conventional fashion, almost without trimming, and with a simple straight skirt. It is the one thing that escapes criticism and that can be worn on almost all occasions. . . . For travelling, nothing replaces it. . . . Dark blue serge has long been the accepted material for the tailored suit which is destined to see much service. . . .'[10]

If romantic nostalgia was finding itself in conflict with the demands of practicality and economy, it had one notable ally in the *couturière* Jeanne Lanvin (1867–1946); her Paris business, like all *couture* enterprises, was producing original clothes of the highest quality, but her distinguishing signature lay in her frequent use of extravagant full-skirted dresses. After 1909 Lanvin expanded from children's to adults' clothes; her taste for fine embroidery and romantic shapes led to her continuation of the shortened pseudo-early Victorian shapes popular in the early part of the First World War, and during the 1920s she established a reputation for these delicately decorated, rather fairy-like dresses in contrast to the straighter and bolder lines characteristic of that decade. They were often referred to as crinolines, although they lacked the separate under-structure of the nineteenth century version. The House of Lanvin provided an opportunity to indulge in nostalgia and an old-fashioned vision of femininity, and by the 1930s, the tide had turned back towards this taste on a wide scale; other *couture* establishments developed collections with similar moods. There was then retrospection and fantasy in abundance, although Jeanne Lanvin retained a reputation for quiet distinction in her designs which were less prone to dramatic or novel experiment than those of some other houses at that time.

What *haute couture* did in Paris affected fashion in London, through the direct influence of wealthy English customers; through copies made in arrangements between Paris and London stores or unacknowledged copies made covertly for a lower rung on the market ladder; and through the more diffuse process of publicity and popularization by the fashion media. For example, one of London's oldest established fashion stores, Marshall and Snelgrove, was an important influence between the wars: they regularly sold designs by Lanvin, Patou, Chanel and so on, and made these a feature of their seasonal collections of less grand names. They helped the attainment of a complete, fashionable appearance by selling accessories and outfits for all occasions, accompanied by generous and informative catalogues and other occasional publications which provided a perspective on the main tendencies in any season.

The fashion media had an influence beyond keeping their readers informed on details and trends; they could act as blue-prints for much more, by disseminating style and taste, the fuels of any fashion. Manners, the smart places, even deportment could be learned from them: 'She stood carelessly, like the women in George Barbier's almanacks, "Falbalas et Fanfreluches," who knew how to stand carelessly. Her hands were thrust into the pockets of a light brown leather jacket – pour le sport. . . . One small red elephant marched across what I could see of her dress, which was dark and not pour le sport.'[11] The spread of style and its ever-evolving vocabulary by fashion publications could help to mould the way people defined beauty; this process adds another dimension to the question of why nostalgia has been so frequently expressed in twentieth century-dress. A pre-war Paris designer might have utilized a nineteenth-century silhouette or feature, who knows for what complex reason or simple whim; it might have sunk without a trace, or it might have been picked up by the media, and so began the long journey of modification from Paris to the English ready-to-wear market. The role of the specialist fashion media should not be underestimated.

Theories about nostalgic indress sometimes seek causes in economic and political conditions, and with hindsight the 1939–45 war would seem to bathe the previous decade in a special light, but ultimately it is

111 The nineteenth-century model for many twentieth-century revivals: Winterhalter 1865.

only possible to observe that a vogue for a Renaissance flavour entered the expensive end of the fashion market in 1932 ('It is smart to look like a troubadour or a page boy – the big sleeves, the tiny cap with an impertinent quill, or a beret, clapped on the side.'[12]) and that in 1939 there was a good deal of talk about bustles and bustle-bows. Beneath these various games with the past lay fundamental shapes as certain and assertive as at any period in fashion, and showing no signs of indecision, whatever the political climate. With all of fashion's past to choose from, the least desirable eras were Elizabethan and seventeenth-century dress; it is possible to find visual references to almost any other period in varying degrees of realism.

The case of the Winterhalter copies show how an apparently simple coincidence triggered off a revival which was to be widely popularized, but which with hindsight now appears an almost inevitable fusion of elements. Franz Xavier Winterhalter (1806–73) was a portrait painter of great skill, under whose brush the Empress Eugénie of France, the ladies of the English royal family and many others blossomed into exceptional prettiness. His most celebrated portraits were done in the 1850s and sixties, when the court and the evening dresses of his sitters were full-skirted, usually sleeveless, with bodies generously draped in gossamer tulle with pretty *corsage* flowers. Jewels at the neck or wrists looked especially splendid in contrast with the airy softness of the dresses to which Winterhalter paid so much attention. As van Dyck *understood* the satin and lace of the seventeenth century, so Winterhalter *understood* the tulle of the nineteenth. In 1937 the new King George pointed out the Buckingham Palace Winterhalters to Norman Hartnell at the time when this English *couturier* was first embarking on dress for Queen Elizabeth's wardrobe. 'His Majesty made it clear in his quiet way that I should attempt to capture this picturesque grace in the dresses I was to design for the Queen. Thus it is to the King and Winterhalter that are owed the fine praises I later received for the regal renaissance of the romantic crinoline.'[13]

The coincidence of the romantic mood of the decade with these revived splendours was an immediate success greatly aided by the state visit to Paris in July 1938. Due to the death of Queen Elizabeth's mother immediately before this visit, the entire wardrobe was reorganized in white. As a royal perogative in mourning, white was correct; as a fashionable gesture in the French capital in high summer it was a *coup de théâtre*. The immense success established an image for royal ladies on state or gala occasions which took firm root; the crinoline outline was continued by the present Queen, and remained little changed until some state dresses began in the 1960s to be designed on straighter lines.

Winterhalter's paintings were the basis for establishing the now familiar 'regal renaissance,' but they have also served as inspiration for numerous designs since those of Norman Hartnell. The crinoline itself, for presentday 'Winterhalters' is replaced by many layers of deeply flounced net so that a full but not entirely bell-shaped silhouette can be achieved, and tulle or lace with a *berthe* are characteristics of what is frequently now simply known as a 'Winterhalter style' [112, 113]. Hardy Amies has observed that there are two fundamental silhouettes which recur, the narrow hem and the wide hem, and that the wide hem is closest to most women's fantasy or vision of themselves: 'Where a woman can give full rein to her desires and let her taste be untrammelled by practical considerations such as when wearing an evening dress, there is no doubt about it that the straight silhouette, with its more than a hint of the hard-boiled, loses heavily.'[14] In what Hardy Amies designated the 'warfare' between these two types, the Winterhalter and other romantic revivals continue to survive, still seen as feminine and perhaps even more desirable since the sexual attitudes embodied in their Victorian prototypes have disappeared.

Of post-war events in *haute couture*, the arrival of the New Look in the spring of 1947 was one of the most formative. Almost at a stroke, Christian Dior (1905–57) altered the look at the top end of the market, and despite waivering trade response in Britain, partly due to sheer disbelief that women in post-war circumstances would accept such a shape, by the end of the same year the New Look was dominant in English women's wear. Its characteristic was an extreme and assertive interpretation of existing trends: resolutely lowered hemlines, full skirts with sometimes astonishing yardage gathered into small waists and a celebration of features which seemed extravagant in the austere post-war days, such as heavy pleating, or layered fabric to catch the eye as the figure moved, and deeply turned back cuffs and carefully planned collars and necklines. The other New Look silhouette was a sheath-shaped skirt, also well below the knee, which also emphasized the hips and pinched waists. The name given to this Dior-inspired change in shape suggests it was thought of as pure novelty; in fact the reverse is also true. Whilst it seemed a refreshingly generous and confident style after the difficult war years, it was also seen as a return to what was then usually called 'womanliness.' Some people thought it was an unwelcome revival of Edwardian luxury and conspicuous excess, at a time when women should have been searching for new roles to play in the reconstruction of post-war life; others thought those same passive traits were desirable and

112 A 1953 revival of Winterhalter at a time when the crinoline was also brought back in softer ways.

113 Winterhalter again without emphasis on crinoline. Princess Alexandra in much-praised gold lace 'Winterhalter' worn to Paris fashion gala, 1978. By Belville Sassoon, London.

long overdue for revival, and enjoyed the prospect of traditional sexual roles being affirmed by such clothes. Yet others saw it as a revival of Victorian shapes and feminine values, a continuation of the revival so dramatically orchestrated by the Hartnell crinolines of the previous decade.

'Crinoline' was a busy word in the late 1940s and early fifties, and it was to be found in the company of other resurrections from the nineteenth century. London *Vogue* noticed in April 1952 'Sweeping Paris by night, an airy sequence of sheer dresses, the favourites, chiffon, organdie,' to which Pierre Balmain's contribution was 'Black penny spots on white chiffon over a crinoline of palest pink tulle, the hip swathing knotted into a soft bustle. Balmain's signature: the corset lacing up the back.' The lacing was an elaborate feature made to be noticed and the crinolines were not separate frames but made of deeply layered underskirts, often helped by wings of stiffening set under the waist of the skirt. As unlike the clothes of pre-1914 days as the New Look may now appear to us, it was in its day regarded as a return to them, to an old-fashioned femininity and a clear revival of former taste. In 1950 Dior and others also introduced wrapped coats and straight, loose jackets for women which were regarded by both the glossy and the trade press as neo-1920s styles; they are hardly discernible as such to presentday eyes, but in 1951 *The Tailor and Cutter*, for example, was breathing a sigh of relief that the imminent danger of a full-scale twenties revival had been averted. Such a revival was not to find serious converts again until the early 1970s.

Post-war women's dress played on several retrospective themes and Paris designers enjoyed what was to be their final decade of dominance through their *haute couture* collections. After Dior's death in 1957 the pattern of influence shifted towards *prêt-à-porter*, and the *couture* collections became more of a testing ground, and publicity enterprise. It was to be Englishmen who helped to change things. In the 1950s it was demonstrated beyond doubt by the neo-Edwardians or Teds that other sources of style existed outside high fashion. The previous reflex against high fashion had been some variation of artistic style and these had formed the pivot in the process of change in dress. The Teds disregarded this particular stylistic process, which was a sort of tug-of-war with no room for another team; they turned their back on this, and played a game of their own.

To win it they not only had to evolve some distinct style, they had to have the conviction that it was sufficient. This they had. The internal meaning of the Ted 'look' has become self-sufficient in lasting its original creators to date the best part of thirty years, with only minor changes, and in winning new converts during the Rock revival of the early 1970s.[15] Teds took over components of a late 1940s revival, in which men had reinstated some Edwardian ideas, such as long overcoats, velvet collars and half-collars. This had been at the expensive end of the market, but by about 1954 the Teds had made these features wholly their own. The borrowed, revived Edwardian overcoat with velvet collar was treated as a long jacket and known by the old jacket name of 'drape'; they also borrowed a simultaneous revival of waistcoats, often with rolled lapels. Their 'drainpipe' trousers and thick-soled shoes known as 'brothel-creepers' or 'beetle-crushers' were quite distinct, and so too was the shoestring necktie. Hairstyles were of central importance, and came in a number of carefully created shapes, some with a faintly Byronic echo. Teddy girls, like

114 Teddy boy in 1954.

115 Teddy boys in 1972.

those within mainstream fashion, did not really develop any of the Edwardian themes. There was an American connection in Teds' dress which also helped to feed ideas. They began as a working class grouping, virtually outlawed by everyone else, but by the time of their 1970s revival they were seen by the press with nostalgic affection.

Outside the Ted look, some waistcoats for men were blooming again; some saw them as Regency revivals, others as Edwardian. In fact they partially resembled both; they were waist length, with lapels, and pockets, and often made of brocade or other decorative material. In November 1951, *The Tailor and Cutter* featured a waistcoat made with six silver buttons, and the trend continued through the decade.

Another revival brought about for practical reasons in men's wear which also lasted the decade was that of elastic-sided boots and shoes; very narrow trouser legs had been adopted in mainstream fashion, as well as by the Teds, and in the early 1960s, sharply cut Italian suits increased the dilemma: a shoe with laces breaks a very straight trouser line, and catches on a narrow trouser leg. A correspondent to *The Tailor and Cutter* in February 1960 demonstrated his solution in lacing his shoes from the top to the bottom, but the same publication noted the likelihood of the revival lasting because of its elegance and commonsense. In that year they suggested that a good pair of elastic-sided shoes could be had for 6½ guineas from Russell and Bromley, and that henceforth there would be no need for men to untie their laces in the cinema, for the new revival would easily accommodate swelling feet. Presumably this last problem was diminishing anyway as in January 1960 *The Tailor and Cutter* had announced an occasional series of features investigating the influence of TV on men's dress because they felt by then it had overtaken the cinemas as a determining factor in masculine fashion.

Men's dress also revived certain Regency features during the 1960s: short coats with high collars made a comeback, not unlike a Teds' long 'drape.' Shirts for evening wear had a vogue for frills at the front and on the cuffs; in 1964 for example, a white nylon frill with a black edge graced a dinner shirt at 45/-, and a 'duelling' shirt in voile was 5 guineas, and both would have been considered acceptable. However, these styles were fairly rapidly dismissed by a quieter and smoother line to men's appearance which was occasioned by a nostalgia for the dress of the 1930s. An interview in 1967 with the trendsetting designer Mr (Michael) Fish revealed that his thirties-inspired dressing gowns could have come from the wardrobe of P.G. Wodehouse,[16] and at the same time other designers and manufacturers were observed 'pillaging' films from the thirties. Another manifestation of the shift from a taste for a romantic Regency look to a less flamboyant thirties one was the opening in May 1972 of a London shop called Grey Flannel, run by ex-Jaeger designer Edward Lloyd. It was an inspired name for a shop, reflecting the revival of pre-war values in quality menswear, and their transfer into a new idiom: 'I like the whole soft slouchy Thirties look, particularly in white.'[17] Sleeveless, V-necked pullovers, baggy trousers, and flat caps were amongst the garments to be welcomed back. Films such as *Bonnie and Clyde* (1967) had helped this trend, and it was confirmed by others such as *The Sting* and *Chinatown*.

Even by the time Grey Flannel exactly caught the tone in 1972, *Grease* was on Broadway, and the film *The Last Picture Show* had been made. What these and others offered was a new emphasis on younger people; in recreating the American high school life of the 1950s such imports provided imagery more suited for revival by the sub-teenagers of the 1970s than did the rather more sophisticated menswear of the thirties. (In this respect it is interesting to note that an amateur survey of Mods and Rockers done in Brighton in 1964 showed that the seeds of confidence sown by the Teds had begun to grow, so as to allow men and boys to cultivate distinct or alternative styles: of those boys asked in 1964 about the main influences on their dress, 80 per cent of both groups said other boys helped them choose clothes, and none of either group were helped by their girlfriends. Other questions established that 45 per cent copied their pop idols, and 30 per cent acknowledged the influence of advertising.[18])

By and large women's fashion has not been so widely influenced by these youth movements, at least not until very recently, but has been instead subject to more diffuse historical revivals, often stemming as much from the will of the fashion media and trade as from any individual expression. There was in 1960 an Art Nouveau revival in textiles which had a very wide appeal, and affected furnishings and interior decorations and graphics as well as dress. It was a designer-inspired phenomenon, in turn arising from a series of museum exhibitions of Art Nouveau in Europe and later in New York. With plenty of imagery thus available, William Poole of Liberty saw the potential concurrence of taste and used the company's own supply of original Art Nouveau furnishing fabrics as a source for redrawing and reprinting designs onto finer dress fabrics, including a variety of silks. Transferred from blocks to screen printing and with a fresh range of colours, these archive prints re-emerged to an enthusiastic reception; they were known as the 'Lotus' range. It was used in *haute couture*, and benefitted from *haute couture* designers because the larger-than-usual size of the prints was at first slightly daunting for less skilled eyes; it was to lay the foundation for other such ventures.

As often in the history of the company this project by Liberty was to be widely imitated. In a press release at the time in 1960, the initial success of the revival was rightly attributed to the high quality of the original designs; this quality could not be attained in the many popularized versions made without the benefit of authentic Art Nouveau sources, and the imitations often drifted well away from the founding spirit. Retrospective textiles for dress obviously had an important role; Liberty revived some of their original Paisleys, and in 1961 developed a range by Martin Battersby inspired by Bakst and Poiret; Bernard Nevill's Art Deco-inspired collection called 'Jazz' followed in 1966. Since textiles do not 'happen' overnight these particular revivals make an interesting area of study because they show a distillation of the process by which some of the taste and judgement of one era is retrieved and modified by another. They are a miniaturization of what occurs on a larger scale in dress and in the other arts too.

The influence of the 1930s on men's dress at the end of the sixties and into the seventies was also seen in women's dress; it encouraged a renewal of interest in long cardigans, shoes with buckles and T-straps, and various features helped to reinstate the longer silhouette after several years of dominance by the 'mini' length. It was also an influence which began to replace the 'wide-eyed schoolgirl' character of women's appearance with a more knowing and discrete air; 1965 for instance had seen the peak of a metallic, silver look, and stark Op Art patterns. In the words of the fashion media it was Op versus Trad, and towards the end of the decade it was clear that Trad had won, helped no doubt by Faye Dunaway as Bonnie Parker, and other film treatments of pre-war themes. By March 1968 London *Vogue* described the robbery: 'Clyde Barrow might have wryly laughed to see his straw hat with a

116 Romantic dresses for professional ballroom dancing competition. Those designed for Latin American sections are more revealing and idiosyncratic.

Banker's suit, but . . . a double-breasted slim back jacket teams with a man's suiting striped pleated culotte skirt – robbing the thirties of more of their best looks and making them immediate.' The luke-warm reception of a recent down-market Op Art revival suggests that what sixties slang called Trad may be with us for sometime yet.

The world of professional ballroom dancing has sustained a convincing re-establishment of mid-nineteenth century taste in dress. It is curious that these gently archaic clothes are part of a system which began at a date when tubular and boyish figures were fashionable, when jazz, cigarettes and bobbed hair were challenging established ideas of feminine behaviour. In 1924 the Imperial Society of Teachers of Dancing formed its Ballroom Branch and under a committee which included Victor Sylvester, set out a syllabus and examination for qualifying teachers of dance. The first British Professional Championship Competition followed as a result in 1928 and from that point the United Kingdom became an important and successful centre of the profession. The competitions at national and international level attract large, loyal audiences and many television viewers. It would be unthinkable to waltz competitively in jeans, or even in a floor-length evening dress as they did before the Second World War, since the action of the feet has to be assessed. Nowadays a particular sort of elegance and decorum are expected, and awarded marks, and the romantic crinoline has come to be almost standard wear for ladies. It is not held out by hoops as its ancestor was, but is dependent on many layers of stiff netting to create an almost circular profile. As if to compensate for its curtailed length, the ballroom crinoline is even fuller than the originals. The top layer is often sequined and decorated in bright colours, especially since the advent of colour television, and recently the skirts have been made less full in the front to allow closer contact with the gentleman partner, but the resemblance to the drifting puffs of the ball-skirts of the 1850s is never far away. Their fragility is only emphasized by contrast with the assertively dark, tailcoated partners [116].

It is notoriously difficult to predict what will happen in fashion, as Marshall and Snelgrove's catalogue wisely acknowledged. It is also very difficult to see the wood for the trees when trying to assess the dominant features of the dress of the very recent past, and the present may elude analysis altogether. What is new,

117 Styles from 1940s and fifties enjoyed revival in 1970s. Distinguished from originals by extreme shoulders, this 1978 swagger coat was worn with higher heels than would have been seen first time round.

118 Inspired by the art of Gustave Klimt. Mysterious but comfortable black dress and jacket spangled from top to toe. Thea Porter, 1977.

however, when it comes to historical revivals, is the sheer bulk and detail of information available to us about the past. Old magazines, photographs, and trade catalogues which might have once gone into the wastepaper basket are now often prized as collectors' items, and museums now collect dress and fashion ephemera as seriously as any other objects. 'The next best thing to being awarded a tomb in Westminster Abbey is surely to have your nearest and dearest possessions enshrined in the Victoria and Albert Museum.'[19] As long ago as the late 1930s C. Willett Cunnington was broadcasting on television about his collection of historical dress, from which crinolines went on display in Selfridges in December 1938. Intrepid individual collectors have formed the basis for several now famous costume museum collections; societies, academic courses and publishers are now involved in preserving and understanding the past of fashion and dress to a degree which is unprecedented; added to which film and videotape provide ready-animated records of the way people are and were dressed. With luck, this abundance of documentary evidence will not deprive us of future unexpected and felicitous revivals, such as that which was played on by some designers in 1956: 'They all belong to a period, to that little bijou, boudoir period of 1910 to 1914; the period of Shaw's Eliza Doolittle, now born again in *My Fair Lady*, the current belle of New York. It is at such moments, when the pieces suddenly fall into place, that the fascination of fashion is felt – of fashion for fashion's sake.'[20]

PART IV Exotic Revivals

16 *Delicious Harmony*

THE SIXTEENTH CENTURY

. . . a most delitious harmony, in full strange notes was sweetly heard to sound . . .

Edmund Spenser, *The Faerie Queene*, 1589–96

When Sir Philip Sidney, in his *Arcadia*, wanted to make a Greek prince especially splendid he put a 'Persian tiara all set down with rows of so rich rubies' on his head. Writing between 1580 and 1590, Sidney was perhaps familiar with the appearance of the Papal Tiara, and with the dress of Persia and various other Middle Eastern countries. One of the sources for such images which he and his contemporaries may well have known was Jean-Jacques Boissard's 1581 book of costume illustrations known as *Habitus Variarum Orbis Gentium*, in which more ordinary Persian figures were shown; available at that date, too, was Nicholas de Nicolay's earlier book called *Les Quatre Premiers Livres des Navigations et Pérégrinations Orientales*, which was published in 1567, and on which later costume books based many of their Middle Eastern illustrations. That these and other illustrated costume books should have been published in the latter half of the sixteenth century is testimony to people's curiosity about the rest of the world; their accuracy often was their least virtue, but they became established source books, convenient windows on the world.[1]

119 One of the many illustrations of oriental dress available in sixteenth-century costume books and echoed in English dress. 1567.

It has already been pointed out that Inigo Jones used two such books in the 1630s, and borrowed from them for his costume designs for masques.[2] He used the Boissard, already mentioned, and another by de Bruyn, a costume book which was published in 1577 and then reissued, slightly enlarged, in 1581. The connections between Boissard's 'Sponsa Thessalonicensis' and the Hatfield portrait of Queen Elizabeth, known as the 'Rainbow Portrait' [122], have already been made. In this case, the elaborately upturned head-dress of the Queen, though superimposed on a fashionable hairshape, closely resembles that supposed by Boissard to have been worn by a bride of Salonica. So, too, has a strong link been observed between the Hampton Court 'Portrait of a Lady' [120] and Boissard's 'Virgo Persica', or Persian maiden,[3] [121]. In this latter case the similarity is not confined to the head-dress; it extends to the silhouette, if not the exact cut, of the full-length robe, and to the shape of the long sleeves. (The stag is echoed by the belled stag which appears at the side of a Turkish religious in Nicolay's *Pérégrinations*.) A later Boissard volume, of 1597, which was called *Mascarades*, elaborated even further in an imaginative way on these oriental features, especially lofty, ornate head-dresses, often befeathered. Strange striped and curled slippers also appear in it, recalling the unusual ones worn in the Hampton Court 'Persian Lady.'

These imported images played a central role in enlarging the vocabulary of English dress: Middle Eastern dress, often being looser and thinner, made attractive, fluid shapes, a welcome alternative to stiff court and well-to-do dress. We know from the 1560

Iniusti Iusta querela
Mea sic mihi

121 Sources for masque and other inventive dress. Boissard, 1581.

inventory of the Office of Revels that a wide variety of versions of exotic garb had been made and worn for court masques, or the other 'Showes,' 'Devyces,' 'Invencions' and 'Histories' which entertained the court, and that its appearance was probably not only confined to the court circle; in 1572 a complaint was made that costumes from the Office were being indiscriminately hired out, to a wedding in Kent for instance, others to London weddings, and some for no stated purpose to a tavern in Cheapside. On these lesser occasions they were subject to a 'grett presse of peple.'[4] Presumably the Turkish, Barbarian or Moorish or other exotic clothes may have been amongst these more widely seen ones.

Exactly what these supposedly foreign garments looked like is open to debate; like most masque or revel dress they must be pieced together from the quantities of fabric and decorations bought for their construction, and from literary and other descriptions. The 1560 inventory listed, for example, 'Turkye' clothes in some detail: six 'longe streighte turkye gownes of redd cloth of gold with Roses and Scallope Shells stripped downe and garded with a brode gard of Redd Dornixe embrodered upon with clothe of gold and Silver threed and edged with blacke silke lace.'[5] (Dornixe or darnick described a cloth originally made in Dornick in Flanders.) These particular long red garments were made over into clothes for another masque, and then again for a masque of barbarians, underlining the fact

120 English 'Persian' dress, rich in allusion. Partly based on Boissard, possibly for a masque, or just for personal pleasure perhaps. *c.*1590–1600.

that they were made of stout and valuable materials. Quite what 'Turkye' indicated is not entirely clear; it may simply have come to mean any foreign style. On another occasion long hanging sleeves, previously worn by 'Venetian Senators' in another masque, were turned into head pieces for other Turks, possibly wound into turbans.

Turkey, the Turks and their empire loomed large in the English mind; for generations the Turks were feared by Europe; they pressed the eastern edge of Christendom, and penetrated as far as Vienna, beseiged by the Sultan in 1529. Despite animosity to the aims of the Turks, there was often a sense of liberation in the English response to their dress, and to those of other Eastern foreigners. Based as it usually was on imaginative reconstructions rather than experience of the real costume, the revived, reanimated costume of a Turk in one revel would probably be the model for others in later events, so tending to produce a static image. This in turn helped the already prevalent view that fashion did not exist beyond the boundaries of western Europe; England, Italy and France were usually thought of as the principal sources and perpetrators of fashionable dress, and its fopperies and follies. Dress from further east was exempted from the criticisms levelled at that of Europe, and was thus even more attractive.

A Frenchman, and milliner, in London, by St Martin's, produced 'Such fans, such ouches, such brooches, such bracelets, such grand ties, such periwigs, such paintings, such ruffes and cuffs, as hath almost made England as ful of proud foppries as *Tire & Sidon* were. . . . Where as our Englishwomen of the Exchange are both better workwomen, and wil affoord a better penniworth.' Articles of dress produced in London by foreigners ('and al other occupations, they are wronged by the Duch and French'),[6] were seen to be as dangerous to home trade as imports of goods made abroad, and the wool and allied trades and other vested interests were anxious to protect their various livings. The following list was made by a merchant adventurer in 1601, keen to demonstrate the range of his confraternity's trade, even from Italy alone; it well shows the nature of the import problem for merchants dependant on home trades: 'Of the Italians, they buye all Kinde of silke wares, Velvittes, wrought and unwrought, Taffitaes, Satins, Damaskes, Sarsenettes, Milan fustians, Clothe of golde and silver, Grograines, Chamlettes, Satin and sowing silke, Organzie, Orsoy, and all other kinde of wares either made or to be had in Italie.'[7]

With Italy acting as a gateway to the East, the variety of wares 'to be had' there must have been considerable, and who, loving dress, could resist such temptations?

It was often thought that beyond western Europe, in effect, beyond Italy, that fashion gave way to a sort of natural state in dress, in which novelty and vanity were replaced by unchanging simplicity and innocence. Philip Stubbes, for instance, asserted in his analysis of dress, in 1583, called *The Anatomie of Abuses*, that the inhabitants of Palestine still wore the same 'coate without a seame' which Christ had worn, and although not necessarily a handsome garb, Stubbes thought 'at the least it was not curious or new fangled as ours is.' Furthermore he asserted 'the Egyptians are said never to have changed their fashion, or altered the forme of their first attire, from the beginnying to this daie. . . . The Grecians are said to use but one kinde of apparell without any change, that is to wit, a long gowne, reaching downe to the ground. The Germaines are thought to be so precise in observing one uniform fashion in apparell, as they have never receeded from their first originall. . . . The Muscovians, Athenians, Italians, Brasilians, Africanes, Asians, Cantabrians, Hungarians, Ethiopians, or els what nations soever under the sunne. . .' did not, according to Stubbes, need dress at all, except 'so it repell the cold and cover their shame,' and they did without 'hosen, shoes, bandes, ruffes, shirtes, or anything els,'[8] except perhaps for the skins and furs of their own finding.

It is interesting that Stubbes should have excused the Italians from the follies of fashion, when most of his contemporaries did not, and amusing to imagine his vision of the rich and urbane Venetians, perhaps, trading very profitably with the Orient, dressed all the while in crude furs and hides.

So, to the English, to revive these apparently unchanging foreign clothes would, to some extent, also be to reclaim the innocence and simplicity which many Elizabethans believed their own country had once possessed but had temporarily, they hoped, yielded up through vanity and greed. When Queen Elizabeth or her court circle wore foreign dress, or exotic accessories, it suggested an elevation above the common round, into a sphere of nobler aims. Besides exoticism enjoyable for its own bizarre sake, images from Persia, for example, merged with associations of antiquity and fabulous imperial wealth; the headdress of the Hatfield 'Rainbow Portrait' [122] signifies not only wealth, but power and a limitless genealogy. In addition to these possible overtones, possession of whole suits or bales of fabric, or jewelled and exotic accessories from distant places implied connections with travellers or embassies, and considerable purchasing power.

From some foreign imagery came the means to personify various attributes; Poetry, at the Kenilworth celebrations in 1575, wore a Venetian gown, and Doubt, in procession in *The Faerie Queene*, wore curious, pendant 'Albanese sleeves,' and nearby Jolly Summer wore 'a thin silken cassock coloured greene That was unlyned all, to be more light.'[9] 'Cassock' did not take on ecclesiastical meaning until the seventeenth century; in the sixteenth it still denoted a long, loose coat or jerkin, with a distinctly foreign flavour; it also had military and theatrical connections. It may even have taken its name from the Arabic and Persian words for the same garment. In this case, Spenser was describing a 'light' garment, which allowed freedom of movement, as well as coolness, because Summer was on his way back from a forest boar hunt. Perhaps his cassock resembled, in shape at least, the long, fringed robe of the Hampton Court 'Persian Lady' [120].

The procession of Time and Mutability in which Spenser put Summer and other figures resembled a masque, where figures in pairs or groups would march, accompanied by musicians and torch bearers. Somewhere between courtly masques and general revels of spontaneous dancing lay a rather poetic or dramatic stance leading onto organized dancing for guests at a wedding or other special occasions. In 1600, Queen Elizabeth was entertained by a masque in a provincial house and was 'wooed' to dance by a Mrs Fetton, one of the eight masquers. 'Her Majesty asked what she was? *Affection*, she said. *Affection*, said the Queen, is false. Yet her Majestie rose and dawnced.'[10] As these various occasions ranged from events in private houses to the court itself, from a local wedding feast to an ambassadorial entertainment at Whitehall, so it is not always possible to pinpoint the exact nature of portraits of people in what seem to be masque costumes of some sort [55]; perhaps the sitter had taken part in a celebration and then held onto the dress for the portrait painter to copy; a portrait could be an integral part of a celebration requiring commemoration such as a wedding. Perhaps masquing attracted as participants people of special imagination, exactly those people to whom exotic and highly fanciful dress would continue to appeal, and who would allow it to play upon their taste in their other clothes. The costumes glittered in torchlit processions, and the music, Spenser suggested, was heady: '. . . the rare sweetness of the melody The feeble senses wholly did confound And the fraile soule in deepe delight nigh dround.'[11]

This sort of experience for the susceptible masquer or guest would surely have made the clothes associated with the event particularly attractive and significant, guaranteeing them a special place in imagination and memory. It is to be hoped that future research will help us unravel more of the meaning of such dress in portraiture and increase our enjoyment of its nuance.

At this period Amazons appeared often in inventions or masques or other entertainments, and were as much

122 Impressive evocation of Elizabeth's power, *c.*1600. Eyes and ears on her mantle, with ornate curved head-dress probably taken from Boissard.

ON SINE SOLE
IRIS

daughters of some fabulous distant land as of the classical Mediterranean. The Amazon in the fifth book of *The Faerie Queene*, exactly as she would have done in a masque and tournament at Whitehall, fought a knight. She wore 'a Camis light of purple silke Woven uppon with siluer, subtly wrought And quilted upon sattin white as milke Trayled with ribbands diversly distraught.'[12] A camis was a surplice-like shift or shirt (the same Arabic word means 'shirt.') Spenser conjures up a brave and airy dress, 'Short tucked for light motion.' If envisaged as a celebration or masque dress, its likely effect on both wearer and viewer, used to the formalities of unyielding dress and starched ruffs, seems close to that described by Wilfred Blunt when he wrote of the attractions of Egyptian dress in the late nineteenth century; he described how they allowed a European city dweller to bathe his 'sick Western soul in the pure healing beauty of the East. . . . One would not be ashamed to appear thus at the Court of Solomon – nay for that matter at the Court of heaven – for are not the angels, themselves, arrayed in precisely these white garments?'[13]

In Elizabethan dress which, for heroes and heroines, produced a remarkable fusion of exotic and historical styles, it is not difficult to sense the wish for angels in shining light. In 1578, the torch bearers clad in long white garments, accompanying Amazons at a masque, overdid the job and managed to set fire to their plumed head-dresses. Spenser's goodly huntress was 'in a Silken Camus lylly white' so bespangled that she 'glistred bright, Like twinckling starres. . . .'[14] The Office of Revels dealt in quantities of silver fringe, copper silver buttons, tassels of copper silver, and sundry other shiney ornaments, and one of the concerns about the indiscriminate hiring out of the Office's costumes was they would lose their 'glosse and bewtye.'

Surely this was one of the most magical periods in English dress.

17 *Farre Fetcht and Deerely Bought*

THE SEVENTEENTH CENTURY

From spacious China, and those Kingdomes East, . . . farre fetcht, and deerely bought. . . .

James Taylor, *The Needles Excellency*, 1631

Travellers came home to publish accounts of their journeys and the exotic sights they saw; often they wrote in minute detail about dress and social customs when these seemed markedly different from their own. Those who travelled in grand style, with an embassy, for example, might even take an artist along to make a visual record. In England there was a wide interest about the rest of the world, and a belief that travel was itself an educational process and, despite physical and moral dangers, that it should where possible be part of every young gentleman's upbringing. Thomas Coryat, for example, who published his book *Coryat's Crudities* in 1611, gave an account of his 1608 journey around Europe, and introduced his book with an essay in praise of travel, in which it was claimed 'in the whole life of man there is nothing sweeter, nothing pleasanter, nothing more delightful than travell.' His book has many sharp observations about the dress of those he saw. Coryat was later to die in India after extensive travels in Turkey, Persia and places east. Another traveller-writer of the period was Fynes Moryson, who produced in 1617 a very readable account of life in Turkey, for example, from which it was possible to have a very clear and detailed idea of what Turks wore; such accounts gave new ideas of alternative means of dressing:

> The Turkish women weare smocks (of which fashion also the mens shirts are) of fine linnen, wrought with silke at the wrests, upon the sleeves, and at the skirts; and a long cote of silke, wrought with needle-worke, and edged, with sleeves close to the arme, and at the breast, with their necks naked [Moryson meant they wore no ruff or handkerchief]. The womens gownes are much like those of the men, for cloth and fashion . . . and they weare linnen breeches as men, by day and night . . . They weave up their haire in curious knots & so let them hang at length, & deck the haire with Pearle and buttons of gold, and with Jewels & flowers of silk wrought with the needle. The women of Syria cover their heads with little peeces of coined moneys joyned together with thread, instead of a linnen coife.[1]

Moryson observed the fact that none of the women he saw throughout the Turkish Empire ever went out of the house without a veil to hide their head and hands.

On Coryat's 1608 journey he had met a Moor and two Turks in France, and had a long conversation with one of the Turks 'in Latin of many things.' Since the inhabitants of the East came to western Europe it was possible to observe them there too; in Venice in 1645, John Evelyn saw Armenians, Persians, Greeks and others all in their regional dress, and in Bologna in the same year he admired 'a Persian walking about in a rich vest of cloth of tissue, and severall other ornaments, according to the fashion of his country, which much

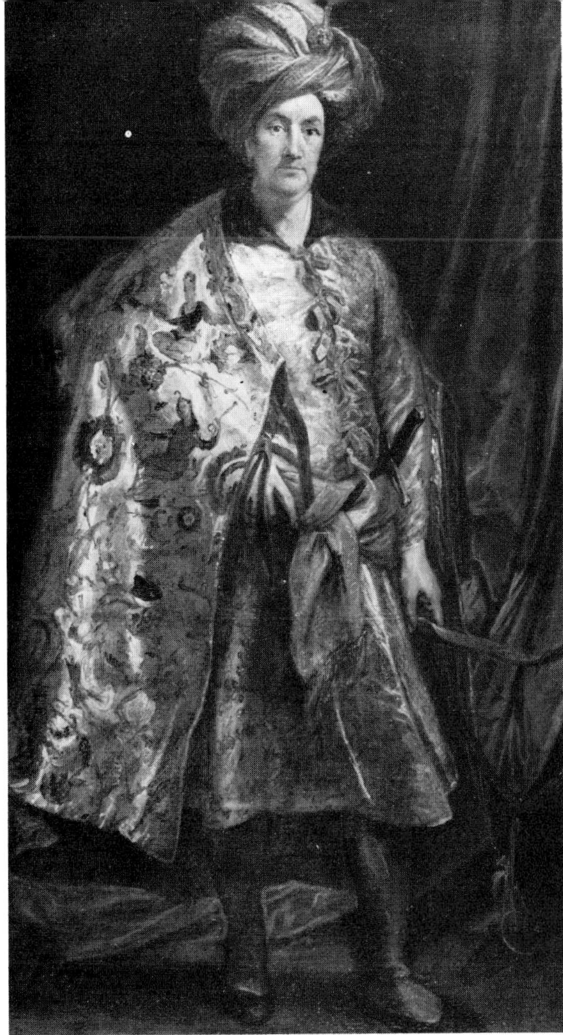

123 This Englishman was ambassador from the Shah of Persia to several European courts, 1622. His Persian knee-length vest may have encouraged later English taste for similar garments (see Plate 19).

pleased me; he was a young handsome person, of the most stately mien.'

As well as the Near and Middle East, the Far East was becoming known from first-hand accounts by European travellers; for example, Vecellio had published an illustration of a Chinese gown in 1590, in 1664 Evelyn saw for himself in London 'Glorious vests' from Japan and China,[2] and details of Indian dress were brought back by the English Embassy to the Great Mogul, in 1622. These were published as *A Voyage to East-India* in 1655 by the Embassy Chaplain, Edward Terry, who was alert to the pleasures and possibilities of the cultures they saw. It is worth pausing over what he wrote, because it illuminated what was to become a long relationship for the English, and in his comments about that curiosity, the apparent absence of fashion, and the timelessness of the dress, Terry was reiterating one of the perennial attractions the English have felt for various non-European styles of dress. (Terry's pen picture of the inside of a perfumed and carpeted tent, or the pleasures of an Indian water garden which 'makes such a pretty murmur, as helps to tie their senses with the bonds of sleep' added to the lure that the best of India was to become for the English.) '. . . The constancy there observed by natives of both sexes, in keeping to their old fashions in their habits, exampled to them by their predecessors in many foregoing generations, and by them still continued, is the great praise of this people, as the commendation of every nation in the world, almost, besides ours, still constant to their ancient fashions in their apparel.'[3]

With a hint of envy, Terry noted that the Mogul's garments were washed after only one day's wear, and that he was coolly dressed in fine white lawn. The English Embassy, however, asserted their own native dress: 'For my Lord Ambassador, and his company, we all kept to our English habits, made as light and cool as possibly we could have them. His waiters in red taffeta cloaks, guarded with green . . . myself in a long black cassock; and the colours and fashion of our garments were so different from theirs, that we needed not, wheresoever we were, to invite spectators to take notice of us.'[4]

The Ambassador's Chaplain let nothing pass without his careful observation; in his long black cassock, Terry watched the apparently classless and unchanging white dress of the Indians: 'their coats fitting close to their bodies unto their wastes, then hanging down loose a little below their knees, the lower part of them fitting somewhat full . . . of white calico . . . Under their coats they have long breeches, like under Irish trousers, made usually of the same cloth, which came to their ankles, and ruffles on the small of their legs. For their feet, they keep them . . . always bare in their shoes.' Of the grander people, Terry observed 'their coats and breeches of striped taffata of several colours, or of some other silk stuff of the same colour, or of slight cloth of silver or gold, all made in that country,' but all to the same shape.[5]

In view of Charles II's later attempt to establish an unchanging dress for himself, which was to be known as the English vest, these earlier observations by Terry were significant; he depicted a great monarch in a garb both unchanging and splendid; the Mogul was 'in his daily unvaried habit, as he is bedeck'd and adorn'd with jewels he continually wears. For the fashion of the habit in which he is . . . it is for the fashion the habit of that whole vast empire; so that he who strictly views this, may see the dress of the men throughout that whole great monarchy.'[6]

Published in London in 1669 were details of dress from China; the Dutch had sent an embassy there, and John Nieuhoff described not only the glimpses they had of the Emperor himself, but the Lammas,' Tartars

and Indians they met waiting at the same audience. The Dutch gave the Emperor a European suit of black velvet, complete with stockings and drawers; they in turn were given amongst other things many packages of rich cloth, a mandarin's gown, and black and blue silk damask coats for their escort. Before this long-awaited encounter, they had met a viceroy 'in a Lemmon-coloured Gown, embroidered with Golden Dragons, and behind in his Cap he wore their Badge of Royalty, a Peacock's Tayl, about his Neck a Chain of White Saphirs of great value. . . .'[7]

These varied Near, Middle and Far Eastern forms of dress were fascinatingly different from the traditional English tailored garments: like the dress of antiquity, they were worn in shapes straight from the loom; or they were curiously cut and fastened, as Edward Terry was at pains to describe in his account of Muslim Indians; or they used combinations of rare and light fabrics not usually seen in England, and the trousers of Turkey and India interested an audience unfamiliar with such garments. (Trousers were not in regular use in England until the early nineteenth century.) Looked at from the point of view of seventeenth century dress alone, it seems odd that it could ever be said that the English are insular in outlook; there was in the seventeenth century an obvious inclination to shed formal or complex fashion for something easier and looser, whenever an opportunity arose, and the borrowing and reanimation of foreign dress for this purpose has been a factor present at most other periods too.

Samuel Pepys was more cautious than most, and always very concerned that he struck the right tone in his appearance. In 1666 he was having his portrait painted by John Hayls in an Indian gown [125] and although that same April he observed that he was getting a good deal richer, he hired this gown, instead of buying it. In December 1663, Mrs Pepys had been presented with a Japanese gown by an acquaintance of her husband, and was very pleased with it. We know what Pepys' garment looked like from his portrait; the earlier Japanese gown was not recorded in paint, but may well have been cut in a similar way. Both would probably have served as a form of undress, suitable for the reception of visitors, for a loose comfort about the house, and possessing perhaps a pleasant hint of artistic taste or oriental panache. Since Pepys, anxious to do the correct thing, had his portrait painted in one, we can assume an Indian gown was a garment with reputation of some substance, and wholly unlike our present dressing-gowns. What Pepys had against buying the fine gown we will never know. It was made

124 Feilding visited Persia and India in 1631–3. Seen here afterwards in pink Indian garb. Pyjamas were copied in the nineteenth century but were rare at this time.

125 Samuel Pepys' brown Indian gown cut like a kimono. He hired it especially for the portrait. Sash visible behind his elbow.

of a glowing brown silk, and was constructed rather like a kimono with wide sleeves and no lapels. (Having already bought himself another Indian gown in the summer of 1661, Pepys may still have been wearing it and so perhaps it was too shabby for a portrait.)

These comfortable kimono-shaped garments were quite common in the seventeenth century; their purchase is listed in surviving account books, and tradesmen became known as 'gownmen,' or Indian gownmakers. They were in use for both men and women, and became established items which remained current for most of the following century. Indian gowns were so-called probably because they were thought to resemble Indian or other oriental dress which may have been imported into England through India; they were by no means always made of oriental fabric. When Pepys saw Sir Philip Howard in his nightgown and turban in 1666 he thought he looked like a Turk. Isaac Newton, among others, was portrayed in an Indian gown; one imagines Pepys settling down at home to one of his innumerable sessions with his account book, or his diary, grateful for the ease of the capacious gown, and pleased to know that possession of such a garment of leisure was saving wear and tear on his precious formal coats.[8]

In contrast to the successful absorption into English

private life of these useful oriental-shaped gowns, a curious occurrence instigated by Charles II showed how difficult some modifications to public dress can be. We have seen how the embassy to India had been impressed by the spectacle of a monarch contriving to appear so splendid in a style of dress which was yet fundamentally uniform with that of his subjects, jewellery excepted, and Terry's account of this journey, although made in 1622, was published in 1655. In 1666 Charles II appeared at court in a style of dress he resolved never to change. John Evelyn, who had admired Persian dress when he saw it previously in Italy, observed that the King's innovation was Persian in spirit, if not in detail, and obviously wondered if his own tract, in which he had described the advantages of Persian dress over the ceaselessly changing French styles adopted at court, had something to do with this remarkable royal gesture. Charles was seen by Evelyn first on 18 October 1666 to 'put himself solemnly into the Eastern fashion of vest, changeing doublet, stiff collar, bands and cloake, into a comely dress, after ye Persian mode, with girdle or straps, and shoe strings and garters into bouckles, of which some were set with precious stones, resolving never to alter it, and to leave the French mode, which had hither to obtain'd to our greate expence and reproch.'[9]

Not surprisingly courtiers immediately bet gold with the King that he would not keep to his resolve. Pepys had seen the King's 'Persian' vest three days before, and had also had an unexpected preview of the Duke of York's vest in the same new mode on 13 October. When Pepys, who was less well travelled than Evelyn, saw the King, he was struck by the smart colours more than by the origin of the construction: 'a long cassock close to the body, of black cloth, and pinked with white silk under it, and a coat over it, and the legs ruffled with black ribbon like a pigeon's leg; and, upon the whole, I wish the King may keep it, for it is a very fine and handsome garment.'[10] For all the admiration of the English for oriental dress, and its seemingly unchanging grandeur, and for all the complaints about the expense and bother of fancy French fashions, would it really be possible for Charles and those courtiers who followed his lead to keep to the 1666 resolution? If they did they would finally be making amends for all the criticism of the English as a fickle nation always searching for novelty in dress, and lacking an identifiable style of their own. Perhaps Charles' ingenious fusion of Persian and English court dress would finally achieve this last goal and prove wrong the complaint that England 'will neither relye on her owne invention, nor compose her selfe to the fashion of anyone particular Nation, but make her selfe an Epitomized confection of all. Thus becomes shee not onely a stranger to others, but to her selfe.'[11]

126 Persian vest seen again at a court masque in 1635.

Needless to say, Charles II did not remain 'fine and handsome' for the rest of his days in the same 'Persian vest'. On the other hand, the idea did not disappear, and a similar garment remained in fairly common use [19]. It was Evelyn who was keen to see the new close-fitting overgarment as Persian, connecting it with what he had seen abroad, but it has also been shown that related garments had been seen in England before,[12] and that the King was amalgamating ideas from the theatre and the hunt, as well as perhaps digesting Edward Terry's account of the Mogul, and Evelyn's tract on Persian dress with which he had previously been presented.

In more general terms, various oriental-style garments appeared in masques which the court and its guests enjoyed during the century, and oriental garments and textiles reached England from trade and diplomatic enterprises. For those who did not have the means or the rank to enjoy these there was always the marvel of a pageant. In October 1678, for example, the splendours of India and other Far Eastern countries were paraded through London in the shape of figures dressed in all manner of garments, such as a robe painted all over with birds, insects, reptiles and animals, surmounted by a coronet of coloured feathers, and a figure representing all Eastern treasure wearing pearls and diamonds, with a crown of sunbeams and a robe 'of all colours, richly interwoven with silk, gold, silver and jewels; a scarf of gold, silver buskins, laced with gold ribon.' How marvellous it all was, glittering and impressive and the worshipful Company of Grocers who were footing the bill, added an extra exotic gesture; a 'negro with a prodigal hand' scattered goodies to the crowd, 'where you might see an hundred persons confusedly scrambling in the dirt for the frail achievement of a bunch of raisins, or a handful of dates, almonds, nutmegs.'[13]

Better still, it might have been possible to glimpse one of the lavish embassies from Morocco or India and elsewhere which arrived in London. For instance, in 1682, the Bantam ambassadors offered yet more exotic possibilities for dress. 'Their garments were rich Indian silks, flower'd with gold, *viz*, a close wastcoate to their knees, drawers, naked legs, and on their heads capps made like fruit baskets.'[14] A replacement official of this embassy who had stopped at Mecca on the way to London was seen in a sash which Evelyn thought was Turkish or Arabic. Pepys saw his first Persian in London in 1668, and thought he was dressed in a very comely manner. Naturally embassies took care to dress well and impress the natives, and so seventeenth-century Londoners were treated to plenty of opportunities of observing and assessing the best of oriental dress at first hand.

18 *A Gold Thread*

THE EIGHTEENTH CENTURY

The grandeur of the Eastern dress, which so far surpasses the European, depends as much on quantity as on costliness.

William Hogarth, *The Analysis of Beauty*, 1753

In his discussion of dress as a factor in defining true beauty, William Hogarth (1697–1764) referred to the quantity of Eastern dress, by which he meant the amount of cloth in each garment or set of garments. He considered loose and free lines to be as imposing in their way as precious fabrics; many portrait painters in the eighteenth century sought to depict rather voluminous or draped cloth on their sitters in order, as they thought, to escape the dating of the portraits by more intricate fashionable garb, and for this purpose some Eastern dress suited them very well. It was, however, not confined to their studios; it was well known and well liked in eighteenth-century England. Notable sources of ideas, fabrics and actual garments were India, China and Turkey.

Costliness, whatever Hogarth thought of it, was a factor in the impressions made on many English minds: for example, from Madras in the 1740s:

. . . her coat was made of fine gold muslin, made close to her, and a short sleeve; a gold vail hung loosely over her head, and the rest went over her body, – all the front of it was trimmed with a row of *large pearls*. She had a girdle, or rather a large hoop, made of diamonds, which went round her waist. . . . I own I thought myself in a dream all the time I was there. . . . There was a fine Moor's coat and a couple of rich veils, and to each of us a present of a Moor's coat and a gold veil. The Nabob's lady put Mrs Binyon's on; so we, in compliment, put on ours, with which she was pleased; and we came back to the Governor's in ours, where we dined and spent the evening.[1]

India as a source of fabrics, particularly printed cottons, and as a centre of accessible and expanding trade, had an important role in English dress in the eighteenth century. Imports from there threatened to overwhelm the home industry. (In order to help Irish weavers survive in the face of the great popularity of Indian products, Jonathan Swift had to write to the Countess of Suffolk in 1726 to remind her of the quality of the non-Indian product, and to suggest a ruse to get it accepted at court; he spoke of copies of Indian cloth 'wherein our workmen here are grown so expert, that in this kind of stuff they are said to excel that which comes from the Indies; and because our ladies are too proud to wear what is made at home, the workman is forced to run a gold thread through the middle, and sell it as Indian.'[2] When asked at court in London where her fine gown came from, the Countess was to be sure it was realized that it came from Ireland, not India.) Orders for cloth commissioned from India were sent to ensure the products were patterned for European taste rather than Indian, but of course the Indian tradition and ideas showed through and the cloth came back to make a distinct and identifiable style which has had a lasting influence on English fabric design.

Men continued to make use of the wrapped night gown, or Indian gown, or banyan as it was variously known. It was of two types in the eighteenth century: a looser one resembling a kimono, and a more complex type constructed to fit more closely to the arms and body, cut with the curves so characteristic of European tailoring and quite unlike the kimono construction which was invariably on straight lines only.[3] The tighter banyan variety with set-in sleeves resembled Indo-Persian garments from the north-west of India. Both these versions of the comfortable, informal night gown or Indian gown filled an obvious need in a gentleman's wardrobe, being a bridge between street clothes and bed clothes, and consequently they were in wide use. The *Town and Country Magazine* noted that banyans were seen outside, in the London streets, in some numbers in the 1780s.[4] Some were imported whole, some made up here of imported cloth, and some, copying the imported originals, were made up here of cloth also made here. The kimono type was usually buttonless, and needed a sash or cord of some sort to keep it wrapped in place, and the tailored type could be fastened by various buttoning methods. These garments, whilst informal and relaxed, could have artistic and scholarly overtones, in portraits and in life, and it was not until the nineteenth century that they receded into a further degree of informality, and therefore privacy, under the name of 'dressing gown.' After a lengthy contribution to the English scene with their welcome mixture of exoticism and utility, the Indian gowns legacy to men's dress, via the dressing gown, is one of the few retentions in male domestic use of the word 'gown'; 'gown' in 'night gown' and 'dressing gown' remained, but the word has otherwise a ceremonial use only. After the Indian gown, men's indoor dress was generally devoid of any garment that was not carefully fitted. Women also wore Indian or night gowns under the same circumstances.

'The *curdee* is a loose robe they throw off or put on according to the weather, being of a rich brocade (mine is green and gold), either lined with ermine or sables; the sleeves reach very little below the shoulders.'[5] This was a description by the celebrated Lady Mary Wortley Montagu (1689–1762) of her own Turkish dress, which she was wearing in 1717 in Turkey whilst with her husband on his diplomatic duty [128]. The fur-lined overgarment which she called a 'curdee' was to get into fairly frequent use in England for both men and women, and like the banyan, it filled a useful function as well as having a likeable foreignness about it and a degree of panache.

127 Man's Indian-influenced house gown in quilted chintz, 1770–80. It has matching waistcoat to be worn underneath.

In many English travellers' descriptions of various customs and costumes of the Eastern world, there was a

128 Authentic Turkish dress on Lady Wortley Montagu whose enthusiasm for it promoted its revival in eighteenth-century England, for men and women. Natural silhouette, furred 'curdee' and caftan were striking in *c.*1717.

recurring fascination with the pervasive luxury of court life they saw there; '. . . we waited on the Emir, and found him in a Chiosque in his garden, reclined upon a Sopha near a fountain, and indolently enjoying his pipe.'[6] Knowledge about Turkey in particular had been reinforced at about the time of Lady Mary's correspondence by the publication of an illustrated book recording a French embassy there, by M. de Ferriol[7]; from this could be gleaned a great deal about Turkish court life and practice, and also about Greeks and others who came under Turkish rule at the time. This level of international contact encouraged the image of a luxurious land of rich and exotic dress in magnificent settings; busy embassies did not always have time to observe closely the other side of life in their host country.

Details of the kind relayed by Ferriol, however, could not match those given by one who was actually wearing Turkish dress; Lady Mary had become intrigued by Turkish life, and had got inside a harem, which was one place the French embassy could not visit, and had even become knowledgeable about the use of Khol, a cosmetic she thought English women would like except for the fact it could be detected in daylight. It is worth completing her description of her Turkish attire, for it conveys something of the pleasure and attraction such exotic garb had always held for the English:

> The first piece of my dress is a pair of drawers, very full, that reach to my shoes, and conceal the legs more modestly than your petticoats. They are of a thin rose-coloured damask, brocaded with silver flowers, my shoes of white kid leather, embroidered with gold. Over this hangs my smock, of a fine white silk gauze, edged with embroidery. This smock has wide sleeves, hanging halfway down the arm, and is closed at the neck with a diamond button; but the shape and the colour of the bosom very well to be distinguished through it. The *antery* is a waistcoat, made close to the shape, of white and gold damask, with very long sleeves falling back, and fringed with deep gold fringe, and should have diamond or pearl buttons. My *caftan*, of the same stuff as my drawers, is a robe exactly fitted to my shape, and reaching to my feet, with very long strait falling sleeves. Over this is a girdle of about four fingers broad, which all that can afford have entirely of diamonds or other precious stones; those who will not be at that expense, have it of exquisite embroidery on satin, but it must be fastened before with a clasp of diamonds.[8]

With others of her Turkish letters, this account of her dress was published after Lady Mary's death in 1763, and the impact was considerable, confirming an already long-standing willingness on the part of the fashionable English to adopt and revise for themselves anything suitable from abroad. The Turkish mode clearly was suitable, for it was modest, flattering and deliciously prone to small details of great magnificence; a velvet cap worn on one side of the head was to be balanced, in Lady Mary's account, with decorations of jewels, heron's feathers, or bouquets of jewelled and enamelled flowers: '. . . 'tis hard to imagine anything of that kind so beautiful.'[9]

Features of this attire gained popularity in England in varying degrees; the drawers or harem trousers were least suitable, but the fur-lined curdee, the caftan with the pendant sleeves, and the under-smock could all be utilized in modified form. It was usually contrived that

129 One of several similar portraits of this date showing modified dress based on Lady Mary's Turkish costume. Worn with hooped petticoat, *c.*1770.

130 Captain Foote (1718–68), East India Company. Authentic Indian dress brought home, with beautiful shawls much sought after by Englishwomen for the next hundred years. *c.*1761–5.

131 Captain Foote's surviving Indian costume, very similar to contemporary English banyans for men, but clearly showing traditional longer sleeve not used in English copies.

one or other of these was combined with the necessary stays. The cap and the heron's feathers appeared too, as did the elaborate girdle or sash, and the slippers. There are numerous portraits said to be of Lady Mary in Turkish dress; although many are without supporting evidence, and are probably of other people copying the new fashion, some properly of Lady Mary, such as that by Richardson at Sandon Hall, show the fusion of the foreign garments with the prevailing shape of current fashion. Painters such as Richardson, Highmore, Reynolds and Liotard included amongst their English clients many men and women who took up this 'turquerie.' It also had a place in masquerade dress, where it reached perhaps its most lavish appearance at the 1768 masquerade given in London by the King of Denmark. Illustrations from Ferriol's book had been reissued in Thomas Jeffery's 1757 *Collection of the Dresses of Different Nations.* The taste was established in the 1770s and continued for most of the rest of the century, although it is more accurate to say that Turkish taste has never entirely left English dress; it has remained in one form or another ever since; for example, Thea Porter is one designer to have played on it in recent years.

The Kashmir shawl was to become one of the most sought-after commodities of the orient, and the English quickly acquired their taste for it during the eighteenth century. It seems to have made its first appearance in the 1760s.[10] The manufacture of shawls in Kashmir had been long established before the English realized their use and value and had been worn by men, although in England they were restricted to women's use. Their characteristic is the impressive warmth and softness achieved with surprisingly little weight, and this is almost inimitable, for it depends not only on the traditional weaving method but on the wool of a central Asian mountain goat; certain sheep give a similar fleece, and wool nowadays known as 'cashmere' has usually very little to do with Kashmir. However, the original imported shawls seen in England were woven in what is known as the twill-tapestry weave, and later, in the nineteenth century,

the woven patterns were imitated by needlework. Once English manufacturers realized the potential competition, they set about copying the shawl, and it is from these first efforts in Scotland and Norfolk that the Paisley and Norwich shawls derived. The rapid expansion of these centres changed the traditional decoration gradually, until what we know as the 'cone' in a Paisley pattern grew from the originally more geometric Kashmir motif. Once the Kashmir shawl makers began to exploit the large, new European markets, they too altered their style.

Brave but doomed efforts were made to import the goats into England, beginning with the attempts by Warren Hastings in the 1770s and eighties. Others tried and failed, and the English weavers had to be content with substitute yarn. Despite this, they manufactured fine goods, which were even exported back to India by the 1820s. Both imitations and imports expanded significantly until the 1870s, after which the trade declined. The end of the Kashmir shawl as a fashionable article did not end the high esteem in which it was held, but it did spell the end of many livelihoods in Kashmir itself, and caused great hardship there. If William Moorcroft had had his way, we might still be enjoying the fruits of this fine tradition, for he had even schemed in the 1820s to naturalize some Kashmir shawl families in Britain.

During the eighteenth century, Chinoiserie was also a considerable factor in dress and textiles, as well as in the other arts. This was a taste which had been developing through the previous century; once Europeans had mastered the art of making porcelain, there were no other real technical barriers to copying what was thought to be Chinese style. The delicate Kashmir shawl began to alter once it began to travel: the taste for things Chinese had been for so long based on a vision rather than real experience of China itself that no such exacting standards had to be met, and it proved a flourishing and endlessly adaptable basis for decoration[11][132]. Within Europe the style developed with its own Westernized values, and being mostly isolated from genuine contact with China, there was very little opportunity to borrow directly from authentic dress. Much Chinese influence in our dress construction has come to us, particularly in the nineteenth century, indirectly through Japan.

132 Pretty muslin apron with white work 'chinoiserie.' Early eighteenth century.

19 *A Sense of Dignity*

THE NINETEENTH CENTURY

The mere act of passing from one's graceless London clothes into the white draperies of Arabia is a new birth. One's soul rises in dignity with the change. . . .

Wilfrid Scawen Blunt (1840–1922), *Arabist*

Wilfrid Blunt travelled extensively in Arabia in the 1870s; he espoused the course of Islam and Egyptian nationalism and lived as an Egyptian in a house on the outskirts of Cairo. He and his wife both dressed as Arabs, spoke Arabic to each other and developed a love for the Arab horse which led to the establishment of the famous Crabbet Arabian Stud stables in Sussex. Blunt's feelings about the freedom and splendour of Arab dress were part of his intimate involvement with the surrounding life, but although he spoke of the dress in mystical terms he was expressing the essence of a traditional response to various forms of Eastern dress on the part of many Englishmen during the nineteenth century. There is also in his words a link with the previous centuries. 'As long as the Eastern world retains its ancient dress, so long will it stand superior morally to the West. The sense of dignity gives dignity, and the Kefiyeh and Aghal add a good six inches to a poor man's moral stature. . . . I enter the pure region of the Eastern tradition as once more I put on its robes with almost religious ceremonial. . . .'[1]

Blunt was to be seen in these robes in Sussex too. Whilst this was not common practice for nineteenth-century England, there was an abiding inclination towards Eastern dress; it gave obvious satisfaction to men who would otherwise be confined in 'graceless London clothes,' and who felt more at home in a

133 Edward Lane (1801–76) in Egyptian dress which he habitually wore there. Navigator, celebrated linguist, author of 1836 English bestseller explaining modern Egyptian life to the West.

djellabah. English women too enjoyed a fashionable flirtation with Eastern forms of attire, as well as establishing some as a permanent addition to the vocabulary of English dress. It should be said that although exotic items and influences were freely, even avidly, absorbed, those nineteenth-century pioneers who fully adopted Eastern dress were likely to earn themselves a name for eccentricity or worse. Challenging an entire system of dress is more difficult than gradually modifying it; one nineteenth-century case exemplified the fine line between the acceptable importation and revision of exotic dress and the unacceptable adoption of the culture from whence it came.

Henry Stanley (1827–1903) became, in 1869, England's first recorded Muslim peer; he had spent the greater part of his earlier life abroad, and his parents in England were alarmed at stories of his behaviour. It seemed that his wearing of Arab dress and close involvement in Islamic life was eventually enough to lose him both his social and his career connections. Mr Stanley, said *The Times*, '. . . like many other intelligent English gentlemen has mixed with the inhabitants of the countries through which he passed, with a desire to become thoroughly acquainted with their manners, language, habits, and religion, and in his intercourse with the natives may have assimilated his costume somewhat to their habits.'[2] But, the paper went on, Mr Stanley would be indignant to think that it might be thought that he had also absorbed their religion. Mr Stanley, however, had done exactly that. To a traditionalist like his father, Henry Stanley had thereby thrown away his honour and his position: '. . . his friends are Arabs, Chinese, or anything but English or Christians, & he lives entirely in their society in a manner at all events unbecoming to an English Gentleman.'[3] The accent of Lord Stanley's criticism was on the impropriety and the degradation of wearing the dress of non-Christians, and the various newspapers' occupation with his son's activities suggest there was in many eyes a potential scandal. 'There is a paragraph in the Morning Post about that wretched fool Henry, saying he was at Penang living entirely with Mahometans & dressed in their dress. He was, it said, living with a certain Sheikh. . . ., speaking Arabic perfectly & avoiding the society of Europeans. Is he mad or what is he?'[4]

Against this sort of response there was no answer, and it can be taken as a fairly typical attitude to circumstances in which alien mores lingered too closely, as it were, in the folds of the clothes. It was all right to adopt foreign attire, but one was not supposed to espouse its culture – so it was implied. The frequent instances in the nineteenth century, of men being acceptable whilst wearing exotic garb, were due to the

134 Lieutenant-General Colin Mackenzie (1806–81). The Afghans called him the 'English Moollah.' Renowned in 1840s for courage in action there. Depicted in fine Afghan costume.

fact they remained reliable 'gentlemen' and were often heroic defenders of the Empire [134]. Indian, Persian, Arab and other attire was frequently brought home and proud owners sat for portraits in Eastern splendour, secure in the knowledge they were esteemed administrators or soldiers about whose religious faith or table-manners there could not be the slightest doubt. Unlike the spirited Stanley or Blunt, these men wore their imported magnificence more as the picturesque spoils of imperialism than as signs of cultural flexibility.

Nevertheless, outside this particular sphere of concern there were numerous occasions when Eastern dress came easily and naturally into sophisticated social circles; the spectacle of Turkish or Greek dress, and natives wearing it in England, were admired: 'I only paid a visit to the Duchess of C. . . . Among her attendants was a beautiful Greek boy in his national costume, scarlet, blue and gold, with naked legs and feet. He was saved from the massacre of Scio by being hidden in an oven. He is now become a perfect Englishman, but has retained something inexpressibly noble and foreign in his air.'[5] When the English wore it themselves they could turn such dress into a badge of taste and artistic sensibility. In these circumstances, it tended to attract less criticism than it did in cases like that of Henry Stanley, and it could be seen as an adoption of a style rather than an unpatriotic shedding of identity. Indeed, in the early nineteenth century, when Greece struggled to independence, most things Greek aroused considerable sympathy. Lord Byron, champion of the Greeks, possessed splendid garments from there, in addition to his famous Albanian costume (now kept at the Museum of Costume, Bath,[6]) and which was later worn in England at a masquerade. Byronic Greek dress was quite fashionable in England. But his greater influence on dress lay in the rather melancholic and negligent appearances given to him by portrait painters. Dark clothes were unusual for men in the early nineteenth century, although they were to become almost standard during Victoria's reign and after, and Byron's imagined and idealized dark, poetic garments in his portraits were widely imitated by both men and women, often with added exotic detail [135].

The authentic regional dress of the eastern Mediterranean was much liked. In an era when men of fashion habitually wore bright colours and embroidered waistcoats, the same features in Greek or Turkish dress were easily assimilated, but it was also the construction and types of garment in such dress that were so appealing. Many English people wore native dress whilst in Turkey as a precautionary disguise, but it was not always an easy attire for the inexperienced: '. . . whenever they went out, they got so entangled in their shaksheers and trousers, their shawls and their papooshes, that our progress might be traced by the mere relics of their habiliments which strewed the road.'[7] This quotation describing Germans in Constantinople is from an extraordinary novel written at the end of the eighteenth century and first published anonymously in 1819. There was much speculation about the authorship of *Anastasius*, a racy, vivid tale of adventure and opportunism in the Near East; some thought it was by Byron who was said to wish he *had* written it. Its author was in fact Thomas Hope who was by 1819 considered a leader of classical Greek taste; the style and contents of his earlier work on neo-classical furniture it was said 'certainly contrast strangely with the glowing impassioned Anastasius, overflowing with thought and feeling. An acquaintance of mine said to me "One thing or the other: either Anastasius is not by him, or the work on furniture."'[8] The novel went into thirteen editions in four languages.

Thomas Hope, like many of his contemporaries, was able to reconcile these two contrasting tastes. His wife, portrayed in 1812 by George Dawe, looking strikingly like a Grecian figure from Hope's book on classical costume, was also painted by Thomas Lawrence in 1826 in a turban and the clothes of a splendid oriental Fatima. Hope himself wore magnificent Turkish dress in his 1798 portrait made by Sir William Beechey [see colour plate], and judging by his appearance there he echoed his hero's feelings in *Anastasius* when donning fine Turkish clothes: 'The species of ease and delight derived from my transformation positively baffles all my powers of description. My chest seemed to dilate, my breathing to acquire a freedom before unknown, and my limbs and gait to have gained a fresh vigour and buoyancy.'[9]

The relationship in Hope's mind between this type of clothing and classical dress of the antique world is evident at a point in the novel when Eastern dress is exchanged for Western dress: 'It seemed to me a sort of degradation to exchange the rich and graceful garb of the East, which either shows the limbs as nature moulded them, or makes amends for their concealment, by ample and majestic drapery, for a dress which confines without covering, disfigures without protecting. . . .'[10] These were also the admired qualities of classical dress. Hope's 'rich and graceful' appearance was echoed in the lavish entertainment described in another novel based on his social circle, *A Winter in London* by T.S. Surr; a masquerade to be attended by the Prince of Wales took place in which a Turkish garden was recreated, and Turkish dress was worn by many of the guests, one of whom commented, 'one might believe oneself actually in Turkey.'[11] It seems likely that on such occasions authentic imported garments were worn, as well as copies and adaptions made up by the dressmakers, or even hired out. The influence of Lady Mary Wortley Montagu, who had died in 1762, was still strong enough for Surr the novelist to insert a quotation from her published description of Turkish female dress, and to have a central character arrive at the masquerade in dress which was said to resemble it in every particular. This was obviously a highlight of the event, since the introduction of the young lady who wore the costume was one of its main purposes. The rest of her family male and female, were equally picturesque.

Similar choices of costume were seen at less grand galas than that described by Surr; for example Disraeli attended a ball in 1835 where 'Lady Chesterfield was a Sultana, and Mrs Anson a Greek, with her own hair lower than the calf of her leg.'[12] Disraeli, like Hope, was one of a succession of men who greatly enjoyed Eastern dress, and for whom its significance went much deeper than occasional fancy dress. Disraeli (1804–81) was twenty-seven when Thomas Hope died, and he

135 An example of oriental taste in the early nineteenth century.

preceded the generation of Wilfrid Blunt; whilst there is insufficient room to list all the travellers and artists and others who took up a taste for Eastern dress, these three men, who span the period from the late eighteenth to the early twentieth century, exemplify certain attitudes. Disraeli travelled in the Near East in 1830–31, and found there a style of dressing exactly suited to his image of himself, and like Hope, Blunt and others he brought echoes of it back home with him. His description of himself fills out some of the feelings which may have prompted the building in larger houses of smoking rooms in the Eastern style: 'I am quite a Turk, wear a turban, smoke a pipe six feet long, and squat on a divan. Mehemet Pasha told me that he did not think I was an Englishman because I walked so slow: in fact I find the habits of this calm and luxurious people entirely agree with my own preconceived opinions of propriety and enjoyment. . . .'[13] (Disraeli added that he detested the Greeks more than ever.) The habit of smoking, first taken up by men only, resulted not only in special smoking rooms, but in loose jackets called simply smoking jackets, and often accompanied by round caps not unlike a flattened fez, with a tassel. Both of these items were often embroidered, perhaps with oriental decorations, and no doubt the after-dinner smoke in relaxing clothes seemed closer to the 'calm and luxurious' East than most occasions in an Englishman's life.

The nineteenth century saw many exotic references in the dress of women too. Turbans, for instance, or turban caps as they were also known, enjoyed a vogue in various forms for most of the century, and have survived into the twentieth; the English ladies' turban was taken from masculine oriental dress and was ready-constructed by the milliner to appear as if it was wound round the head. It could combine with other styles quite happily; for example, during the early part of the nineteenth century it could be part of an otherwise plain ensemble: 'A turban cap, lined with pink, ornamented with roses in front' was recommended for wear with a brown muslin dress by *The Ladies Monthly Museum* in October 1807; in April 1812 the same magazine was to rejoice in the variations possible within fashion as it observed the fragmentation of the purely classical idea, and it remarked that 'the whole habitable world is ransacked for bodily adornment. The wool of Cachimere, the turban of the east, and the plaid of the north, lend their assistance, while the Turk, the Pole, and the Indian, lay their treasures at the feet of the fair.'

In these years Lady Hester Stanhope (1776–1839), niece of William Pitt the Younger, was making herself a reputation as an intrepid traveller. She was eventually to be disowned as a bothersome eccentric. A correspondent wrote in 1812 to stress that he was not following Lady Hester's example, nor that of Hope and others: 'You must not imagine I am deck'd out in Oriental finery, like Lady Hester Stanhope. I preserve my independence and European over-alls. She displays hers by Turkish trowsers, and rides *à la Marmeluke* on a fine Arabian given her by the Pacha of Cairo, with an alarming number of pistols in her girdle.'[14] In her own letters, Lady Hester detailed her costume, and it was partly because of her extrovert and strong-minded manner that she was not to be so lionized by fashionable people as Lady Mary Wortley Montagu, who had kept well within the limits of the modesty of her time. Lady Hester did not: 'You have heard, I suppose, that I am dressed as a man; sometimes as Chief of Albanians, sometimes as a Syrian soldier, sometimes as a Bedouin Arab (the famous robbers in the desert), and at other times like the son of a Pacha. . . .'[15] In Cairo she wore two very valuable cashmere shawls, one as a turban and the other as a girdle, and in the Holy Land she travelled in a burnous and trousers. Although she considered such dress more decent than the dress of women in England, Lady Hester's use of trousers was not to be popular in England.

Amelia Bloomer (1818–94) became a celebrity in her attempts to popularize trousers for women. The bold few followed her lead, but there was an outcry against her ideas in England, and she was not to achieve much success in her native America. Advocates of her ideas to shorten skirts and free women from the cumbersome crinoline stressed that the full and bifurcated pantaloons or 'Bloomers' to be worn with the new clothing were modest and sanctioned by centuries of use by very docile women in the East. Mrs Merrifield considered that however correct this line of

136 Amelia Bloomer's supporters argued that bifurcated garments were worn by respectable women all over the East, but Bloomers were often ridiculed in England.

argument was, especially in view of the fact that long bifurcated pantaloons had been worn in the West *under* skirts for years anyway, the experiment failed because it was introduced too suddenly, and was accompanied by a large hat which many people took to be an integral but unacceptable part of the deal. Ugly prints appeared frequently in the Bloomer costumes which were offered for sale in the shops, and these also contributed to the failure. Mrs Merrifield described the ensemble in sympathetic terms:

> . . . the short dress, a polka jacket fitting the body at the throat and shoulders, and confined at the waist by a silken sash, and the trousers fastened by a band round the ancle, and finished off with a frill. On the score of modesty there can be no objection to the dress, since the whole of the body is covered. On the ground of convenience it recommends itself to those who, having the superintendence of a family, are obliged frequently to go up and down stairs, on which occasions it is always necessary to raise the dress before or behind according to circumstances. The objection to the trousers is not to this article of dress being worn, since that is a general practice, but to its being seen. Yet we suspect few ladies would object on this account to appear at a fancy dress ball in the Turkish costume.[16]

Charles Reade tried to lend his support to this potential reform with a scene in his short story, *The Bloomer*, published in 1857 with others under the heading *The Course of True Love never did run Smooth*. His American-based heroine Caroline put on an elaborate pageant to extol the Bloomer costume, a style in which she herself frequently appeared. After a parade of examples of inconvenient historical and modern dress, two women in Persian dress appeared; in their roomy trousers and splendid decorations they affected amazement at the other styles of dress, whilst Caroline addressed her audience on the fact that half the women of the world wore trousers, and that Western women were foolish to pretend they were more modest or more feminine than their Muslim sisters. Reade switched horses halfway through this story; counter-arguments about the logic of wearing veils with such costumes were heard, and although Caroline's Bloomer costume was instrumental in saving her husband-to-be from drowning, she gave up the costume and the crusade a year after her marriage.

Other reformers seeking to improve dress in England during the nineteenth century looked to Eastern dress in other ways. Mrs Merrifield had observed, for example, that to see beautiful feet unspoiled by tight shoes one would have to go to Egypt or India. Once international transactions with Japan became more frequent after the 1850s, Japanese dress attracted some reformers' attention. In 1889 the Rational Dress Society was presented with a male Japanese garment described as a silk divided skirt, and, in its *Gazette* of July that year, told how a member of the Society had some years previously obtained a cotton version of this useful garment, and used it as the foundation of a divided skirt called a 'Wilson.' In October 1888 the Society's *Gazette* documented an open letter written by some American women to the women of Japan urging them not to adopt Western dress, since their own traditional dress was exemplary from the point of view of economy of fabric as well as grace and utility. They were concerned that the corset would travel to Japan, as indeed it did very quickly, so that, far from the Society's aims succeeding, the European dress they were trying to change found yet more converts in Japan.

Fashion magazines unsympathetic to reform were keen on much more modified foreign dress for women which would add a piquant detail or some attractive nuance to current forms, and would decorate rather than alter the status quo; for example, small pouches of velvet or silk, worn suspended from the waistband, became fashionable in the 1860s; they were described by one periodical as being somewhat oriental but also somewhat Scotch. Occasionally a sense of fatigue entered the fashion columns as commentators found themselves overwhelmed by the range of foreign-inspired items:

> This year's fashions seem to borrow something from the number of foreign costumes that are seen in Paris since the opening of the Great Exhibition. Amongst these the most eccentric are those that meet the most favour. Thus we have Chinese sleeves, Egyptian girdles, Turkish jackets, Russian touquets. It becomes more difficult than ever to dress really well and in good taste, and to avoid these fashions which are too much exaggerated to be ladylike.[17]

Of course the magazines steered a ladylike way through this maze for their readers and also continued to remind them of the service they were rendering them in doing so.

The Arab burnous was one of these 'eccentric' imports; it stayed to become a very serviceable addition; being wholly untailored, with the simplest of fastenings and variable in size and length, it could serve as a comfortable covering to envelop both the very wide bells of crinolines in the 1850s and sixties, and the big, fussy bustles of the next two decades. After that it remained popular as an occasional alternative to other outdoor garments. In its native habitat the burnous serves as a voluminous wrap of great importance in desert conditions due to its warmth and protection from blowing sand. It can be turned back over the shoulders, its tasselled hood lowered for warm days, and its very looseness acts as a cooling device. Or it can be wrapped like a cosy blanket with the hood almost entirely covering the face for cold nights. These extreme conditions did not concern the lady of fashion in England, but the burnous proved not only flexible in accommodating her changing of silhouette but its hood was convenient protection for elaborate coiffures in an era when it was a natural gesture to cover one's

137 The burnous proved a useful and attractive over-garment for fashionable English women at this time and has remained so. This triple-tasselled example was recommended for spring 1862.

head out of doors. Nor was there any need to confine the garment to its traditional cloths; in April 1862, the *Englishwoman's Domestic Magazine* described one 'of white muslin . . . trimmed with green silk ruching, and three handsome green and white tassels.' This [137] was to accompany a white muslin dress for a picnic.

Although Arthur Liberty did not open a separate costume department in his shop until 1884, he had previously sold individual oriental garments imported along with the silks and other fine objects for which his shop was renowned. The original name of the store at 218A Regent Street when opened in 1875 was East India House. By its importation of and then its creative imitation of the finest cashmeres, silks, muslins and so on, Arthur Liberty's company had from its beginning a powerful effect on English taste. Since the history and beneficial role of this company has been so well documented,[18] it may be amusing to note how very exacting its customers could be; Edward Burne-Jones addressed the shop on the matter of his dressing gown:

> I return the Japanese Dressing Gown sent on approval, with thanks, but with regret. . . . Will you allow me to urge upon you most seriously to import only *genuine* Oriental colours & materials. Nothing can replace the beauty of the things that used to be bought over from China & Japan, but which it is almost impossible to find in the market now. . . . With gratitude for what you have done in the past by bringing lovely and precious materials & colours over. . . . I am sure a return to the original colours might be made – if we would trust the Oriental workman as he deserves. . . . The importance of the subject is my reason for troubling you.[19]

20 *Aladdin's Cave*

THE TWENTIETH CENTURY

> Europe is almost thrown into the shade by the temptation of the Orient, that fairyland which seems to have completely captivated the imagination of the Western people lately, and of which they cannot have enough to satisfy their desires.
>
> Florence Winterburn, *Principles of Correct Dress*, New York, 1914

The Japanese presence has continued in the dress of men and women, and is now established as a familiar if variable component, from *haute couture* to the High Street. Dress reformers who, in the 1880s, were worried lest Japan, once within Western influence, would lose its graceful indigenous dress would now be gratified to see that the process of influence has been partly reversed: not only has the kimono, with other traditional forms, been widely accepted in English dress, but more recently, contemporary Japanese designers of fine clothes have come to the fore with other

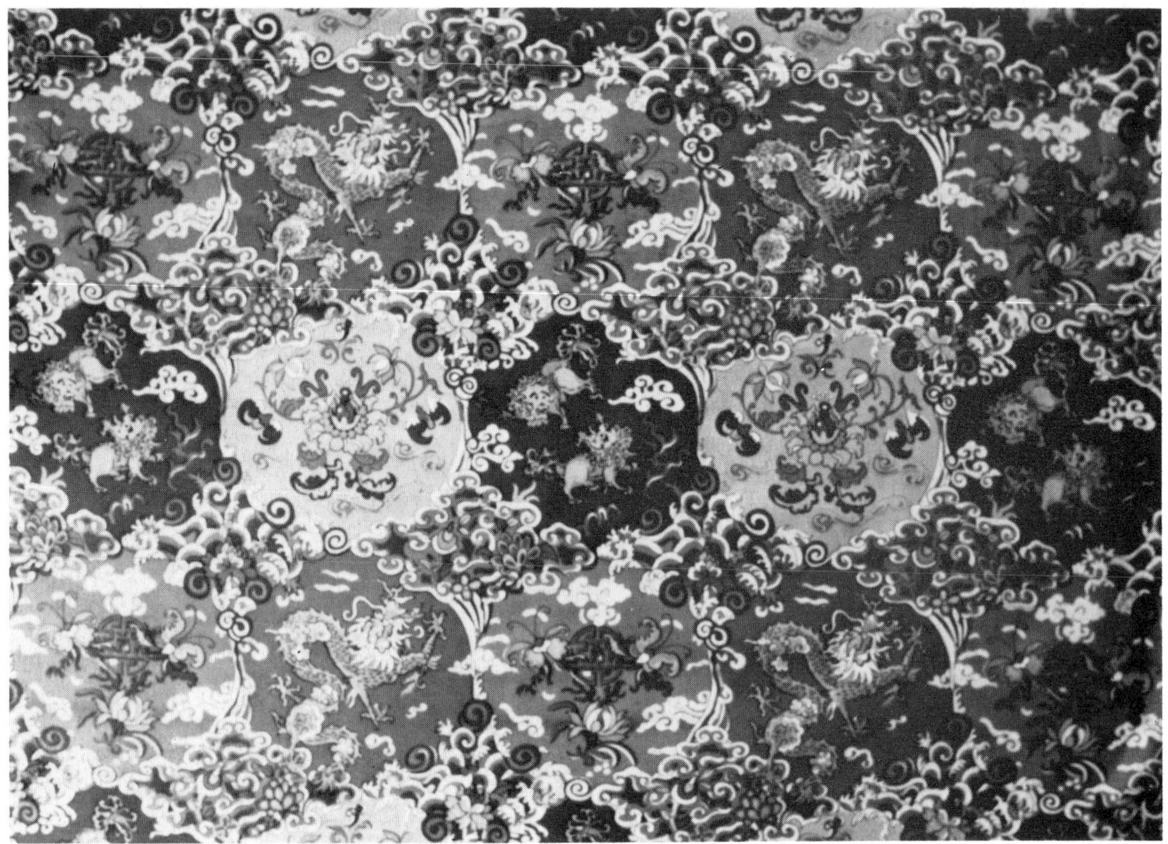

138 Liberty silk print with *c.*1900 dragon-and-dog design, 1980. Winston Churchill was said to have had a dressing gown in this print.

139 Internationally worn judo suits help to preserve virile image of oriental original in countries where such loose dress would otherwise be unacceptable for men.

successful mergers of old and new and these are having a beneficial impact at the mass market level.

After the celebrated events of 1909 and 1910, when a remarkable convergence of elements including the Russian Ballet and the enterprising *couturier* Paul Poiret excited the world of fashion into a cult of hybrid orientalism, concerns such as that of Edward Burne-Jones about authentic Japanese colours were overshadowed: orientalism in English dress was no longer the privilege of an artistic minority, nor was it principally to do with the importation of genuine fabrics or garments, for it was to develop its own momentum and its own Westernized renaissance. However, in the early years of this century there was a lull before this cult spread; the kimono, for instance, could be seen translated into sedate and elegant indoor use in this country. True to the original, it was worn by both sexes, and had an air of propriety, quite unlike the versions Poiret and his imitators were later to launch. For men, imported kimonos and the use of the kimono construction made a leisurely addition to 'undress'; to call them 'dressing gowns' seems unfair since in recent years that has become a devalued term unsuitable to the splendid versions then available to men of fashion. Just as it is used today by Japanese men who may work in a Western business suit, but may prefer to wear traditional clothes at home in the evening, the kimono and its copies gave the Englishman a comfortable release from his suit. Smoking jackets or dressing gowns might follow not only the construction but also the exotic decoration and fabric of the Eastern originals; dragons might have been taboo in the office, but they could stalk freely over leisure wear. The jacket form of the kimono is also usefully adopted for beach or bathroom, as well as it was for the now almost extinct smoking wear. Popularization of judo in the West has helped to demonstrate the utility of the wrapped kimono construction, and has in addition helped to preserve and promote the virile image it always had in its original form but which does not always sit easily with loose, full or unstructured garments in England and the West generally.

Women, too, took up the kimono and its imitations as teagowns and dressing gowns, in their sitting

INTERS
JUDO-WM
253
1975 - WIEN

rooms and boudoirs; it is testimony to the almost infinite flexibility of this oriental garment's construction that it could satisfy a wealthy Edwardian lady's sense of sedentary elegance and can also fit the self-image of an athletic young man of today. The difference of course is in the fabric. An early twentieth century teagown was a fragile and airy thing, and the kimono shape was much liked for its capacity to enfold a lady gracefully without revealing whether she had or had not succumbed, *cinq-à-sept*, to a brief release from her corset. At such moments, the weight of fashion could be shed. The Rational Dress Society had in the 1880s declared its disapproval of any clothes which weighed, without shoes, more than seven pounds, and it is unlikely that any fully dressed follower of pre-1914 fashion would have been able to achieve such lightness except in her night clothes and at home 'undress.' Those women whose incomes and lifestyles did not include the luxurious pause in a teagown before dressing up again for dinner could still come home after work and exchange the fitted exactitude of their suits and corsets, and the restraints of the classroom or the office desk, for something more comfortable with a welcome hint of the orient. For example, in 1903 a dressing gown, or house robe, was described as being 'in shape very suggestive of the kimono of Japan, which effect would be heightened were a wide sash draped tightly round the figure. The beauty of this gown is that it preserves a straight outline whether worn with or without corsets, and it can either be finished with a girdle or worn loose. . . .'[1] In 1909, Selfridges were offering Japanese quilted jackets in silk with 'Chinese Mandarin Sleeves,' at a very reasonable price,[2] which were also available in full-length versions, and Liberty continued with their oriental department making its own special contribution, occupying the unique position it still holds today.

So things might have remained, if Paris had not so energetically embraced its own brand of orientalism in the years after about 1909. Nothing so diffuse occurs so suddenly, but 1909 was the year in which Sergei Diaghilev (1872–1929) succeeded in organizing his ballet company's first appearance in Paris; Russian music and opera had been successfully performed in both London and Paris before, but it was the ballet which made the most dramatic impact on European orientalism; the Russian Ballet did not appear in London until 1911, but its influence was felt almost as soon as it was in Paris. Diaghilev employed several designers, but Léon Bakst's (1866?–1924) work made perhaps the most vivid impressions on the new audiences. He used a range of vivid colours and rich overtones which were virtually unprecedented, and the first performances to use his designs were sumptuous: *Schéhérazade* in 1910 was probably the most influential on dress. Paul Poiret, in his autobiography published in English in 1931 as *My First Fifty Years* firmly denied that Bakst had any part to play in his couture interpretation of orientalism, and Poiret's kimono coat called 'Confucius' had certainly appeared in 1906, well before Bakst and the Ballet arrived. Nevertheless these two names are linked closely in the development of the new exoticism, Bakst's clothes on the back of the astonishing Nijinsky and his fellow dancers, and Poiret's seen amongst the beau monde, and in the work of the best French fashion illustrators.

Skilled at publicity, Poiret produced two lavish albums of his clothes in 1909 and 1911, illustrated by Paul Iribe and Georges Lepape respectively and they remain as rightly celebrated evidence of the quality and imagination to be found in fashion illustration and design at that time. (They clearly demonstrate the Western experiment with the 'floating world' of Japanese art, and the important effect of Matisse and Les Fauves on the decorative arts.) In 1909, Poiret was in London at the invitation of Margot Asquith, wife of the Prime Minister, and a considerable storm was provoked by her unpatriotic purchase of foreign clothes; this too extended his reputation with no ill-effect. The information that he purchased fabrics from Liberty was used to redress the balance. Poiret's oriental phase of these years was aided by an inspirational visit to see the Indian turbans in the Victoria and Albert Museum.

Turbans of various designs for women enriched with aigrettes, jewels and rich fabrics were a frequent feature of his design collections from 1909, and were rapidly copied and worn elsewhere; they made a dramatic contrast to the enormously wide hats of less adventurous fashion. Harem trousers appeared in 1911, after Poiret's famous '1002nd Night,' a lavish party (curiously similar to that held in 1804 in T.S. Surr's novel, *A Winter in London*, at a time when the same mix of classicism and orientalism held sway over fashion). These were also known as pantaloon gowns or trouser skirts, and caused both offence and envy. 'Duchesses are ready for Paul Poiret to dress, undress, and costume them. All they care about is to be the beloved favourite, the silk and fur pillow covers, the lampshades, and the cushions in the harem of the sultan in vogue.'[3] The harem trousers were made with generous quantities of fabric and allowed more movement than Poiret's hobbleskirts which noticably restricted the gait, but on the whole Poiret was not concerned with affecting or reflecting progress in women's dress, and although some of his designs appeared relatively simple in comparison to other highly ornate clothes of the day, utility was not an aim.

Poiret created a world of his own, in which women wore his fantasies, just as in 1911 he had a whole oriental market reconstructed for his party, when he also provided garments so that all his guests should look the part, and he himself was dressed as a sultan, his wife as the harem favourite. These were not only expensive tastes, they were also not modern enough in spirit to survive the deep changes forced by the First World War. When Poiret died in 1944 he was long spent as a leader in fashion design; although he had remained in business until 1929, his most memorable innovations were those of the pre-1914 years of firstly Hellenic styles, and secondly the oriental phase. His vigorous personality and flair for publicity allowed him to put his mark on the taste of those days, and he brought a number of renewed Eastern elements to the last days of a lifestyle which ended with the war.

With Poiret and the influence of the Russian Ballet no longer central to the generating of fashionable ideas, the oriental taste was less extreme, but no less popular. The increasingly lean silhouettes of the 1920s were flattered and softened by voluminous kimono-type overcoats and wraps, burnouses and shawls. Fine embroidered Chinese shawls were often made so large, with such deep fringes, that they entirely enveloped their wearer from neck to floor, and functioned as cloaks; 'London theatres on a fashionable first night when the stalls are as gay as a July flower border with the exquisite embroidered Chinese and Manila shawls worn by the women playgoers. . . .'[4] In the early 1920s there was much use made of sashes, and an 'Eastern sash' was a frequent item. Headbands, handbags, shoes, and other accessories often added some exotic detail. Going back to first principles, Chinese ideas enjoyed a vogue: pagoda sleeves, for instance, and head-dresses based on authentic imperial Chinese originals. As the ideal female shape got longer in the waist, so-called 'coolie' blouses and jackets appeared which fell straight from the shoulder to the hip.

Pyjamas as evening and beachwear for women were fashionable for most of the decade [140]; they had been partly helped to the fore by Poiret's much publicized trouser-skirts, and also by outfits promoted during the 1914–18 war, when efforts were made to make work clothes attractive: whilst factory work and other tough jobs put working women into trousers for the war effort, readers of London *Vogue* were, by the introduction of charming clothes, encouraged to get out into their gardens and cultivate potatoes. Mandarin hats and tasselled overblouses were accompanied by sensibly wide trousers cut to well above the ankle, and the magazine noted that once permitted to wear such

140 'How to be different. Don't wear pyjamas at the Lido.' Summer 1929.

attractive trousers for the war efforts in the vegetable patch, most women would be reluctant to give them up when the war ended. *The Queen* was usually alert to the dangers of certain fashions for some of its readers, and gave helpful, tactful suggestions about the pyjama suit once it was established after the war. It noted that whilst it could be prettily 'Aladdinish' such a suit drew attention to itself by being very skimpy in cut and bold in colour. 'Made in brightly patterned silks they appeared last year on the Lido as beach suits, their success increasing during this year's summer season. The popular version of these suits had Chinese trousers of black satin and a long jumper top of gay silk . . very appropriately worn by those of the slender, shingled, rather boyish type.'[5] Many versions of trousers teamed with loose tops have remained popular for women since the 1920s; mixing the Chinese and Indian, female and male, smocks, wrap-over tops, or over-blouses, they have variously come and gone from fashion both as evening and day wear. Once likely to be thought of as unusually Aladdinish or Eastern, they seem now to be indigenous. Recent variants have included trousers, sometimes called 'harem,' sometimes 'jodphur,' using widely cut legs narrowing to the ankles; even serviceable denim jeans can be seen cut in this shape, but their oriental origins are now forgotten. Gone too, are the days when bifurcated garments for women caused earnest arguments.

During the 1930s a fresh wave of confidence seemed to appear in the work of *haute couture* designers, which allowed amusing details and experiments, and a new tone in the fashion media which enthusiastically greeted events such as the oriental phase of 1934. The Anglo-French designer Edward Molyneux and some other designers had collections that year at which fashion writers were in ecstasy:

> And such prints! Riots of Korean blossoms, wistaria, lilacs, poppies, hollyhocks – all as colourful as old Japanese flower panels. There are vivid swathed sashes, too, and bamboo buttons and bamboo coloured accessories, gay bordered tunics and hems, trains like dragon tails, narrow tubular skirts with slits, and even Japanese wing-draperies instead of sleeves. . . . Above these placid Chinese necklines, these celestial flowing lines, sit giant coolie hats. Often the crowns are cone-shaped exactly like those of the boys who trundle your jinricksha in Tokio. It's these huge cartwheels that give the final filip to the exciting Oriental silhouette.[6]

The magazine writer spoke of the fusion of East and West, and there was evidently also a fusion of East and East; Korean (a dignified traditional dress surprisingly little used by Western designers), Japanese, Chinese imperial and Chinese peasant and so on, all mingled happily. The collar we now know as 'mandarin' was useful in the 1930s and the 1950s in the search for a long neck look. Unexpectedly the masculine fez of Turkey was utilized for that purpose: in the early thirties a flattened version came into fashionable use, often decorated with additional buttons, and worn at a rakish angle, usually of felt but sometimes even knitted or cröcheted: 'The fez is now among the most firmly established features of the new mode and will probably become one of those things that mark an epoch. It is all part of the new ambition to appear tall, to do everything we can to exaggerate a vertical look, and in some mysterious way this extra inch or two on your head seems to produce that long-necked effect even if you are not actually swan-like.'[7]

During the war, heirlooms of fine, old Indian shawls were put to good use against the cold, and in the 1950s women's millinery enjoyed a marvellous renaissance with sharp, often witty inventions balancing the after-effects of the bold New Look, using coolie hats, parasol hats and flights of vague oriental fancy based on shallow conical shapes which completed the small-waisted and long-skirted outfits so influenced by Dior's 1947 dictate. Textile designers continued of course to utilize oriental imagery but it was not until the 1960s that any interpretations as radical as those by Poiret came to the fore.

The 1960s' use of orientalism originated in the United States, and in the hippy movement in particular. 'Hippy' is an awkward word; it came to mean something quite separate from the adjective 'hip' and has as yet no comfortable generic noun such as 'hippydom' or 'hippyness': the word remains individual, which is characteristic of the mood which generated this democratization of the exotic. Like the London Teds before them, the American hippies asserted the right of ordinary people to their own expressive taste. Style was no longer a privilege. Specifically, the hippies emerged from a configuration of events on the west coast of America, and, with the help of the largely unsympathetic press, had by about 1967 become an acceptable if quaint part of the English scene. By that time the anarchy of the original American drop-outs, high on drugs and love, had been defused, and Flower Power had been taken over by the mass market. Before this commercialization had occurred the hippies' political dissatisfaction, anti-materialism and espousal of Third World issues were all expressed in clothes which sinned against the commandments of post-war taste: they were untidy, often barefooted, both sexes often bare chested with unstyled shoulder-length hair. Their sheepskin coats and jackets, 'Afghans,' were calculated to offend traditionalists used to wearing fine English sheepskins, for they were often badly cured or speckled with embroidery to cover the holes. The point of deliberately wearing such badges of poverty during the boom years

141 Black and red satin evening wear in Japanese style, with red rose on the skirt. 1951.

of the 1960s was lost on their detractors. Hippies liked beads and headbands, and bracelets, for both sexes, and wore an assortment of oriental robes or wide-hemmed trousers which flapped and flowed in picturesque impracticality, whilst followers of fashion imitated the short spotless angularities of Pierre Cardin or André Courrèges.

Hippies dared to reject what their own culture was offering them; this offended some but one feels that Disraeli would have understood their search. He thought the Eastern life of the 1830s, reposing on couches smoking fine pipes, was 'a far more sensible life than all the bustle of clubs, all the boring of drawing rooms,'[8] and he saw beauty in the smallest Eastern item of personal decoration. 'A common pair of slippers that you push on in the street is tinged of a vermilion or a lake so extraordinary that I can compare their colour to nothing but the warmest beam of a summer sunset.'[9] The original hippies saw their ideas gradually spread; as teachers of Eastern meditation techniques were sought out or imported, pop and film stars went East, young people hitch-hiked the trail to Afghanistan and India, and a bevy of shops opened to cater for those who could not make the trip but who still wanted cheap oriental clothes and other goods. However, when in 1968 London *Vogue* featured Lady Antonia Fraser, photographed by David Bailey, as one of a series of 'Entertainers in Vogue,' the game was up: sitting *on* her dining table, in a gold and purple Indian tunic and trousers with elaborate Indian earrings, Lady Antonia was signalling the end of the real hippies and the rise of their fashionable imitators. Lady Londonderry figured subsequently in the same series, and was seen in antique Indian paisley made up into trousers and waistcoat by Thea Porter, a designer who had by then earned a justifiable reputation for extending bizarre or exotic images into a softer and more sophisticated mode.

142 Clothes and religion from Tibet, seen in a London shop front.

American Indian decorations had first been borrowed by the hippies, but proved so attractive that they too were taken up by the mainstream of fashion. By 1968 this was noted: 'For such a naive form of decoration, fringing has acquired a remarkable chic. As part of the hippie look, it was jumbled up with beads, floating scarves and flapping trousers. Fashion designers, coming up in the wake of hippiedom like a starchy nanny tidying up a dishevelled child, got rid of the rest of the paraphernalia, herded Minnehaha and Pocohontas firmly back into the reservation, and made fringing their own.'[10] Designers who revived this Indian idea included Bill Gibb, and the French *couture* house of Patou. A curious side-effect of the subcontinental Indian styles which some hippies had worn was the men's Nehru jacket. This was a smart style taken from the Indian Prime Minister's typical appearance, and was a respectable garment acceptable as an alternative to the suit jacket, although for some men who wore it with beads, it represented a half-way house between conformity and hippydom. It was in vogue from 1966 until about 1968, and was an American idea.

Of the several designers who took delight in the impetus begun by the hippy movement, Yves St Laurent is perhaps the one most responsible for extending the oriental ideas and giving them new meanings for Westerners. St Laurent set up in Paris on his own in 1962 after difficulties in continuing his work for the house of Dior on that designer's death. St Laurent has since successfully followed the two distinct lines of a basic wardrobe for women, such as blazers, trousers and suits, and a seemingly inexhaustible reanimation of traditional peasant and Eastern clothes. He has expressed the view that pursuing these two approaches can liberate women from annual fashion changes altogether. 'Whatever the fashion might be – one could suddenly decide on a Russian influence, for example – there would always be behind it this classic wardrobe. If a woman wears trousers as a man wears his, she's lost. But wherever she goes, whatever the year, she'll never be out of fashion.'[11] St Laurent claims credit, probably rightly, for making what he called 'flea market' clothes perfectly chic – vast burnouses, kaftans, harem trousers, richly draped scarves and sashes around heads and hips. St Laurent's successful use of all these has given a chance for more flexible and relaxed attitudes in combining the best of various oriental garments, which can be as opulent or as casual as one's pocket allows. Like Poiret before him, St Laurent, born in Algeria, has used the traditions of North Africa in his work; he lives at present in both Paris and Morocco. In common with most surviving Paris *couturiers*, he depends on the international *prêt-à-porter* market through which his eclectic and generous mix of

143 One of a French couple living the simple life in Italy, *c.* 1965. Hippy life and looks quickly became international, combining orientalism and Rousseau in both.

exotic idioms is readily seen. Those who cannot afford to be his customers eventually find their own level of imitation; his long-term influence in bringing diverse traditions together can hardly be over estimated. It is partly in an effort to convey this process that fashion writers have taken during the last decade to using the word 'ethnic' to denote a *mélange* of borrowings not from whole racial groups but from localized traditional forms of dress.

Since the 1960s the Japanese influence has been very evident in avant-garde *couture* and in *prêt-à-porter*, and has spread through into the mass market too. It has brought an imaginative use of prints, more inventive ways with women's trousers, and new interpretations of traditional Japanese clothes which have always combined discretion with sensuousness. The success of

144 Kimono on offer, 1980. Now popular as dressing gowns.

this source of ideas is due in part to the tendency of some of the Japanese designers to produce styles which encourage their wearers to mix and assemble their own image. Kenzo Takada, for example, has been called the greatest designer in the world,[12] and is known as a much-copied but little-acknowledged source of ideas for manufacturers of both clothes and textiles. His is a benign influence, contributing to a renewal of women's confidence which may now release them from their former restraints under the sort of stylistic duress which has been fairly common from the press and the industry generally. Kenzo Takada has said 'I dress people with imagination,'[13] and no doubt that double meaning is intentional. The spirit of Mr Shimada is perhaps pleased at this development; he was the editor of a Tokyo newspaper and in 1889 had talks with the Rational Dress Society in London about the best way to help traditional Japanese costume into the new industrial world. It was felt that something halfway between European and traditional Japanese would be the best solution, a dual dress as it was then named, which Mr Shimada undertook to promote in his newspaper. It seems that something approaching that has at last emerged.

Notes

Introduction

1 For a fuller, illustrated account of the dress of the ancient Greeks, Romans and Egyptians see M. Davenport, *The Book of Costume*, New York, 1948, pp. 15–88.
2 Edmund Spenser, *The Faerie Queene*, in *Poetical Works*, Oxford, 1929, Book II, p. 69.
3 Lord Chesterfield, *Letters to His Son*, London, 1919, p. 47 (22 February, 1748).
4 *The Rational Dress Society's Gazette*, July 1888, p. 6.
5 Lady Mary Coke, *The Letters and Journals*, Bath, 1970, vol. III, p. 249.
6 William Cowper, *The Task* in *Poetry and Prose*, selected by B. Spiller, London, 1968, p. 479.
7 Ibid., p. 480.
8 *The Spectator*, ed. D. Bond, Oxford, 1965, vol. II, p. 12 (Saturday, 28 July 1711).
9 Mary Russell Mitford, *Our Village* (1824–32), London, 1936, p. 302.
10 A.W. Schlegel, quoted in H.G. Schenk, *The Mind of the European Romantics*, Oxford, 1979, p. 33.
11 Alexander Pope, *A Discourse on Pastoral Poetry* in *Poetic Works*, ed. H. Davis, London, 1966, p. 10.
12 W.F. Monypenny, *The Life of Benjamin Disraeli*, London, 1910, vol. I, p. 232.
13 Ibid., p. 157.
14 This is a checklist of the sixteenth-century costume books, including some not referred to in the main text. For further information on these remarkable compilations or *Trachtenbücher* see J. Olian in the Guide to Further Reading at the end of this book.

1) J. Amman, *Habitus Praecipuorum Populorum*, Nuremberg, 1577.
2) J. Amman, *Gynaeceum Siue Theatrum Mulierum*, Frankfurt, 1586.
3) F. Bertelli, *Omnium Fere Gentium*, Venice, 1563.
4) Pietro Bertelli, *Diversarum Nationum Habitus*, Padua, 1589.
5) J.-J. Boissard, *Habitus Variarum Orbis Gentium*, Maline, 1581.
6) Robert Boissard, *Mascarades Recueillies*, Valenciennes, 1597.
7) R. Breton, *Recueil de la Diversité des Habits*, Paris, 1562.
8) A. de Bruyn, *Diversarum Gentium Armatura Equestris*, Cologne, 1577.
9) A. de Bruyn, *Habitus Variarum Gentium*, Antwerp, 1581.
10) Nicholas de Nicolay, *Les Quartres Premiers Livres des Navigations et Pérégrinations Orientales*, Lyon, 1567.
11) A. de Fabri, *Diversarum Nationum Ornatus*, Padua, 1593.
12) J. de Glen, *Des Habits, Moeurs, Cérèmonies, Façons de Faire Anciennes & Modernes du Monde*, Liège, 1601.
13) Cesare Vecellio, *De gli Habiti antichi et moderni di Diverse Parti del Mondo*, Venice, 1590.

15 A recent study by Jennifer M. Scarce, *Turkish Fashion in Transition*, discusses change in dress once thought by west Europeans to be timeless. It usefully examines the process in detail, and is very well illustrated. Its references make it a good starting point for anyone wishing to explore further. In *Costume*, 14, 1980, pp. 144–67.
16 Wilfrid Blunt on being in the Egyptian desert; the Earl of Lytton, *Wilfrid Scawen Blunt*, London, 1961, p. 67.

Chapter 1

1 This link is described in a definitive book: Frances Yates, *Astraea: The Imperial Theme in the Sixteenth Century*, London, 1975.
2 John Nichols, *The Progresses and Public Processions of Queen Elizabeth*, London, 1823, II, pp. 159–64, quoted by Enid Welsford, *The Court Masque*, Cambridge, 1927, pp. 154–5. Both these books are very important for the Elizabethan period. Welsford also includes seventeenth-century masques.
3 A. Feuillerat, *Documents Relating to the Office of the Revels in the Time of Queen Elizabeth*, London, 1908, p. 20.
4 Nichols, op. cit., I, from *Laneham's Account of the Queen's Entertainment at Killingworth Castle.*
5 Ibid.
6 Ibid.
7 Robert Greene, *A Quip for an Upstart Courtier*, London, 1592, reprinted in *Life and Complete Works in Prose and Verse of Robert Greene*, ed. A.B. Grosart, the Hutch Library, 1881–3, XI, p. 239.
8 Philip Stubbes, *The Anatomie of Abuses*, London, 1585, p. 65. First published 1583.
9 *The Defence of Conny Catching*, London, 1592, reprinted in *Life and Complete Works in Prose and Verse of Robert Greene*, see note 7, pp. 94–5.
10 Ibid., p. 95.
11 *Kemp's Nine Daies Wonder*, 1600, reprinted for the Camden Society, London, 1840, p. 17.
12 J. Ashelford: see Guide to Further Reading.
13 Philip Sidney, *The Countess of Pembroke's Arcadia*, Oxford, 1973, pp. 26–7.
14 For full names and details of these costume books, usually known simply by their compilers' names, see note 14 of the Introduction.
15 Sidney, op. cit., p. 376.
16 Feuillerat, op. cit., passim.
17 Ibid., p. 286.
18 Edmund Spenser, *The Faerie Queene* in *Poetical Works*, Oxford, 1929, Book V, p. 295.

Chapter 2

1 Francis Bacon, *Works*, ed. Spedding, London, 1858, VI, p. 467.
2 Ben Jonson, quoted by Enid Welsford, *The Court Masque*, Cambridge, 1927, p. 267.

3 Henry Peacham, *The Compleat Gentleman*, London, 1622, Chapter XII, reprinted Oxford, 1906, pp. 107–8.
4 *The Education of Young Gentlewomen*, London, 1699, Chapter X.
5 Thomas Fuller, *The Holy State and the Profane State*, 1648, reprinted London, 1840, p. 288.
6 Sir William d'Avenant, *Dramatic Works*, London, 1872, II, p. 323.
7 F.W. Fairholt, ed., *Lord Mayors Pageants*, London, 1844, II, p. 118.
8 D. de Marly, 'The Establishment of Roman Dress in Seventeenth-Century Portraiture,' *The Burlington Magazine*, July 1975. Key study of this subject. Deals with male and female dress, with 21 illustrations and useful notes.
9 Samuel Pepys, diary entry for 17 August 1667.
10 Pepys, diary entry for 15 January 1666.
11 John Evelyn, diary entry for visit of 9–10 October 1671.

Chapter 3

1 Quoted in J.P. Malcolm, *Anecdotes of the Manners and Customs of London during the Eighteenth Century*, London, 1810, II, p. 321–2.
2 Ibid., p. 328.
3 Richard Rush, *Residence at the Court of London*, ed. B. Rush, London, 1872, pp. 106–7.
4 Mary Granville, Mrs Delany, *The Autobiography and Correspondence*, ed. Lady Llanover, London, 1861, II p. 28.
5 J.-J. Rousseau, *Emile*, London, 1974, p. 330.
6 Ibid., p. 335.
7 Ibid., p. 336.
8 Ibid.
9 William Cole, *A Journal of My Journey to Paris in the Year 1765*, London, 1931, p. 84.
10 Catherine Hutton, *Reminiscences of a Gentlewoman of the Last Century*, ed. C.H. Beale, Birmingham, 1891, p. 65.
11 F.W. Fairholt, ed., *Satirical Songs and Poems on Costume*, London, 1849, p. 264.
12 Quoted in P. Byrde, *A Frivolous Distinction: Fashion and Needlework in the works of Jane Austen*, Bath City Council, 1979, p. 5.
13 Malcolm, op. cit., p. 355.
14 Beaujolais Campbell, *A Journey to Florence in 1817*, London, 1951, p. 125.
15 Ibid., p. 171.
16 Mrs Jameson, *Diary of an Ennuyee*, London, 1826, p. 240–41.
17 Ibid., p. 268.
18 Ibid., p. 346.
19 T.S. Surr, *A Winter in London or Sketches of Fashion*, London, 1807, II, p. 176.

Chapter 4

1 *The Ladies Monthly Museum*, August 1809.
2 Ibid., April 1812.
3 E. Hall ed., *Miss Weeton, Journal of a Governess, 1807–1811*, London, 1936, I, p. 285.
4 *The Rational Dress Society's Gazette*, October 1888, p. 3.
5 *The Young Englishwoman's Domestic Magazine*, September 1865.
6 Elizabeth Gaskell, *North and South*, London, 1970, p. 35.
7 Charles Reade, *Christie Johnstone*, London, 1853, pp. 28–9.
8 *Rational Dress Society's Gazette*, October 1888, p. 3.
9 Ibid., p. 4.
10 Ada Ballin, *The Science of Dress in Theory and Practice*, London, 1885, pp. 260–67.
11 Mrs Merrifield, *Dress as a Fine Art*, London, 1854, p. 11.
12 Mrs Oliphant, *Dress*, London, 1878, p. 68.
13 Henry Holiday, 'The Artistic Aspect of Dress,' *Aglaia*, July 1893, p. 15.
14 Ibid., p. 28.

Chapter 5

1 *The Sunday Times*, 17 August 1975.
2 Isadora Duncan, *My Life*, London, 1928, p. 123.
3 Ibid., p. 134.
4 D. Watkin, *Thomas Hope, 1769–1831, and the Neo-classical Idea*, London, 1968, p. 257.
5 *The Daily Mirror*, 4 June 1913, p. 10.
6 *The Ladies Realm*, vol. XXII, 1907, p. 117.
7 Palmer White, *Poiret*, London, 1973, p. 31.
8 This photograph is reproduced on p. 158 of Diana de Marly, *The History of Haute Couture*, London, 1980, and on p. 19 of the catalogue to the Scottish Arts Council/Victoria and Albert Museum exhibition *Fashion 1900–1939*, London 1975. Both also contain other illustrations of Vionnet and Grès designs.
9 Cecil Beaton, *The Glass of Fashion*, London, 1954, p. 183.
10 Micki Forman, 'Tutmania', *Dress*, Journal of the Costume Society of America, vol. IV, 1978. This article contains several illustrations of 1920s 'Tutmania' clothes, and also some of the subsequent revivals in the later 1970s inspired in the United States by the travelling exhibition of 'Treasures of Tutankhamun.'

Chapter 6

1 John Nichols, *The Progresses and Public Processions of Queen Elizabeth*, London, 1823, I, from *Laneham's Account of the Queen's Entertainment at Killingworth Castle, 1575*.
2 W.B. Rye, *England as seen by Foreigners in the days of Elizabeth and James the First*, London, 1865, p. 28.
3 *Manuscripts of his Grace the Duke of Rutland*, Historical Manuscripts Commission, HMSO 1905, IV, p. 376.
4 Nichols, op. cit., I, from *An Account of Queen Elizabeth's Visit to Greenwich Park on 10 July 1559*.
5 Ibid., I, from *An Account of Princess Elizabeth's Visit to Richmond, 1557*.

6 D. Meads, ed. *Diary of Lady Margaret Hoby 1599–1605*, London, 1930, p. 181.
7 Philip Stubbes, *The Anatomie of Abuses*, London, 1585, p. 88. First published 1583.
8 Nichols, op. cit., III, from *Queen Elizabeth's Visit to Bisham.*
9 *The English Courtier and the Cutrey-gentleman*, London, 1586, p. 66.
10 Ibid., p. 67.
11 Edmund Spenser, *The Faerie Queene* in *Poetical Works*, Oxford, 1929, Book VI, p. 342.
12 A. Feuillerat, *Documents Relating to the Office of the Revels in the Time of Queen Elizabeth*, London, 1908, p. 193.
13 Philip Sidney, *The Countess of Pembroke's Arcadia*, Oxford, 1973, p. 37.
14 Ibid., p. 190.
15 Spenser, op. cit., Book VI, p. 376.
16 Stubbes, op. cit., p. 43.
17 Ibid., p. 44.
18 Feuillerat, op. cit., p. 193.
19 Samuel Rowlands, *The Melancholie Knight*, London, 1615, reprinted by the Hunterian Club, 1874, pp. 5–6.

Chapter 7

1 *Manuscripts of his Grace the Duke of Rutland*, preserved at Belvoir Castle, Historical Manuscripts Commission, HMSO, 1905, twelfth report, Appendix V, vol. II, p. 102.
2 Nicholas Breton, *The Court and the Country*, London, 1618, reprinted by The Roxburghe Library, 1868, p. 183.
3 Ibid.
4 Richard Brathwait, *The English Gentlewoman*, London, 1641.
5 Richard Brathwait, *The Shepheards Holy-day* in *The Shepheards Tales*, London, 1621.
6 F.W. Fairholt, ed., *Satirical Songs and Poems on Costume*, London, 1849, p. 104.
7 Ibid., p. 145.
8 Thomas Fuller, *The Holy State and the Profane State*, 1648, reprinted London, 1840, p. 132.
9 Samuel Pepys, diary entry for 14 July 1667.
10 *Letters from Dorothy Osborne to Sir William Temple*, London, 1942, p. 85.
11 Thomas Overbury, *A Faire and Happy Milkmayd*, in *Works*, ed. E.T. Rimbault, London, 1856, p. 118.
12 Pepys, diary entry for 26 August 1664.
13 *Rutland Manuscripts*, op. cit., vol. IV p. 227.
14 John Evelyn, diary entry for 9–10 October 1671.
15 Pepys, diary entry for 11 August 1667.
16 Thomas Coryat, *Coryat's Crudities*, London, 1611, republished Glasgow, 1905, I, p. 228.
17 Pepys, diary entry for 6 August 1667.
18 E. Boswell, *The Restoration Court Stage*, Cambridge, Mass., 1932, p. 327. This book reprints in detail the costume accounts for *Calisto*.

Chapter 8

1 Mary Granville, Mrs Delany, *The Autobiography and Correspondence*, ed. Lady Llanover, London, 1861, II, p. 147.
2 Lady Mary Coke, *The Letters and Journals*, III, p. 152.
3 Delany, loc. cit.
4 Ibid., p. 492.
5 Miss Berry, *Extracts of the Journals and Correspondence*, ed. T. Lewis, London, 1865, II, p. 382.
6 P. Kalm, *Account of his visit to England in 1748*, ed. J. Lucas, London, 1892, p. 85.
7 *The Spectator*, ed. D. Bond, Oxford, 1965, I, p. 62.
8 J.P. Malcolm, *Anecdotes of the Manners and Customs of London during the Eighteenth Century*, London, 1810, p. 331, quoted from the Weekly Register, 10 July 1731.
9 Samuel Richardson, *Letters from Sir Charles Grandison*, 1754, reprinted London, 1815, I, p. 57.
10 Delany, op. cit., II, p. 363.
11 Kalm, op. cit., p. 327.
12 Ibid., p. 326.
13 *The Public Advertiser*, 6 June 1791.
14 Delany, op. cit., II, p. 1.
15 Horace Walpole, *Correspondence*, Yale, 1944, XI, p. 290.
16 *The London Chronicle*, 21–3 June 1791.
17 *St James Chronicle*, 7–9 July 1791.
18 Dudley Ryder, *Diary*, ed. W. Matthews, London, 1939, p. 310.
19 Malcolm, op. cit., p. 336.
20 Walpole, op. cit., p. 272.
21 *Ladies Monthly Museum*, June 1807.
22 Richard Rush, *Residence at the Court of London*, ed. B. Rush, London, 1872, p. 324–5.

Chapter 9

1 *The Ladies Monthly Museum*, November 1806.
2 Ibid., November 1808.
3 Mary Russell Mitford, *Our Village*, (1824–32), London, 1936, p. 220.
4 P. Kalm, *Account of his visit to England in 1748*, ed. J. Lucas, London, 1892, p. 154.
5 Miss Berry, *Extracts of the Journals and Correspondence*, ed. T. Lewis, London 1865, vol. II, pp. 366–7.
6 Ibid., p. 381 (entry for 8 June 1809).
7 Mitford, op. cit., p. 308.
8 Ibid., p. 309.
9 Ibid.
10 Ibid., p. 286.
11 *Miss Weeton: Journal of a Governess*, London, 1936, I p. 70 (1808).
12 Ibid., p. 285 (1810).
13 Ibid., p. 261 (1810).
14 *Elizabeth Ham by herself 1783–1820*, ed. E. Gillett, London, 1945, p. 69.
15 Beaujolais Campbell, *A Journey to Florence in 1817*, London, 1951, pp. 34–5.
16 Charles Reade, *The Bloomer*, p. 38. This story was published with others under the title *The Course of True Love Never did Run Smooth*, London, 1857.
17 *The Queen*, 21 February 1885.
18 Richard Jefferies' article in *Longman's Magazine*, July 1883.

19 Ibid.
20 George Ewart Evans, 'Dress and the Rural Historian,' *Costume*, 8, 1974, p. 39.
21 *The Ladies Cabinet of Fashion, Music and Romance*, March 1835.
22 Robin Doughty, *Feather Fashions and Bird Preservation*, Berkeley, 1975, p. 25.
23 Adern Holt, *Fancy Dresses Described or What to Wear at Fancy Balls*, London, 1887 (5th edition).
24 W.H. Hudson, *Nature in Downland*, London, 1900, quoted in A.L.J. Gossell, *Shepherds of Britain*, London, 1911, p. 20.

Chapter 10

1 Cecil Beaton, *The Glass of Fashion*, London, 1954, p. 64.
2 Ibid., p. 12.
3 *The Morning Standard*, 13 September 1909.
4 Jean Worth on dress, in Florence Winterburn, *Principles of Correct Dress*, New York, 1914, p. 222.
5 Selfridges' advertisement, *The Gentlewoman*, spring 1913.
6 The slow but gradual change of fashion's conscience on the question of respect for bird life is fully documented in Robin Doughty, *Feather Fashions and Bird Preservation*, Berkeley, 1975.
7 J.C. Flugel, *The Psychology of Clothes*, New York, 1969 (paperback edition), pp. 124–5.
8 Romilly John, *The Seventh Child*, London, 1932, p. 3. For an illustrated and fuller account of Dorelia's clothes see Malcolm Easton, 'Dorelia's Wardrobe: There goes an Augustus John,' *Costume*, 8, 1974.
9 Frances Jennings, *A Tour in a Donkey Cart*, London, 1921, p. 25.
10 Description of Carrington, whilst resident with Lytton Strachey, c.1920. Leonard Woolf, *Downhill all the Way*, autobiography of the years 1919–39, London, 1970, p. 69.
11 Beaton, op. cit., pp. 155–6.
12 Evelyn Waugh, *Decline and Fall*, London, 1966, p. 75.
13 Vogue *Real Life Fashion Guide*, London, 1979.
14 London *Vogue*, early April 1917.
15 Elizabeth Gaskell, *North and South*, London, 1970, p. 96.
16 London *Evening Standard*, commercial property review, 15 March 1976.
17 James Laver, *A Letter to a Girl on the Future of Clothes*, Home and Van Thal Ltd., no location given, 1946, pp. 19–20.

Chapter 11

1 Roy Strong, *The Cult of Elizabeth*, London, 1977, p. 161.
2 Edmund Spenser, *The Faerie Queene* in *Poetical Works*, Oxford, 1929, Book III, p. 225.
3 Francis Bacon, *Works*, ed. Spedding, London, 1858, VI, p. 468.
4 This painting can be seen reproduced as plate 42 of Strong, *The Cult of Elizabeth* [see note 1].
5 Spenser, loc. cit.
6 Strong, op. cit., p. 140.
7 Philip Stubbes, *The Anatomie of Abuses*, London, 1585, p. 17. First published 1583.
8 John Nichols, *The Progresses and Public Processions of Queen Elizabeth*, London, 1823, I, from *Laneham's Account of the Queen's Entertainment at Killingworth Castle, 1575*.
9 Ibid.
10 Ibid.
11 Stubbes, op. cit., pp. 36–7.
12 Ibid., p. 46.
13 Ibid., p. 69.

Chapter 12

1 Henry Peacham, *The Truth of our Times*, London, 1638, reprinted by The Facsimile Text Society, New York, 1942, p. 66.
2 Ibid., p. 64.
3 Ibid., p. 73.
4 Anthony Wood, *Life and Times 1632–1695, described by himself*, Oxford, 1890–91, I, p. 423.
5 Francis Sandford, *The History of the Coronation of James II*, London, 1687.
6 Samuel Pepys, diary entry for 22 April 1661.
7 Enid Welsford, *The Court Masque*, Cambridge, 1927, p. 244.
8 Sir William d'Avenant, *Dramatic Works*, London, 1872, p. 311.
9 Ibid., pp. 274 and 286.
10 Ibid., p. 278.
11 *Manuscripts of his Grace the Duke of Rutland*, Historical Manuscripts Commission, HMSO, 1905, pp. 508–9.
12 Ibid., p. 492.
13 F.W. Fairholt, ed., *Lord Mayors Pageants*, London, 1844, p. 157.
14 Pepys, diary entry for 29 October 1663.
15 Ibid., 29 October 1664.

Chapter 13

1 Horace Walpole, *Correspondence*, Yale, 1944, XVII, p. 338.
2 Mary Granville, Mrs Delany, *The Autobiography and Correspondences*, ed. Lady Llanover, London, 1861, II, p. 1.
3 Walpole, loc. cit.
4 Ibid.
5 P. Kalm, *Account of his visit to England in 1748*, ed. J. Lucas, London, 1892, p. 65.
6 Quoted in A. Buck, p. 37, see Guide to Further Reading.
7 Mrs Cowley, *The Belle's Stratagem*, London, 1813, p. 75.
8 Roy Strong, *And when did you last see your father?*, London, 1978. Appendix pp. 155–168. This book is a full study of the eighteenth and nineteenth centuries' sense of the past through art, including sections on the principal costume historians and their influence. Copiously illustrated, some colour.
9 Joseph Strutt, *Complete View of the Dress and Habits of*

the People of England, London, 1796. Introductory 'Address to the Public.' The 'improved' 1842 edition of this book, ed. by J.R. Planché, was reprinted in 1970 by Tabard Press Ltd., London.
10 Thomas Hope, *Costume of the Ancients*, London, 1841, I, p. xiii.
11 P. Rameau, *The Dancing Master*, first published London, 1728, reprinted 1931, p. 31.
12 F.W. Fairholt, *Satirical Songs and Poems on Costume*, London, 1849, p. 231.
13 Ibid., p. 237.

Chapter 14

1 J.R. Planché, *History of British Costume from the Earliest Period to the Close of the Eighteenth Century*, London, 1847, p. xiv. (First ed. 1834.)
2 Roy Strong, *And when did you last see your father?*, London, 1978, pp. 155–168.
3 F.W. Fairholt, *Costume in England. A History of Dress from the Earliest Period till the Close of the Eighteenth Century*, London, 1846, p.x.
4 Planché, op. cit., p. 321.
5 Ibid., p. 403.
6 J.R. Planché, *Souvenir of the Bal Costumé*, 12 May 1842, Buckingham Palace, London.
7 Fairholt, *Costume in England*, op. cit., p. 123.
8 Ibid., p. 399.
9 *Ladies Monthly Museum*, August 1808.
10 *Young Englishwoman*, 25 November 1865.
11 Walter Scott, *The Abbot*, London, 1895, p. 19. (First published 1820.)
12 Ibid., p. 197.
13 *Ladies Monthly Museum*, September 1808.
14 Giles Gossip, *Coronation Anecdotes*, London, 1823, p. 285.
15 F.W.H. Cavendish, *Society, Politics and Diplomacy 1820–1864*, London, 1913, p. 44.
16 Peter Buchan, *The Eglinton Tournament and Gentleman Unmasked*, London, 1840, p. 42.
17 For a full account of the tournament see Ian Anstruther, *The Knight and the Umbrella*, London, 1963. See also Stevenson and Bennett in Guide to Further Reading.
18 Buchan, op. cit., pp. 34 and 35.
19 Ibid., pp. 41–2.
20 Ibid., p. 58.
21 *Ladies Monthly Museum*, March 1809.
22 *London Illustrated News*, 21 June 1851.
23 *The Queen*, 8 January 1898.
24 Ibid., 1 January 1898.
25 Quoted in Shonfield, see Guide to Further Reading.
26 E.M. Ward, *Memories of Ninety Years*, London, 1924, p. 54.
27 Vernon Lee, *Miss Brown*, London, 1884, I, p. 6.
28 Ibid., p. 299–300.
29 Mrs H.R. Haweis, *The Art of Dress*, London, 1879, p. 102.
30 Ibid, p. 103.
31 Quoted from *The Queen*, 1879, by Alison Adburgham, *Liberty's: A Biography of a Shop*, London, 1975, p. 31.
32 Haweis, op. cit., p. 110.
33 Adburgham, op. cit., p. 51.
34 Haweis, op. cit., p. 94.
35 M. Swain, see Guide to Further Reading.

Chapter 15

1 *The Daily Mirror*, 12 September 1912.
2 Liberty and Co., *Dress and Decoration*, London, 1905.
3 Ibid.
4 Ibid.
5 *The Ladies Realm*, 1907.
6 Lady Cynthia Asquith, *Diaries 1915–1918*, London, 1967, p. 11.
7 F.H. Winterburn, *Principles of Correct Dress*, New York, 1914, p. 211.
8 Asquith, op. cit., p. 75.
9 Arthur Marwick, *Women at War 1914–1918*, London, 1977, tables between pp. 166–169.
10 Winterburn, op. cit., p. 191.
11 Michael Arlen, *The Green Hat*, London, 1924, p. 9.
12 London *Vogue*, 20 January 1932.
13 Norman Hartnell, *Silver and Gold*, London, 1955, p. 94.
14 Hardy Amies, *Just So Far*, London, 1954, p. 173.
15 The Teds, revived and original, are featured in the following: Chris Steele-Perkins and Richard Smith, *The Teds*, London 1979; This is a book of photographs and has a text which includes conversations with Teds. For an account of Teds within the framework of other post-war youth cults, see Dick Hebdige, *Subculture: The Meaning to Style*, London, 1979. This latter book is not illustrated; both books usefully concentrate on much else besides the dress, so giving it a fuller context than is appropriate here.
16 *The Tailor and Cutter*, 1 September, 1967.
17 Ibid., May 1972.
18 Ibid., 16 May 1964.
19 Alison Adburgham, *The Guardian*, 5 October 1960; reprinted in *View of Fashion*, London, 1966., p. 249.
20 Alison Adburgham, *Punch*, 15 August 1956; reprinted in *View of Fashion*, London, 1966, p. 125.

Chapter 16

1 For their authors and titles see note 14 of the Introduction.
2 E.E. Veevers, 'Sources of Inigo Jones's Masquing Designs,' *Journal of the Warburg and Courtauld Institutes*, XXII, 1959, pp. 373–4.
3 Frances Yates, *Astraea: The Imperial Theme in the Sixteenth Century*, London, 1975, pp. 220–21.
4 A. Feuillerat, *Documents Relating to the Office of the Revels in the Time of Queen Elizabeth*, London, 1908, p. 409.
5 Ibid., p. 20.
6 Robert Greene, *A Quip for an Upstart Courtier*, London, 1592, p. 288.

7 Quoted by R.H. Tawney, ed., *Tudor Economic Documents*, London, 1924, III, p. 284.
8 Philip Stubbes, *The Anatomie of Abuses*, London, 1585, pp. 13–14. First published 1583.
9 Edmund Spenser, *The Faerie Queene* in *Poetical Works*, Oxford, 1929, Book VII, p. 403.
10 Quoted by Enid Welsford, *The Court Masque*, Cambridge, 1927, pp. 156–7.
11 Spenser, op. cit., Book III, p. 206.
12 Ibid., Book V, p. 295.
13 Earl of Lytton, *Wilfrid Scawen Blunt*, London, 1961, p. 167.
14 Spenser, op. cit., Book II, p. 83.

Chapter 17

1 Fynes Moryson, *An Itinerary*, Glasgow, 1907, IV, pp. 226–7.
2 John Evelyn, diary entry for 22 June 1664.
3 Edward Terry, *A Voyage to East India*, London, 1777, p. 205. (First published 1655.)
4 Ibid., p. 205.
5 Ibid., pp. 201–2.
6 Ibid., p. 347.
7 Jan Nieuhoff, *An Embassy from the East India Company of the United Provinces to the Grand Tartar Chan Emperour of China*, London 1669, p. 45.
8 For more information see Swain, Guide to Further Reading.
9 Evelyn, diary entry for 18 October 1666.
10 Pepys, diary entry for 15 October 1666.
11 Richard Brathwait, *The English Gentlewoman*, London, 1641.
12 See Diana de Marly, *King Charles' own Fashion*, Guide to Further Reading.
13 F.W. Fairholt, ed., *Lord Mayors Pageants*, London, 1844, pp. 161 and 153.
14 Evelyn, diary entry for 19 June 1682.

Chapter 18

1 Mary Granville, Mrs Delany, *The Autobiography and Correspondence*, ed. Lady Llanover, London, 1861, II, pp. 171–2.
2 The Countess of Suffolk, *Letters*, London, 1824, I, p. 210.
3 See Swain, Guide to Further Reading.
4 See Tarrant, as above, p. 94.
5 Lady Mary Wortley Montagu, *Letters and Works*, ed. Lord Wharncliffe, London, 1898, I, p. 174.
6 Robert Wood, *The Ruins of Balbec*, 1757, reprinted London, 1971, p. 4.
7 M. de Ferriol, *Receuil de Cent Estampes representant differentes Nations du Levant*, Paris, 1714.
8 Montagu, op. cit., pp. 173–4.
9 Ibid., p. 174.
10 John Irwin, *The Kashmir Shawl*, HMSO, 1973, p. 19. An illustrated, comprehensive account of the history, technique and influence of the Kashmir shawl on which I have leaned gratefully.
11 Hugh Honour, *Chinoiserie: The Vision of Cathay*, London, 1961. This is the fullest account of the origins and development of the style, and is well illustrated. Furniture, architecture, ceramics and textiles are all included. There is still room for a full-length study of Chinoiserie and orientalism in dress.

Chapter 19

1 Earl of Lytton, *Wilfred Scawen Blunt*, pp. 67–8.
2 *The Times*, 16 November 1859.
3 Nancy Mitford, *The Stanleys of Alderley*, London, 1939, p. 224. Lord Stanley to Lady Stanley, 7 September 1859.
4 Ibid., p. 223. As above, 4 September 1859.
5 *A Regency Visitor.* The English tour of Prince Pückler–Muskau described in his Letters 1826–8. London, 1957, pp. 218–9.
6 See Doris Langley Moore, 'Byronic Dress,' *Costume*, 5, 1971, pp. 1–13, for a detailed and illustrated account of all aspects of Lord Byron's real and idealized dress.
7 Thomas Hope, *Anastasius*, or *Memoirs of a Greek*, London, 1836, vol. I, p. 119.
8 *A Regency Visitor*, op. cit., p. 94.
9 Hope, op. cit., vol. II, p. 321.
10 Ibid., p. 371.
11 T.S. Surr, *A Winter in London* or *Sketches of Fashion*, London, 1807, vol. 2, p. 219.
12 W.F. Monypenny, *The Life of Benjamin Disraeli*, London, 1910, p. 303.
13 Ibid., p. 159.
14 Miss Berry, *Extracts from the Journals and Correspondence*, ed. T. Lewis, London, 1865, vol. II, p. 522.
15 *The Life and Letters of Lady Hester Stanhope*, London, 1914, p. 144. (22 January 1813, from Syria.)
16 Mrs Merrifield, *Dress as a Fine Art*, London, 1854, p. 83.
17 *The Englishwoman's Domestic Magazine*, March 1867.
18 For Liberty's centenary in 1975 two publications appeared which detail and illustrate the history of the company and its products fully: Alison Adburgham, *Liberty's: A Biography of a Shop*, and the catalogue to accompany the Victoria and Albert Museum's July–August exhibition, *Liberty's 1875–1975*.
19 Westminster City Victoria Library, Liberty Archives 788/164, letter 6, a, 17 December 1897.

Chapter 20

1 *The Lady*, 15 January 1903.
2 *The Daily Express*, 22 November 1909.
3 From the diary of Jean Cocteau, quoted by Palmer White, *Poiret*, London, 1973, p. 93.
4 *The Queen*, 14 January 1925.
5 Ibid.
6 London *Vogue*, March 1934.
7 Ibid., March 1933.
8 F.W. Monypenny, *The Life of Benjamin Disraeli*, London, 1910, p. 170.
9 Ibid., p. 169.
10 *The Observer Magazine*, 10 November 1968.
11 Ibid, 5 June 1977.
12 Prudence Glynn, *The Times*, 26 October 1978.
13 London *Vogue*, 15 April 1976.

Guide to Further Reading

This selected and annotated bibliography is intended to be used with those more detailed sources already pointed out in the notes to the text.

General

Quentin Bell, *On Human Finery*, London, 1976. This revised and enlarged edition of a 1947 classic provides a stimulating survey of the theories and mechanics of fashion. It illuminates revivals in some detail by the light of chapters such as 'Vicarious Consumption – Archaism' and 'Sumptuosity.' Forty-three illustrations, plus an illustrated survey of fashion from the fifteenth to twentieth century drawn by the author, and four colour plates.

Millia Davenport, *The Book of Costume*, New York, 1948. Now available in a single volume, this basic source book has 3000 illustrations. Few specific examples of revivals, but essential background reference.

Sarah Stevenson and **Helen Bennett,** *Van Dyck in Check Trousers: Fancy Dress in Art and Life 1700–1900*, Scottish National Portrait Gallery, 1978. Lively thematic look at revivals with many Scottish references. Separate section on fancy dress balls. Well illustrated, some colour, including some rarely seen pictures and photographs. Very useful addition to Eglinton Tournament illustrations.

Raymond Williams, *The Country and the City*, London, 1973. Important account of attitudes in English literary history which underpin meaning of rural and pastoral dress.

Sixteenth century

J. Ashelford, 'Female Masque dress in late sixteenth-century England,' *Costume,* 12, 1978. Illustrated account of main changes and influences in this delightful little-known subject.

S.M. Newton, *Renaissance Theatre Costume and the Sense of the Historic Past,* London, 1975. Unusual, scholarly account of this related subject, covering northern and southern Europe and including the fifteenth century. Over ninety illustrations.

J. Olian, 'Sixteenth Century Costume Books,' *Dress*, vol. 3, The Costume Society of America, 1977. Well-illustrated, only published source dealing exclusively with the costume books. Clarifies an otherwise complex field.

Roy Strong, *The Cult of Elizabeth: Elizabethan Portraiture and Pageantry*, London, 1977. Valuable book on the context and meaning of much Elizabethan imagery, including some details of dress. Accession Day Tournaments are fully described. Ninety illustrations, some colour.

Roy Strong, *The English Icon: Elizabethan and Jacobean Portraiture*, London, 1969. Useful for dress with over three hundred portraits illustrated, some colour, and essays on general topics relevant to dress: Elizabethan neo-mediaevalism and romantic melancholy.

Cesare Vecellio, *Vecellio's Renaissance Costume Book*, New York, 1977. Readily available American paperback of all five hundred woodcuts taken from the 1598 edition of *Habiti antichi et moderni di tutto il Mondo*.

Seventeenth century

M. Louttit, 'The Romantic Dress of Saskia van Ulenborch: Its Pastoral and Theatrical Associations,' *The Burlington Magazine*, May 1973. Interesting detailed study of Dutch romantic dress; complements English ideas in this little known area. Illustrated.

D. de Marly, 'King Charles II's Own Fashion: The Theatrical Origins of the English Vest,' *Journal of the Warburg and Courtauld Institutes*, 1974. Illustrated article which establishes sources and spread of Charles's 1666 venture.

D. de Marly, 'Undress in the Oeuvre of Lely,' *The Burlington Magazine*, November 1978. Short, illustrated description of main types of classical and Arcadian dress, and Indian gowns.

O. Miller, *Sir Peter Lely*, National Portrait Gallery, 1978. Catalogue to N.P.G. Lely exhibition. Over ninety illustrations, some colour. Useful guide to many aspects of seventeenth century dress, including pastoral and classical styles.

Eighteenth century

Janet Arnold, 'The Classical Influence on the Cut, Construction and Decoration of Women's Dress *c.*1785–1820,' in *The So-Called Age of Elegance, Costume 1785–1820*, from the fourth Annual Conference of the Costume Society 1970. With very carefully chosen illustrations and contemporary fashion sources, this article usefully clarifies important details of female dress in the neo-classical era. This Costume Society volume also contains several other essays of general interest to anyone exploring the dress of the period from the point of view of revived classical style.

Anne Buck, *Dress in Eighteenth Century England*, London, 1979. Over ninety illustrations, some colour. Establishes variety of dress possible at one time and also attitudes to fashion. Section on masquerade dress. Useful bibliography.

E. Miles, *Thomas Hudson 1701–1779*, Greater London Council, 1979. Bicentennial exhibition catalogue. Fully illustrated survey of the work of one of the portrait painters most involved in the van Dyke revival.

J.L. Nevinson, 'Van Dyke Dress,' *The Connoisseur*, November 1964. Nine illustrations including surviving garments.

M.H. Swain, 'Nightgown into Dressing Gown,' *Costume*, 6, 1972. An illustrated study of men's night gowns in the eighteenth century but also includes seventeenth-century examples. Valuable appendix of location of surviving specimens.

N.E.A. Tarrant, 'Lord Sheffield's Banyan,' *Costume*, 11, 1977. Illustrated analysis of background and construction of garment in Buckinghamshire County Museum.

E. Ribeiro, 'Some Evidence of the Influence of the Dress of the Seventeenth Century on Costume in Eighteenth Century Female Portraiture,' *The Burlington Magazine*, December 1977. Very useful survey of origins and development of this revival. Eighteen illustrations.

E. Ribeiro, 'Hussars in Masquerade,' *Apollo*, February 1977. Popular Hungarian style of male masquerade dress in the eighteenth century, not included in this book. Eleven illustrations and useful notes.

E. Ribeiro, 'Turquerie: Turkish Dress and English Fashion in the Eighteenth Century,' *Connoisseur*, May 1979. Generously illustrated short survey of the Turkish influence.

M. Webster, *Johan Zoffany 1733–1810*, National Portrait Gallery, 1976. Many illustrations to useful exhibition catalogue, providing both general costume background and various revivals.

Nineteenth century

S.M. Newton, *Health, Art and Reason. Dress Reformers of the Nineteenth Century*, London, 1974. Nearly seventy illustrations. Full account of the reform movement. Very useful notes and bibliography.

L. Ormond, 'Female Costume in Aesthetic Movement of the 1870 and 1880s, *Costume*, 1 and 2, 1967–8, reprinted 1970. Brief illustrated survey, supplemented with relevant contemporary quotations.

Z. Shonfield, 'Miss Marshall and the Cimabue Browns,' *Costume*, 13, 1979. Illustrated. Unusual documentary insight into Aesthetic dress from manuscript diary of Jeanette Marshall (1855–1935).

R. Smith, 'Bonnard's Costume Historique – a Pre-Raphaelite Source Book,' *Costume*, 7, 1973. Well-illustrated investigation of the uses by artists of one of the century's grandest costume history books.

M. Swain, 'Mrs Newbery's Dress,' *Costume*, 12, 1978. Story of one individual's contribution to artistic dress. Illustrated with contemporary photographs. Period includes early twentieth century.

Twentieth century

D. de Marly, *The History of Haute Couture, 1850–1950*, London, 1980. Fully illustrated, some colour. Includes information on many designers instrumental in various revivals this century.

P. Glynn with **M. Ginsburg,** *In Fashion*, London, 1978. Good, general background to fashion this century, with some revivals mentioned. Many illustrations. Some colour.

G. de Osma, *Mariano Fortuny: His Life and Work*, London, 1980. Many illustrations, several in colour. Includes select bibliography and useful list of museums containing Fortuny exhibits.

Index